WHEN PEACE BROKE OUT
+ BRITAIN 1945 +

London: HMSO

Researched and prepared by Reference Services, Central Office of Information.

© Selection and introduction Crown copyright 1994
Applications for reproduction should be made to HMSO's copyright unit
First published 1994
Second impression 1995

ISBN 0 11 701860 0

Published by HMSO and available from:

HMSO Publications Centre
(Mail, fax and telephone orders only)
PO Box 276, London SW8 5DT
Telephone orders 0171 873 9090
General enquiries 0171 873 0011
(queuing system in operation for both numbers)
Fax orders 0171 873 8200

HMSO Bookshops
49 High Holborn, London WC1V 6HB
(counter service only)
0171 873 0011 Fax 0171 831 1326
68–69 Bull Street, Birmingham B4 6AD
0121 236 9696 Fax 0121 236 9699
33 Wine Street, Bristol BS1 2BQ
0117 926 4306 Fax 0117 929 4515
9–21 Princess Street, Manchester M60 8AS
0161 834 7201 Fax 0161 833 0634
16 Arthur Street, Belfast BT1 4GD
01232 238451 Fax 01232 235401
71 Lothian Road, Edinburgh EH3 9AZ
0131 228 4181 Fax 0131 229 2734
The HMSO Oriel Bookshop
The Friary, Cardiff CF1 4AA
01222 395548 Fax 01222 384347

HMSO's Accredited Agents
(see Yellow Pages)

and through good booksellers

Acknowledgments

We would like to thank the staff of the British Library Newspaper Library at Colindale for their ready and cheerful assistance and co-operation. *Good Housekeeping* kindly granted us access to their archives. The staff of the library of the Imperial War Museum have been most helpful in showing us their files of unpublished war diaries and obtaining permission, from the copyright holder, to quote from the diary of Mr J.D.F. Mudford, RNVR. We have been unable to trace the copyright holder of the diary of Miss N.V. Carver. We also owe special debts to the Mass Observation Archive at the University of Sussex in Brighton, the University of Sussex Library and Brighton Central Library. Copyright in the extracts quoted generally belongs to the newspapers and magazines concerned, and to their successors in business. Present owners have been most kind in granting permission to quote, as have Reuters Ltd.

The photographs of President Roosevelt's memorial service published in *The Times* on 18 April 1945 are (first left) © Associated Newspapers Ltd and (third from left) © the Hulton Deutsch Collection; the other two were taken by the Graphic Union. The photographs on pp. 24 and 54 are © Imperial War Museum.

We would like to thank our colleagues in COI Pictures Section for helping us to choose the photographs for this book.

The books that have provided valuable background are listed at the end of the introduction.

PREFACE

By Sir John Mills

When Peace Broke Out commemorates 1945 – a watershed in British history: the end of a six-year war and the start of dramatic changes in all our lives. It conveys the flavour, and feeling, of life during the final months of the war and the first months after it, and the euphoria of the peace itself. Our dreams about what it would be like to live in peacetime again at last became reality. But the war had left terrible scars and many families still had sons and husbands unaccounted for.

It still seems amazing what we had to put up with. How much we take for granted today! We were advised to take food and soap on holiday. We were told that Nissen huts were to be converted into dwellings to relieve the housing shortage. There was even a proposal that housing estates should be set up in the royal parks. Advertisements for Robinson's patent barley went on apologising for its not being available. There was a seemingly permanent sense of crisis about food shortages. News items about food must have fascinated, galled or frustrated us. What did we make of ministerial announcements in October that bread might have to be rationed during the winter and in November that there was 'a little food in hand' and therefore we would be allowed extra rations of sugar, chocolate, butter and meat at Christmas?

Press headlines (especially the tabloids) were just as good as those of today. Racy and interesting titbits informed the London evening press. There were the usual family dramas and petty crime. Homelessness was widespread. One still detects deference for local magnates, top politicians and big stars. Comment on the defeated Axis powers was harsh and mainly unforgiving. One of the most moving reports was on the horrors of Buchenwald from the MP Mavis Tate, a woman much honoured in her day. The greatest shock of all was the defeat of Churchill in the general election and the landslide Labour victory.

Watch out for more than a tinge of truth being stranger than fiction. In April troops of the 36th Division clearing the jungle in Burma found the Mahadevi of Mongmit (Mabel Phillips from Cambridge), English wife of a Shan chief who had refused to leave her husband's side during the years of Japanese invasion and occupation. In August dancing was banned in Vienna, 'to remove any possible cause for the useless dissipation of energy' – when that energy was needed to clear rubble and refuse from the streets.

The provincial press provides a fund of stories: the great Yorkshire batsman Herbert Sutcliffe lecturing to a packed audience in Ripon; the Cornwall vicar who found £500 in notes wrapped in brown paper left in his church one night as a thanksgiving gift; the Queen of Albania turning up at a Northamptonshire church fête; the man arrested for being drunk on horseback in Kensington; the careless post-war destruction of Nottingham's oldest building; Kathleen Ferrier singing Handel and Mozart at a concert in Hereford.

Humour was never far away – often understated. The *New Statesman's* This England corner provided marvellous press snippets – try the one from October about the defective housing in Wilby. *Punch* featured exquisite cartoons, especially on petrol rationing, the atomic bomb and taxi shortages.

To those who were not yet born, some things may come as a surprise; other things – the way people are capable of behaving at their best and worst, or the minute concerns of local communities – have not changed all that much.

The book is a mixture of the serious, the unusual, the fascinating, the flippant, the quirky, the sad, the cruel, the tragic, the pathetic and the funny. It does not pretend to follow a scheme or formula. We hope that it will make people think, make them smile, and perhaps remember.

INTRODUCTION

After the successful campaign in Normandy in the summer of 1944, hopes rose among the British people for a speedy end to the war as British and American forces raced across France and Belgium in August and September. The British defeat at Arnhem, however, braked the advance and during the winter of 1944–45 the Allies were held up in the Ardennes region by the last German offensive of the war in December–January.

Shortly after the D-Day landings there was an uncomfortable reminder that British civilians were still in danger. In mid-June a menacing new noise was heard over southern England as the first of the many thousands of Hitler's revenge weapons – the V1 flying bombs (or doodlebugs) – began to drop. Over 6,000 civilians were killed and over a million houses were seriously damaged. Some 2,800 people were also killed by the V2 rockets which, unlike the doodlebugs, were the first ballistic missiles. As 1945 opened, thousands of building workers from all over the country were repairing London's damaged houses. At least one person had the answer to the doodlebug. Shortly after one dropped close to Lords cricket ground in July 1944, the Middlesex batsman Jack Robertson hit the first ball after play's restart for six!

Rationing and shortages intensified in the last few months of the war, giving rise to war-weariness among the population. Festive food offered for Christmas in one West End hotel was dried egg omelette and cold apple tart.

Yet there were moves towards a more normal life. In September 1944 it was announced that pre-war fitted curtains and blinds could be used again. By December cars could driven without headlight masks. And on 20 April 1945 the abolition of the black-out was announced by Home Secretary Herbert Morrison. One observer noted on VE Day:

> What impressed me most . . . were the lit-up trams and buses on the Brighton Road – this was a wonderful sight and I should have been quite glad to have stood there and seen the buses and trams shine past for quite a long time.

VE Day finally came a week after Hitler's suicide. On 2 May German forces in Italy surrendered, followed two days later by their surrender in Denmark. On 7 May the nation waited for news with great expectation, but there was a sense of anti-climax when it was announced that Winston Churchill would not be broadcasting until 8 May, which would be Victory in Europe Day. The Board of Trade did its bit to uplift the nation:

> Until the end of May you may buy cotton bunting without coupons, as long as it is red, white or blue and does not cost more than one and three a square yard.

Crowds poured into Trafalgar Square and Whitehall on 8 May in anticipation of Churchill's 3 o'clock broadcast announcing the unconditional German surrender. Present in Palace Yard was the MP and former diplomat Harold Nicolson, who recorded in his diary:

> I decided to remain there and hear Winston's speech which was to be relayed through loudspeakers. As Big Ben struck three, there was an extraordinary hush over the assembled multitude, and then came Winston's speech. He was short and effective, merely announcing that unconditional surrender had been signed, and naming the signatories.

The Prime Minister then went to the House of Commons and repeated the news to a packed House. After a meeting with the King, Churchill and the War Cabinet appeared on a balcony overlooking Parliament Square to loud and enthusiastic applause.

Elsewhere in the country people celebrated VE Day with thanksgiving services, street parties and bonfires, as one observer in Bourneville noted:

> At the end of Old Barn Road there was a party round a bonfire in the road, with the women dressed up in fancy clothes, mainly red, white and blue, and plenty of dancing. There was a piano in the road, and a barrel of beer.

Another reported from Sanderstead:

As it was getting dark, I saw through my bedroom window the glow of bonfires . . . the bonfires were a focal point for sightseers and around one big fire children and youths were dancing in a wide circle and singing songs.

A Cardiff woman gave an account of the celebrations:

We gathered together on our bomb site and planned the finest party the children ever remembered. Neighbours pooled their sweet rations, and collected money, a few shillings from each family . . . and our grocer gave his entire stock of sweets, fruit, jellies etc. All the men in the neighbourhood spent the day clearing the sites. The church lent the tables, the milkman lent a cart for a platform and we lent our radiogram and records for the music. We all took our garden chairs for the elderly to sit on . . . Black-out curtains came down to make fancy dresses for the children.

Victory was sweetest for the long-suffering inhabitants of the Channel Islands, who were not liberated from German occupation until May 1945. Over 2,000 islanders were deported during the occupation, although some were allowed to return. In addition, between 70 and 100 islanders served sentences in Nazi prisons and concentration camps and at least 20 died in captivity. Many were imprisoned for offences such as listening to illegal radio sets.

Shadows were cast on the rejoicing in Britain by the horrific newsreels of conditions in concentration camps such as Buchenwald, Belsen and Dachau, which left a permanent impression on those who saw them. Members of a British parliamentary delegation to Buchenwald also publicised their findings widely in the media, adding to the sense of shock, incomprehension and bewilderment aroused by the atrocities.

Shortly after victory had been declared in Europe, the wartime coalition broke up; a general election took place on 5 July. The main issues were social reform and a desire for an end to the mass unemployment of the 1930s. Although the coalition had concentrated its efforts on winning the war, lively political debate took place throughout the period on issues like social security, housing and health, the public giving a massive endorsement to the 1943 Beveridge Report, which called for a remodelled social welfare system and a free health service. Pressure groups and think tanks produced blueprints on issues like town and country planning. The coalition government had recognised the need for change; the Butler Act of 1944 made major changes in the education system by guaranteeing secondary education for all. A government White Paper also accepted the principle of a comprehensive health service for everyone.

The 1945 election result surprised most observers, given Churchill's popularity in the war years, a feeling encapsulated by the Conservative party slogan 'Help Him Finish The Job'. The Labour party won nearly two-thirds of the Commons seats and formed the first majority government in its history under the leadership of Clement Attlee. Public opinion polling was then in its infancy compared with later general election campaigns and little attention was paid to it by the media. Yet the percentage of votes cast for the various parties closely mirrored the final Gallup poll taken before election day.

Although the war had finished in Europe, British, Australian, New Zealand and American soldiers were still fighting the Japanese in the Far East and the Pacific. At the July Potsdam Conference between Britain, the United States and the Soviet Union, the latter agreed to enter the war against Japan. A joint British–US statement demanded the unconditional surrender of Japan, whose cities were subject to massive air attacks.

The war with Japan ended in August, after intervention by the Soviet Union and the dropping of atomic bombs on Hiroshima and Nagasaki by the US air force. The massive civilian casualties caused by the atomic bomb led to serious debates about the morality of its use. Supporters of the bomb's use claimed that it had shortened the war by avoiding the need for an Allied invasion of Japan, while opponents maintained that the nature of the destruction caused by a single bomb was unacceptable.

Victory over Japan was celebrated throughout Britain on 15 August, which was proclaimed a public holiday. The State opening of the new Parliament took place on the same day, MPs voting an address of thanks to the King on the ending of the Japanese war. Later in the day the King, the Queen, Princess Elizabeth and Princess Margaret

appeared on the balcony of Buckingham Palace before the crowds. Elsewhere the scenes of VE Day were repeated, with dancing and bonfires, although feelings were mixed, as an observer in Leicester noted:

> Joy that the slaughter is over, hope that this may be a new era, but doubts and fears as to whether man is equal to the task which lies ahead.

Further Reading

Of the many books published about the experience of World War II in Britain, the following are particularly illuminating and informative:

Addison, Paul. *The Road to 1945*. Pimlico, 1994.

Belsey, James and Reid, Helen. *West at War*. Redcliffe, 1990.

Calder, Angus. *The People's War*. Pimlico, 1992.

Hawkins, Desmond. *War Report: D-Day to VE-Day*. BBC, 1994.

Kee, Robert. *1945: The World We Fought For*. Sphere Books, 1986.

King, Peter. *The Channel Islands War 1940–1945*. Robert Hale, 1991.

Last, Nella. *Nella Last's War*. Sphere Books, 1983.

Longmate, Norman. *How We Lived Then*. Arrow Books, 1977.

Nicolson, Nigel (ed.). *Harold Nicolson: Diaries and Letters 1939–1945*. Fontana Books, 1970.

Sheridan, Dorothy (ed.). *Wartime Women*. Mandarin, 1991.

JANUARY
1945

FARTHINGS AND COINS FOR THE RED CROSS

Sir,—The amount of farthings collected in Ripon now totals 12,698. The Cathedral Infants' School, per Miss Kay, 5,204; the Cathedral Girls' School, per Miss Marston, 3,100; other sources 4,394. £130 has been sent to the Chairman of the fund in London. This amount has been made up from 71,262 farthings from Bradford, together with Ripon's collection and the proceeds from the broken and unwanted silver, together with gifts of money. I should like to take this opportunity of thanking all those who have so kindly helped with this collection.

All coins, farthings and broken and unwanted silver can be left at Messrs. Gowland and Young, North Street, Ripon.—Yours,
  HUGH TOLSON.
2, Trinity Close, Ripon.
January 15, 1945.

Ripon Gazette

Comdr. Bower, the Tory M.P., denounced in House of Lords

COMMANDER R. T. BOWER, the Tory M.P. for Cleveland, who recently made a violent attack on Russia, was denounced as "reactionary and irresponsible" in the House of Lords yesterday.

Viscount Samuel, the Liberal leader, said protests should be made against the action of this "little known M.P."

"I sincerely trust," he added, "that our friends in Russia will realise the complete unimportance of that speaker, who is known, I think, only for his prominence as one of the most reactionary and irresponsible of our M.P.s."

Daily Mirror

Commander Bower's speech made on January 10 has already been criticised sharply by the Soviet paper *Pravda*.

He spoke of the Soviet Union "stabbing Poland in the back," and "cynically betraying" the people of Warsaw.

Lord Templewood (formerly Sir Samuel Hoare) said that nothing could be more magnificent than the achievements of our Russian Allies, but he was somewhat disturbed about the recent political developments.

One by one the difficult issues of Europe are being shattered, for the most part piecemeal, unilaterally and without the consultation or the full approval of the populations concerned."

He added that the time had come for the Allies to have a programme for the liberated areas.

Lord Cranborne, the Government spokesman, had a sugar-coated pill for the Press when he spoke about the Greek situation.

"I believe we owe a deep debt of gratitude to the Press for the courage and restraint shown, and the British Press stands high in reputation

Plenty of Eggs for the children's supper

What shall I make for the children's supper is a question many housewives ask. Let dried eggs solve the problem. They're easy to digest — even at bedtime — and a nourishing egg dish can be made in a matter of minutes. Why not let the children make their own pancakes, or scramble? Modern children like to know how to cook modern food, and the golden powder in the brown packet, the greatest food discovery of the war, is modern food indeed — easy to *get*, easy to *cook* and easy on the *purse* as well.

SAVOURY PANCAKES

Ingredients : 4 oz. flour, a little salt, 1 level tablespoon dried egg (dry), ½ pint milk and 2 tablespoons water (or milk and water to this amount). Chopped bacon, or any savoury filling.

Method : Mix dry ingredients then add sufficient liquid to make a stiff batter. Beat well, then add the rest of liquid and beat again. Cook each pancake in a little hot fat, browning it on both sides. Put savoury filling in centre, roll up and put on a hot plate.

Woman's Journal

NEW TOWNS

MILLIONS of people whose homes are on the outskirts of large cities but whose employment is close in to the centre travel at least twenty miles a day, a costly business in time, energy and money.

Many put up with daily travel simply to avoid the heavy expense of central rents, and in order to have a garden and wider home life than a flat offers. Is there any way of having these privileges without paying for them by laborious travel? The people who have just worked out a new plan for developing Greater London think they have a better alternative to offer.

Their plan is to develop eight or ten self-contained small towns in a ring outside London. Each town would have about sixty thousand inhabitants and be self-contained—that is, have its own factories, shops and places of entertainment. But these would not be isolated communities; by road, rail and air they would be linked with London and the whole country.

The scheme is attractive in many ways. It stops the ugly sprawl of Outer London; it preserves open country round the great city and between the new towns; it encourages people to work and live without long hours of travel.

But will people want to move out of the cities and put their heart and energy into these new towns? The indication is that they will. Between the wars over half a million people drifted away to the outer suburbs of London; it is reckoned that hundreds of thousands more would follow if the new towns offer good homes, good jobs, accessible country—and quick, easy access to London for pleasure.

This is not only London's problem—Glasgow and Manchester have it too. And other great cities are heading in the same direction.

The Editor

Woman

Hurrah for Spa

—it's a *wonderful toothbrush*
NYLON OR BRISTLE

JOHN FREEMAN & Co., Ltd.,
Spa Brush Works, Chesham, Bucks.

WHAT WOMEN ARE DOING AND SAYING

FAMOUS novelist *Daphne du Maurier* finds that bringing up her family of three and writing novels leaves her with very little time on her hands. In the photo above, taken at her home in Cornwall, you see her helping *Flavia* and *Tessa* with their lessons while *Christian* looks on. Daphne du Maurier is married to *Lt. General Browning*, of Arnhem fame, Chief of Staff at SEAC H.Q.

"YOUNG couples ought to have house priority. If they don't get a good start they don't get a good finish." *Mrs. Evelyn Hill*, of Didsbury, member of Manchester City Council, county borough organiser of W.V.S., housing and reconstruction authority, one of busiest workers in north.

BRITISH post-war air lines will have uniformed hostesses, long popular in U.S.A. First here is *Miss Millicent Curran*, of Liverpool, ex-Y.W.C.A. worker. But for present hostesses will work only at air ports, on motor coaches between them and railway Air Services H.Q.

CAN you think of a more adventurous job than doing intelligence work among Assam tribes in Burma frontier jungle? *Miss Ursula Graham-Bower*, of S. Kensington, London, has done that for 5 years, organizing scouts, questioning captured spies, suppressing looting, supervising arms training, tending wounded. Has native Naga bodyguard; is becoming known as woman "Lawrence" of Assam.

WHAT girl does not dream of getting a leading film part with £20,000 contract? That stroke of fortune has come to *Jill Evans*, discovered by Sidney Box in Llandrindod Wells repertory, given star role in *Acacia Avenue*.

JILL, 17, hails from Bournville, went to Edgbaston College, Birmingham, took part in school shows from age 7, studied at London School of Dramatic Art, Webber Douglas School, joined Llandrindod company at 16; was playing there in *Murder Without Crime* when Sidney Box invited her to London for screen test. One more triumph for ambitious young actresses who do not shirk hard work of "rep."

Woman's Own

Did you MACLEAN your teeth to-day?

M P   M P

Yes, they're like 'Snowdrops'

Macleans Tooth Paste—one size during war, 1/1 tube

Honours for Workers

The second part of the New Year Honours List, published to-day, epitomises the story of the work of millions of civilians whose toil helped make " D " Day possible. In the forefront of those who receive awards are the men who controlled and organised work at the ports and the railways leading to them. Of the twenty-two million men and women mobilised for war work, more than a thousand are singled out for honours in this list. There are two hundred awards of the O.B.E., of which eighteen go to women; 371 become M.B.E.s, including seventy-seven women; and fifty-nine women also are included in the list of 489 persons who receive the British Empire Medal. One of the recipients of the B.E.M. is Mrs. Kay Summersby, driver to the Supreme Commander of the A.E.F., the only British woman to hold a U.S. Army commission and still retain her British citizenship. An M.B.E. is awarded to Miss Eily Tolley, who is described in the Gazette as " the principal trainer of women crews for canal boats." She had never handled a boat until 1941, and at present is pursuing her patriotic endeavours on a canal somewhere between London and Birmingham. Men and women in all branches of the munitions industries have been chosen for honours. A Lancashire cotton worker, a woman aged eighty-four, with seventy-one years service in the industry, receives the B.E.M. for doing her " bit "; and Alfred Porter, who has been a rope worker in the Midlands for sixty-five years, is similarly honoured. Thus the men and women who have striven on the Home Front receive recognition. It is good that they are named for signal service; better still to recognise they are, so to say, " samples."

Birmingham Post

Coffin lids charge

William Hirstwood (49), joiner and undertaker, and Paul Bowman (59), furnaceman at a crematorium, were remanded on bail at Darlington yesterday, charged jointly with the larceny of ten coffin lids from the Darlington crematorium, and with conspiracy to steal other coffin lids.

News Chronicle

DEAR LEONORA EYLES,

"We have been happily married for a number of years and have a little girl. For a year now my husband has been getting good money, after years of struggle, but he has taken to drinking and going about with another woman whose husband is fighting overseas. It is making me desperate and I keep on nagging at the child, though I know I shouldn't. Ought I to leave him and take her with me and try to be happy?"

I DON'T think you would be happy, my dear. No doubt his folly will pass in time, when the husband comes back; also he may not go on earning such big wages much longer. You must try to be patient; get out more and see friends, and go to the cinema with your little girl. And do try to pull yourself together where she is concerned; it is terribly unjust to make her suffer for her father's fault, isn't it? I should have thought your present loneliness and unhappiness would make you love her all the more.

WON'T BE ALONE

"Early in the war I married a foreigner, and we are very happy together. But now the time is coming when he is planning to take me back to his country, and I am appalled at the prospect of leaving everything I know and starting in a strange country where they don't even speak my language. Please help me."

THIS is a problem a great many girls have to face. First, you are not starting alone—you are with the man you chose to spend your life with—and he, and all his friends in his own country, will try to make things easy for you. Secondly, I think you would be very well advised to make an earnest effort to learn his language; you can't get on without talking. And, thirdly, remember that communications after the war will gradually become much easier—you may be able to get home for holidays as easily as, before the war, you could get to the North of England from London.

TERRIBLE MISFORTUNE

"I am eighteen and have a problem which is ruining my life. I have a squint and have to wear glasses; sometimes I think I would rather risk my sight than wear them, though I know how silly that is. The doctor says I can get my squint cured by an operation, and Mother and I have begged and pleaded, but Father won't give his consent. I can't tell you how miserable I am."

IT is incredible that your father won't consent. A squint is always a misfortune to any girl, and I do urge you to get the doctor to talk to your father. If this does not convince him, the only thing you can do is to wait till you are twenty-one and then

LEONORA EYLES' address is c/o "Woman's Own," Tower House, Southampton Street, London, W.C.2. A stamped, addressed envelope ensures a postal reply, but please do not be impatient if you have to wait a few days for an answer. Mrs. Eyles' postbag is heavy, and a little delay is often inevitable. Please note that problems about war service jobs and careers are dealt with by Victoria Stevenson. (See pages 9-10.)

have it done, or if it is the cost that troubles your father, ask the doctor if you cannot be a free patient.

LIKES DISCIPLINE

"I loved being in the W.A.A.F.s. It was the kind of life I adored, and now I have had to leave and come back home to live I am thoroughly unhappy. I have not been awfully well and am now better, but I won't be able to join up again. But I hate having to make up my own mind about things; I like having someone tell me to do them."

THAT was the reason you liked being in a disciplined life where all your time was arranged. You must learn to stand on your own feet and make up your mind for yourself, my dear, or how will you ever be able to take a good place in the brave new world? Don't be afraid of your own decisions; you are capable of arranging your life for yourself.

SIMPLE PROBLEM

"Some of us were talking and we decided to write to you. We have all got very happy and friendly together during the war, we share the same copy of "Woman's Own," and once a week meet and talk about the things that turn up and worry us. There are five of us, and three will, after the war, have husbands back and homes running as normal. We are very happy at the prospect, naturally, but all three of us are worried about the same thing. We are all in our thirties, and we don't want to start a new family—our children are now at school-going age, and we feel we've done our bit. Can you advise us about this?"

THIS seems a problem that worries lots of women, and yet it is one of the simplest in the world to solve. Send me a stamped addressed envelope, and I will advise you. I think your idea of meeting together once a week is excellent; so often one person has some nagging little worry or problem that another person can solve as soon as it is mentioned.

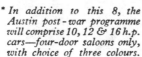
Correspondence

HUNS IN PALACE -ROAD

Sir,—It was with very deep disgust that at approximately 4 p.m. on Sunday, I observed three Huns walking down Palace Road in company with an unarmed British soldier. Yes, I said un-armed. Surely it has come to a queer pass that such a state of affairs should be allowed to exist, and to make matters worse the Huns were "camouflaged" with a Red Cross armlet. Maybe the war is over? That our enemies are allowed such latitude, one would think so, when one sees how the Italians have just about taken possession of "ye ancient cittie." It makes me terribly afraid that all this "ca ne fait rien" attitude is going to lead to a repetition of the years following 1914-1918.

Is there no one with enough guts, to clamp down on these specimens of barbarity, with the big stick and enough barbed wire and pad-locks to stop their meanderings.—Yours,

INCREDIBILIS.

Ripon Gazette

★★ BACK TO REAL LIFE

NORAH C. JAMES gives you another lively point of view on a subject which affects most women

WHAT will be the most important among all the post-war problems for women? I think the central one will be the reinstatement of the home as a family unit. The home and the family have always been an essential part of our life and no war can alter that fact.

What has happened to the average home since 1939? Chiefly, its dispersal. When peace comes that dispersal will not cease because the bells of victory ring out. It goes far deeper than the mere physical return of the family.

It seems to me most essential that women should prepare themselves now for the future. For the members of the family coming home will not be quite the same as those who went away. A husband, a son or daughter, who has been away for anything up to five years will, inevitably, have changed a little.

Women must be prepared to readjust their outlook. They are going to meet husbands who, before they went away, led quiet, regular lives. Since then they have faced the dangers of the battlefield, and passed through experiences so gigantic that they are bound to have left their mark on them.

It may well be, too, that there is a change in the women themselves which they must learn how to control. Quite possibly, they have become more independent since their husbands went away. They have had to shoulder responsibilities that would not have been theirs in normal times. Some women may even have learned to enjoy the independence of salaries of their own. Giving these up may not be too easy.

Spectators Only?

All these adjustments will need courage and the realization that life alters constantly. But change and development are the very salt of life; if that were not so, the world would never make any progress at all. All of us have had new experiences, pleasant and otherwise, that have changed us a little from the people we were in 1939. I think that, at first, these changes may not be apparent. Getting into civilian clothes, taking up peace-time jobs, etc., will obscure them. But in a little while they will begin to show, either in a divergence of interests, or in an apathy that will be hard to combat. It is at this point that the wise wife or mother will squarely face the problem and overcome it.

She should remember that, when peace has had time to make good the most glaring ravages of war, homes will be far easier to run than before. The labour saving devices we are promised will substantially reduce the burden of housekeeping, so that we shall all have more leisure.

Now leisure is a very precious thing, hard to get and easy to waste. The war has not helped to teach people to use it—rather the reverse : everyone has had more than enough work to fill their days.

The wise woman must know how to develop the faculties for leisure in her family. She must encourage them to pursue any hobbies they have, and bear with the enthusiasms of the amateur. I feel very strongly that it is better for people to *do* things themselves rather than remain the spectators of other people's activities.

Hobbies and Horse-racing

It is far wiser to view with a lenient eye the wood shavings and saw-dust of the experimenting carpenter, and to ignore the smells caused by the budding scientist, than to encourage the study of race-horse form or too great an interest in football pools. Sport is a fine way of spending leisure, but let it be a sport in which the enthusiast can participate rather than just watch.

There is so much to interest people these days. Such pursuits as reading literature, the study of local government, gardening, amateur theatricals and so on, are far more creative than feverish attendance at the cinema. They teach the genuine pleasures of leisure, whereas the latter is merely a way of avoiding the boredom which comes from not knowing how to use leisure.

I think that one of the things which probably does more to unite a family than anything else is a common interest. One of the happiest families I ever knew were all keen supporters of the same political party. Another family loved the open air, and planned their walking-tour holiday during the winter evenings. It is obviously not possible for all families—particularly large families—to like the same things, but when an interest is shared by more than one, the intelligent mother will endeavour to encourage and take part in it.

One thing war has done for many people is to give them a far wider social consciousness. They have learned that England cannot exist alone, that the world is made up of very many more countries than they realized before. They have learned, too, the narrowness of their old point of view. The vision they have achieved out of the pain and hurt of war can be one of the most valuable factors in the re-building of post-war England.

I am certain that, for those who have understood the comradeship of a community life, it is essential, if the family is to retain its importance—and it must—that a new community life must be developed from the family unit.

That is woman's main task in the reconstruction of life after the war. She will be the main-spring of a new and better way of living.

Woman's Own

vogue

JANUARY 1945

ANNUS MIRABILIS

ANNUS MIRABILIS, the wonderful year—this is what 1945 may be to Europe; the year of delivery, the year of peace. That earlier "Annus Mirabilis" celebrated by Dryden, was dedicated to the city of London, in terms which have a startling contemporary ring. . . .

". . . that City, which has set a pattern to all others of true Loyalty, invincible Courage and unshaken Constancy. Other Cities have been prais'd for the same Virtues, but . . . their Fame has been won them by cheaper trials than an expensive, though necessary, War, a consuming Pestilence, and a more consuming Fire . . . To you therefore this *Year of Wonders* is justly dedicated, because you have made it so. You, who are to stand a wonder to all Years and Ages; and, who have built yourselves an Immortal Monument on your own Ruins. You are now a *Phoenix* in her ashes. . . ."

In this, London may well stand representative of the cities of Europe, sisters-in-arms. Her trial has been long as theirs has been sharp. Warsaw and Rotterdam, their physical features obliterated, the spirit imperishable; Athens and Paris—twin stars, the one of ancient, the other of modern civilisation—their bodies little harmed, the blows struck deep at the heart within. These cities believe that before the year has run its course, they will again have taken wing from their ashes; and that to their dearly purchased freedoms may be added those of cities where, at last, Hope dares to raise her voice. . . .

There'll come a time...

when once again in a peaceful world a generous fire burns brightly in the grate. What a welcome there is in the quiet of this pleasant room. How cheerfully that old copper kettle gleams in the flickering firelight; so brightly — thanks to Brasso — that it almost seems as if the kettle itself were aflame.

BRASSO

Brasso brings brightness wherever it goes

C4

AN ESSENTIAL OF WARTIME DIET

Stored in this tiny capsule are two vitamins without which it is impossible to maintain health. They are 'protective' vitamin A and 'sunshine' vitamin D and, unfortunately, they are not always readily obtainable in a wartime diet. A daily dose of Crookes' Halibut Oil— one of the richest natural sources of these vitamins— will build up your resistance and stamina and prove of inestimable value during this sixth winter of war.

CROOKES' HALIBUT OIL

OBTAINABLE ONLY FROM CHEMISTS

Isle of Man Examiner

Melting Pot

MAY CLAPHAM OUT EAST

There must be hundreds of Island residents with the happiest recollections of May Clapham, talented pianist with "The Gay Dogs" in Douglas for many years.

Well, Miss Clapham—"Our May" to her many Manx friends—has lately been doing a grand job in entertaining "the boys" in the Middle East, and we are obliged to Mrs. Kane, of the Howstrake Hotel, for letting us see the latest air-mail letter card from this clever artiste.

Writing from G.H.Q. Mediterranean Expeditionary Force on December 12th, Miss Clapham said: "I am so glad I made the decision to leave Town for a while. I am having such a very interesting time. Have been to Cyrenaica, from Tobruk to Marble Arch.

"The tour took me through the battlefields — El Alamein, Tobruk, Benghazi, Agidabia, Marble Arch, and lots of other places in between. The roads were shocking, having been bombed and shelled to smithereens.

"I flew back from Marble Arch to Cairo, 750 miles non-stop, my first flight and I loved every minute of it. Since then I've flown 11,500 miles —Cairo to Khartoum and right through to the Sudan.

"The natives wear marvellous headdresses, and carry spears and knives, but have never heard of clothes. I've got some interesting snaps!

"When flying to Juba, we flew low over the African jungle, looking at giraffes, elephants and hippos. I love flying, and am really nervous of the traffic in Cairo.

"From the Sudan I went to Eritrea and after living and working with an average temperature of 110 degrees, it was a treat to sleep under blankets. From Eritrea we went right into intense heat again— Massawa and then to Aden.

"From Aden right across the Arabian coast and played at all the outposts in Saudi Arabia; back to Aden and from there to the Persian Gulf as far as Baghdad. Flying every day and working every night left very little time to see each place. At Salallah I got up at 6-30 a.m., went to the coconut groves, which were most interesting. I saw about twenty porpoises right in on the beach. Had breakfast at 8-15 and took off to another place at 9 o'clock armed with a dozen fresh coconuts.

"I am now in Cairo, and will be here until after Christmas—just going into the wards of hospitals with a little piano and three other artistes to give the wounded 'a smile and a song.' It's a nice job of work and I find the boys enjoy talking to an English woman.

"I've flown over the Red Sea, the Arabian Sea and the Gulf of Aden to a remote little island in the Indian Ocean, so have certainly covered some ground."

Good work, May—and don't forget to fly to the Isle of Man at your first opportunity. We'll all be delighted to see—and hear—you again!

* * *

WHEN YOUR MAN IS BACK AGAIN

Ways are being discussed now to make his return to civilian life as easy as possible

I HAVE received many letters from you about setting up in small businesses of your own, and they all have a point of view in common. You realize that you and your husband will have to go through a period of adjustment once more. You have both been through it before! You have readjusted yourself to running your home alone; he has adjusted himself to Service life.

You both feel that in a business of your own your second readjustment will be easier. He can work at his own speed, in his own time, and if he wants a day off *you* can carry on!

Similar problems will arise if your husband goes back to factory life, and wives as well as their serving husbands will be interested in a leaflet I have been reading. It is based on a lecture given by an Army welfare officer who gives his personal view of how the soldier should be treated in "big business" when he returns to it.

It is suggested, for instance, that a light rein should be given at first, and time off in the early days might stave off a complete breakdown. Given time, your soldier-husband will get back to the regular routine and not miss the "spells of very rapid and strenuous activity" which fall to the lot of every soldier.

It suggests that the additional skill your husband will bring back with him should be used. It points out the differences between the discipline in the Army and the discipline in a factory. It contains lots of interesting advice to foremen and works managers who have not been in uniform.

The Army team spirit is mentioned —the team spirit that makes five soldiers do the work of fifty. Can this be harnessed? It suggests that the great personal interest Field-Marshal Montgomery takes in all his men should be copied in "big business."

Army life gives very real comradeship which will be missed unless it is replaced in the factory by the formation of clubs and educational facilities.

Starting Again

Lastly, your problems as a wife have not been forgotten. It is pointed out that you will have to find a home, and buy furniture with the small savings from your husband's pay. He may have to buy tools to help him in his job. Lost relatives will have to be traced.

Settlements for air raid damage will have to be arranged, and permits obtained for all sorts of things. Firms may decide to deal with these problems or hand them over to a social service organization, but they have to be solved.

It is encouraging to wives and wives-to-be to know that the problems are being aired and discussed now when there is time for experiment before the thousands of men come marching home.

Write to Joan Lambert about your job and post-war plans

Woman

FILMS IN BIRMINGHAM

BREAD AND CIRCUSES

The average American Technicolor musical film is at once a wonder and a warning. It indicates both the possibilities of the screen, should it ever get into the hands of artists, and the perversities that result when it does not. "Bathing Beauty," in its second week at the Forum, is a case in point. This film must have cost a million dollars. Photographically it is superb. The ingenuity with which its many spectacles are contrived is astonishing. The time, labour and material that must have gone to its assembly indicate a priority amazing in a world engaged in total war. Yet, with all its resources, "Bathing Beauty" offers nothing more than pleasant waftage.

The story round which this expensive pageant rotates is childish: it follows the puerile courtship of Esther Williams by Red Skelton. About four times every hour the film pauses to stage a spectacle that has nothing to do with the story, a spectacle that is just a little too lavish and too expensive to be in good taste. The opulence of what we see and the poverty of what we hear are in startling contradiction: and this preponderance of material resource over mental provision induces long thoughts that lead to disturbing conclusions. Again and again one has agreed that a war-weary world needs its spells of easy enchantment, but the persistence with which the vapid and the trivial are decked out in plumes that should be reserved for the witty and the intelligent leads one to wonder whether Juvenal's tag about bread and circuses may not be tied as fittingly to the twentieth century as it was to the first.

Much more hopeful is the outlook indicated in "The Great Moment," at the Futurist. Preston Sturges is a director with a mind of his own; a mind which realises that there is a place for slapstick and a place for wit, and that nothing is gained and much lost by confusing the two. His use of humour to lighten the history of Dr. Morton, discoverer of Lethon, is both discerning and in character. He realises that the story of the discovery of anæsthetics must occasionally skirt painful incident if the narrative is to capture its native hue and not bask in the borrowed glow of Technicolor. The wit is sharp and salty, and the acting of Joel McCrea, as Morton, the dentist, is both faithful and brisk. All this is not to say that films about painless tooth extraction are to be preferred to, or are inherently better than, pictures about bathing beauties; but rather that, be the film heavy or light, there are rules of construction, that there should be artistic integrity even in a Technicolor musical, and that the present attempts at films which "have everything" will lead ultimately to pictures that have nothing.

T.C.K.

Birmingham Post

GOVERNOR EXONERATED

Did Not Go Back On His Word

TYNWALD REVEALS INFORMATION WITHHELD FROM KEYS

LAND ARMY CONSCRIPTION TO CONTINUE

TYNWALD on Tuesday rejected Mr. E. W. Fargher's long-standing resolution that no more women be conscripted for the Land Army.

A feature of the debate, which lasted about three hours, was the revelation that the War Committee was fully acquainted with the manner in which the Reserved List was being administered with the result that His Excellency the Lieut.-Governor was fully exonerated from the charge levelled against him in the Keys last week that he had "gone back on his word."

"It is a grave matter," said the Attorney-General in the course of the debate, "to make such a charge against the King's Representative," and later in the discussion, Mr. Gerald Bridson, who made the allegation in the Lower House, said that from the information presented to the Keys, he thought His Excellency had gone back on his bargain, but His Excellency had suffered a raw deal owing to the lack of information.

"This policy of secrecy," continued Mr. Bridson, "is absurd and unnecessary, and why the Keys' members of the War Committee remain quiet when charges are being made against His Excellency, passes my understanding."

The Attorney-General said he was glad the hon. member had exonerated His Excellency, "and in doing so, he has also exonerated the Secretary of the House and myself."

This remark, which was challenged by Mr. Fargher, had reference to a suggestion in the Keys that the Attorney-General and the Secretary (in his capacity of High Bailiff) had taken leading parts in the prosecution of Land Army defaulters who, in the nature of their occupations, were presumed to be within the Reserved List.

Isle of Man Examiner

Woman killed by tyre burst

The bursting of the tyre of a motor lorry led to the death of Mrs. Ruth Soloman (50), wife of an Army major, on Chelsea Embankment yesterday.

The burst caused the steel rim of the wheel to become detached. It rolled across the road and struck Mrs. Soloman on the head.

News Chronicle

Mr. Rank's purchase

Mr. J. A. Rank has bought the Denham film printing laboratories, built by Sir Alexander Korda. The price has not been disclosed.

News Chronicle

"How soon are they getting married?"
"Well—she's got her icing-sugar."

Punch

CHEERED AFTER 12-GOAL DEFEAT

By FRANK COLES

The attraction of Cup-tie football was again shown on Saturday when the second qualifying ties of the League Cup, a war-time competition, were played. Thirty thousand spectators watched Sunderland beat Newcastle 4—3 at Roker Park; 20,000 saw the battle of the two Sheffield teams—United and Wednesday; and 13,000 enjoyed the goal riot staged by Liverpool against Southport.

Liverpool's 12—1 victory was the biggest this season. At the end of it, Southport's 19-year-old goal-keeper, Birkett, collapsed from sheer exhaustion and was carried off unconscious.

He did not hear the big cheer which the crowd accorded him—not out of sympathy but for a really valiant display. He saved at least as many potential goals as were scored.

West Ham did well to beat Queen's Park Rangers in League South, for early in the game they lost Jones, Welsh international left-back, with a dislocated shoulder.

Though they only gained one point at Portsmouth, Tottenham Hotspur continue in the lead, with Chelsea, with two games in hand, in a strong challenging position.

Daily Telegraph

TO-DAY'S THE WEDDING DAY (writes the Stroller) of actress and actor Sheila Sim and Richard Attenborough, stars of the R.A.F. film "Journey Together." She was in the film "A Canterbury Tale" and he was in the play "Brighton Rock" and the film "In Which We Serve."

Evening News

Wants court to STOP wife working

A Nottingham husband went to complain about his wife at a local matrimonial court yesterday. He said:

"She gets up at 7.30 a.m. and from that hour until sometimes two o'clock in the morning she is working all the time. I am getting thin and so is she. There are 13 people in the house, including two other women, and my wife does all the work."

"I love work," said the wife.

The Chairman: "Not many men complain that their wives do too much housework."

The husband is 19 and the wife 20, and the magistrates adjourned the case for a month for the probation officer to intervene.

News Chronicle

LADY CAROLYN HOWARD

—charming daughter of the Earl of Carlisle, was a driver with the A.T.S. until recently. She always uses Pond's preparations. She writes: 'I'm like a miser with my Pond's now. No unnamed concoctions for my skin !'

To Relieve Housing Shortage

Nissen Huts As Dwellings

Nissen huts may be converted into dwellings to relieve the housing shortage.

A circular issued by the Ministry of Health and Local Government to local authorities stating that permission to utilise huts no longer required for Service and other departments will be granted.

It is pointed out that while Nissen huts do not provide a high standard of comfort or amenity, the concession, being by way of giving temporary housing accommodation, is made in response to the wishes of many local bodies.

It is also stated the Ministry is advised that it is unlikely to be an economic proposition to remove huts of the Nissen type for re-erection on another site, and that schemes under the provisions of the circular should, save in exceptional circumstances, be confined to existing camp sites.

Among the general conditions laid down in the circular is that the land upon which huts stand should be of a type and in a location suitable for permanent housing, and that local authorities must undertake to acquire the land for housing purposes.

The Ministry will allow Councils the use of the huts and services free of charge, the Councils to be responsible only for the annual requisitioning compensation for the land and the cost of adapting and maintaining the huts during the continuance of the arrangements. Rents will be received by the Councils.

Small-scale adaptation schemes in Lisburn and Carrickfergus can be inspected by arrangement with the respective town clerks.

It is learned that there are few huts inside Belfast boundary. The circular will come before the Corporation Estates Committee to-day.

Irish News

LADY CAROLYN HOWARD IS FINED 1s.

'She's Been Good' Report

When Lady Carolyn B. D. Howard, of Tite-street, Chelsea, 25-year-old daughter of the Earl of Carlisle, appeared on remand at Bow-street to-day she was fined 1s. for breach of recognisances.

The superintendent of the remand home, from which she is said to have absconded when sent there after being put on probation on a drunkenness charge, said in a report to-day : " I have nothing but good to report about Lady Carolyn since she returned to us three weeks ago."

The magistrate (Mr. McKenna) said that it was most satisfactory to have such a good report and suggested she should return to the home until they thought she was fit to go out to a job.

Lady Carolyn : Thank you. I will.

Evening News

ROSITA FORBES speaking from U.S.A.

I SOMETIMES think that lots of Hollywood films show a very strange sort of America to the outside world ! Would you ever have guessed, from seeing American films, that in the country, at least, very few people are afraid of being old-fashioned in family life? And in this village, typical of many, in which I am now staying, most people go to church as a matter of course.

I was interested in the family aspect of the congregation. There were good-looking young couples, very rich some of them, not at all rich others, with the usual American family of two. There were middle-aged husbands and wives with sons in uniform or married daughters. There were plenty of young men from a neighbouring camp. Church seems to me a regular habit with heaps of American families; and families appear to be much more together than in certain sections of modern Britain.

Easier for America

Of course, the war has broken up a great many British homes and disrupted family life to an extent undreamed-of in America. There is the destruction caused by bombing; the fact that in Britain we go where our jobs send us. But, long before the war, it seems to me that family life was, in some cases, getting a bit frayed. Lots of us went off on our separate businesses, using home

The best of all American habits is one Britain might well copy

as no more than a springboard. We prided ourselves on being individuals, owing more to ourselves than to anyone else. So, I think, we brought considerable loneliness and disappointment to our parents, besides laying up a store of discomfort for ourselves.

Families are Important

In America, sons and daughters do come back home a great deal. Birthdays, Christmas, Mother's Day—all are regularly remembered by gifts.

A family is a good, sound buffer, it seems to me, between oneself and a lot of unnecessary hurts. Of course, if you haven't taken any trouble about your own people for months or years, you have no right to expect much of them. But why be careless with the two biggest assets in your counting-house of life—your family and your church?

Faith is never old-fashioned. Nor is love. These are eternal and universal in their different forms. On what we make of these, our characters are based. As Britain stood after Dunkirk, for what she believed and how she lived, so we must stand, if we are worth anything at all, holding fast to family and church.

Woman's Own

WHITER BREAD

" When the bran is extracted from the wheat for the new whiter bread, is Vitamin B1 also removed ? "

No. Owing to quite a new process of milling, Vitamin B1 is retained in the new flour. This was recently explained by the milling expert of the Ministry of Food. Vitamin B1 is also found in breakfast cereals, pork, mutton, beef, liver, kidneys, pulse (dried beans, peas and lentils), all the cabbage family, egg yolk, boiled beetroot, fish and certain vegetable-yeast spreads.

We'll Tell You Why

Since the Ministry of Food asked us to eat more herrings, several readers have written to our WARTIME FOOD SERVICE, asking which is the correct side to open a herring for stuffing. It should be opened down the paler side, the belly

OLIVE OIL

" Shall we soon now be able to buy olive oil, since chemists no longer require a permit to obtain it ? "

It is true that chemists no longer require a permit to obtain olive oil, but there is no likelihood yet of it being available for ordinary use. All the olive oil that is being imported will still be needed for medical purposes

NEW FROZEN COD

" What, please, is the best way of boiling these new quickly frozen cod fillets ? "

Get some cooking parchment. Wet a sheet of it. Place the fillets in the centre, add a sprinkle of salt, pepper, a bay leaf, parsley and a tiny sprig of thyme. Tie up into a bundle and drop into boiling water. Boil for 20–30 minutes, according to the thickness of the fillets. The liquid in the bag will make a perfect sauce.

WHY BAKING SODA ?

" Why do so many wartime cake recipes call for both self-raising flour and bicarbonate of soda ? Is this correct ? "

Bicarbonate of soda is not advised to be used in conjunction with self-raising flour, except in recipes where golden syrup or black treacle has been introduced to replace some of the sugar normally used.

LOOK AT THE LABEL

" What advantage will there be, from the housewife's point of view, in the new labelling of packeted foods ? "

The advantage is great. It is this : she will be able to assess the value of the food in the packet and should, therefore, be in a better position than ever before to choose intelligently the food she gives her family.

CORNFLOUR AND CUSTARD POWDER

" Why is it that I can seldom get any cornflour or custard powder, in spite of the assurance that there is plenty of them about ? "

There is plenty about ! Actually, 90 per cent of the pre-war supplies of cornflour, custard powder and blancmange is available for the general public. The explanation of any shortage is simply this : more people are using these foods, because of the disappearance of other commodities from the market.

SOUPS

" I am a business woman with very little time for cooking. My husband likes soup every night in winter, but I'm finding difficulty in buying tinned soups. Is there any reason for this ? "

Indeed, there is ! Owing to the shortage of tins, production had to cease in the spring. Manufacture was resumed in June—but at only 50 per cent of the planned rate. It is unlikely that this rate will be exceeded for the time being. There is, however, a good supply of powdered soups. Why not try them ?

CHILDREN'S HEALTH

" What is there so vital in codliver oil that makes the Ministry of Food insist on children having it ? "

The Vitamin D in it enables the body to utilize calcium and phosphates which are essential to good bone structure. By giving our children their full daily allowance of codliver oil, as well as the other essentials for growth, it will be possible in one generation to eradicate dental decay in the teeth of young people, and rickets, too

USING UP

" My old parents cannot eat the crusts of bread and these do accumulate. Have you any suggestions, please ? "

Bread and milk is one of the finest nightcaps for old folks. Heat the milk. Cut the crusts into small dice and steep them in it for 5–10 minutes. They will then be very soft and of better flavour than the centre of a loaf. Pleasantly flavoured bread puddings are also good. You can make very good and nourishing forcemeat balls by browning the crusts, putting them through a mincing machine, then mixing them with herbs, sausage meat and dried egg.

RATIONS FOR ONE

" My wife and children are evacuated inland. I find it very difficult to manage on my rations. I'm an office worker but I do some A.R.P. work. Couldn't we, who live alone, be given a little more ? Catering and cooking for one is very difficult, and restaurants are so expensive."

They are. If your firm runs a canteen, that's an extra ration in itself. But, in any case, there are several British Restaurants in your district where you can get inexpensive food. Why don't you have a meal at one of them several times a week ? Canteens and British Restaurants increase the rations we receive.

Anything you don't understand about rationing ? Then write to our Wartime Food Service, The Fleetway House, London, E.C.4, enclosing a stamped, addressed economy label for our reply.

FEBRUARY
1945

HOME FROM ABROAD.

Aberystwyth Girl Arrives From Overseas.

RECALLS EXPERIENCES IN FOREIGN LANDS.

Miss Elvera Burbeck, "Courtlands," Queen's-road, Aberystwyth, an officer serving with the First Aid Nursing Yeomanry Corps, arrived home recently from abroad, after seeing service in North Africa and Italy. She is believed to be the first girl from the town to have returned from overseas.

It falls to the lot of few people to stand on the balcony floor of a Dictator's palace, but many adventures have happened to Miss Burbeck during her nine months' service overseas.

Leaving this country in May last, along with her companions she embarked for North Africa and was one of three privileged to fly part of the journey in a Mitchell bomber. "I was absolutely thrilled with the flying," said Miss Burbeck, "it was grand to see the tops of the mountains appearing through the white clouds." The coastal belt of North Africa, with its various colourings, was no less a thrilling spectacle.

In between working hours and on furlough, Miss Burbeck turned her leisure time to good effect in studying the customs of the natives and seeing places of historic significance. From May until October last year she was stationed near Algiers. In October she was posted to Italy and saw all that was possible.

The voluntary organisations, said Miss Burbeck, were doing a grand job of work, and most appreciated by the men were books and news of home.

Miss Burbeck arrived back in this country without previous intimation, except a phone call from her to her parents.

Cambrian News

Telegraphic Tips

Household tasks made easier— with Hilary's help

WRITE to me if you want any advice on your household problems. A loose, twopenny halfpenny stamp enclosed will bring my solution by post. Address your letters to Hilary, c/o "Woman's Own," Tower House, Southampton Street, London, W.C.2. Hints, written on postcards, sent to the same address stand a chance of winning the weekly prize of 10s. 6d. for the best one published.

EASIER WASHING.—When washing very dirty articles, put them through the wringer once before the final rinse, this expels the dirty water and makes the last rinse easier. Especially good, this, for heavy things that hold the water. Beetroot dropped on the tablecloth makes a bad mark, cover the stain at once with a piece of bread soaked in water and leave until it draws the colour out. Playing cards are scarce and expensive, you can clean up your old ones very easily by rubbing them lightly both sides with a rag dipped in spirits of camphor.

MAKING DO.—A good substitute for a steamer is a sandwich tin that fits your saucepan with holes punched in the bottom, and a cake tin turned upside down for a top. Don't throw out an old cretonne curtain, wash it, square it and bind with bright bias tape and use it as a breakfast cloth, matching napkins can be cut from the extra length you chopped off when squaring.

THIS WEEK'S PRIZE HINT.

Don't discard Baby's matinée coat when it gets too tight. Cut out the sleeves and open up the side seams for about an inch to make a larger armhole, bind with narrow ribbon and the little coat will make a nice woolly waistcoat to wear over a dress or under a nightie, when Baby feels the cold.— *Mrs. Mullard (Preston).*

Woman's Own

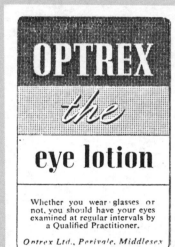

Chorus of "come home to us" offers greet refugees

By Your Special Correspondent

QUEUES of men and women stood round the railway station barriers in Coventry yesterday eagerly volunteering to take into their homes the Dutch refugee children who arrived in the city.

But the 440 pathetic young victims of Hitler's Europe are in such a condition that they will have to go to a hostel for at least two months' intensive feeding and medical care.

After that they can join their foster-parents.

When the refugee train arrived, the children leaned out of the carriage windows and waved flags and a few began to sing.

One good meal on the way of stew and chocolate on the journey from the port of arrival had begun to revive their spirits, but other children were not strong enough to walk, and several had to be carried off the platform.

One was brought off on a stretcher and went straight to hospital suffering from acute malnutrition.

Among the generous people of Coventry who waited for hours in the hope that they could take home one of these little Dutch arrivals was Mr. Bernard Barker, a millwright, of Steppingstone-lane.

He had his own two children along with him—as eager as he was himself to help these tragic youngsters.

Then there were Tiny and Betty Wainwright, who stood clutching a large box which held their sweet rations for six weeks.

Daily Mirror

LLANGAMMARCH WELLS.

The christening took place at the Calvinistic Chapel, on Sunday, Rev. Trevor Williams officiating, of Eleanor Joyce, infant daughter of Mr. and Mrs. Austin Davies, Gwarceiros. Mrs. Watkins (grandmother) was the godmother.

A competitive meeting was held n the C.M. Chapel on Monday evening by the Young People's Guild members. Rev. T. W. Williams conducted. Adjudicators were:—Music, Mr. R. E. Davies, Llanwrtyd Wells; literature, Mr. J. Davies, Garth. Competitions and winners were as follows:—Solo under 10 years, Colin Meal; recitation under 10, Gareth Jones, 2, John Lloyd; novice solo, Ruby Daft; recitation under 16, Eileen Phillips, 2, Betty Jones; best limerick on "Rations," Patsy Lloyd; sweetest singing, Ruby Daft; six questions, general knowledge, Ruby Daft and James Preedy; best love letter, Mary Daft; whistling duet, Ifor Jones and James Preedy; open solo, Donald Jenkins; singing in unison, Donald Jenkins and Bryan Lander; best sentence, Mrs. Williams, Troedrhiwcwarel. A hearty vote of thanks was proposed to all by Mr. Bryn Jones, and endorsed by Mr. Emrys Jones.

Brecon and Radnor Express

BAYONET RUSH CRACKS HUNS

From GEORGE McCARTHY
Before Gennep (Germany),
Sunday.

THIS is the spirit of our men in Field-Marshal Montgomery's new push into Germany from Holland.

British troops, fighting their way forward down the main road to Gennep, a town near the River Maas, found the way barred by strong detachments of the enemy, who were strongly entrenched in the fringe of the Reichswald Forest, with their guns commanding the road.

For a time the whole advance was delayed and the order came: "Open that road tonight."

Scottish troops were given

Bagpipes used as "terror weapon"

the task. They already knew the difficulties.

They had fought their way through the fir trees and the brush of the forest, and they knew how strong the enemy positions were.

It was decided to rush them with the bayonet. The orders were issued. Among them were the words:

"The pipe-major will bring up the pipes, and they will be used as a terror weapon."

When darkness came down, the pipers in the front line began to play their wild music, skirling above the thunder of the guns.

And while they played the troops worked round to new positions. They crept round until they had the entrenched Germans from the rear.

Then the bagpipes listed to a new tune. That grim forest rang to the martial music of "Cock o' the North," a call they knew in other wilder moorlands.

As though it had been a signal, the Scots charged. Their bayonets gleamed in the faint light of artificial moonlighting, and as they ran further, sound mingled with the wild call of the pibroch.

It was the shout of 300 charging men.

Daily Mirror

Woman

"Fred just can't stand privacy any more"

Scottish Rugby Triumph

England ... 11 Scotland ... 18

AFTER four successive defeats in Service internationals, Scotland beat England at Leicester by three goals and a try, to a goal, a penalty goal, and a try on Saturday. No one among the crowd of 20,000 could have doubted the justice of the result.

The almost new Scotland team had to make late changes, which included the playing of J. B. Nicholls, normally a forward, on the wing, but the whole side worked together much better than England.

Youthful as they were, the Scottish pack held their own in the tight with the infinitely more-experienced English eight, and were the better in the open.

D. D. Mackenzie and Black, the halves, created a fine impression, and Maclennan and Henderson, the centres, not only displayed solidity in defence, but a dash and pace that often disconcerted their opponents.

Good Kicking

Geddes at full back, too, committed few errors, and, like Ward at the other end, kicked an admirable length.

While the English three-quarters were none too well together, and frequently had to rely upon kicking to make progress, the New Zealander Goddard brought off some capital runs in the centre, and Ruston late in the game bore a hand in both tries for his side.

McClure, Hastie, and the Dominion second-row forward R. M. McKenzie and Wilhelm were the pick of the Scottish forwards, with Doherty and Weighill perhaps the best for England.

R. M. McKenzie put Scotland ahead in eight minutes with a try that Geddes converted, and although Ward responded with a penalty goal, Grant increased the advantage before the interval, Geddes placing another goal.

In the second half, Maclennan added a try for Scotland. Ward dashed in with one in reply, then in the last few minutes Orr crossed for Scotland, Geddes converting and Goddard raced in for England's second try. Kilthorpe kicking a goal.

Sporting Life

And now... while Parliament sits far into the night debating the problems of peace and removing the restrictions of war, Ford Dealers are hard at it too — giving help and advice to motorists eager to get their Ford cars ready for the road again.

FORD MOTOR COMPANY LIMITED, DAGENHAM, ESSEX

Isle of Man Examiner

HE'S GOT A FLAT !

When Driver Philip L. Corkill, repatriated Manx prisoner of war, alighted from the steamer a fortnight ago and was welcomed by the Mayor of Douglas (Coun. S. A. Quirk) and Mr. A. D. McEvoy (Manx Legion) he told them they could do something for him "You can get me a house" he said.

Well Philip is lucky; he has got his house, or at least a flat, the Corporation, we gather having arranged for him to take over the tenancy of a flat that has become vacant in King Street. Congratulations to Driver Corkill!

PUNCH HOSPITAL COMFORTS FUND

(Registered under the War Charities Act, 1940)

AUDITOR'S CERTIFICATE

I have audited the books of the PUNCH HOSPITAL COMFORTS FUND for the year ended 31st December 1944, with the vouchers relating thereto.

I certify that the whole of the expenses of administering the Fund have been defrayed by the Proprietors of PUNCH and that all payments made from the Fund have been for the purchase of goods for distribution.

(Sgd.) J. G. MESSENGER,
Chartered Accountant,
Auditor.

37 Norfolk Street, Strand, London, W.C.2.
1st February, 1945.

Mr. Punch would like to take this opportunity of thanking all Subscribers to his Fund. Their great generosity has made it possible to send cigarettes and large quantities of warm materials for making up into comforts, not only for British men and women, but also for the men and women of the Allies. There is an immense amount still to do and more money is urgently needed. Donations will be gratefully received and acknowledged by Mr. Punch at PUNCH COMFORTS FUND, 10 Bouverie St., London, E.C.4.

Punch

Men, it is reported, have blackened their cricketing boots for civilian wear. That's all right, but we doubt if the Members' Stand at Lord's would approve of players wearing black boots whitened for cricket.

Cinemas.

THIS WEEK'S ATTRACTIONS.

Set in Poland before and during the war, the story of "In Our Time," showing at the Coliseum on Thursday, Friday and Saturday of this week concerns a young English girl who marries into a Polish family, brings new ideas to the peasantry of that country, and shows her tradition-bound husband (Paul Henreid), member of an aristocratic family, the way to democracy.

Mary Beth Hughes is an orphan who becomes a singer and faces the usual fight between love and a career in "Men On Her Mind," the supporting attraction. She also becomes involved in a murder.

The story of American draftees who enlist before the war, "The Eve of St. Mark," on Monday, Tuesday and Wednesday of next week, contains some vivid war sequences. The men are sent to an isolated atoll in the Pacific, there to cover themselves with glory manning a gun which liquidates Japanese reinforcements. The romantic interest is supplied by Anne Baxter and Michael O'Shea.

Don Ameche, Gloria Stuart and the Ritz Brothers are the stars of "The Singing Musketeer" in support.

THE PALACE.

"Frontier Marshall," the chief attraction on Thursday and the remaining two days of this week, features Randolph Scott, Nancy Kelly and Binnie Barns. In support is "Steel Against the Sky," a drama of the men who risk their lives constructing great suspension bridges. Lloyd Nolan, Craig Steven and Alexis Smith star.

The Marx Brothers indulge in another spate of crazy laugh-raising antics in "A Night At the Opera," the main film next week. In this uproarious comedy the trio leave Italy to enter grand opera business in New York City. There is a romance between two brilliant singers, Kitty Carlisle and Allan Jones.

Craig Stevens is a young attorney who becomes a counter-espionage agent and breaks up a powerful Nazi spy ring in "Secret Enemies," the supporting drama. He is handicapped by his infatuation for Faye Emerson, a night club singer, who is a member of the ring, but wins through after she has engineered, through his information, the escape of a number of spies who were being taken by train to Washington for trial.

Brecon and Radnor Express

"He refuses to confess where he bought the elastic."

Punch

WHAT WOMEN ARE DOING AND SAYING

Westmorland Gazette

DON'T reproach a girl for being a "book-worm." *Miss Helen Margaret Burness*, 26, of Cheam, Surrey, was always studying; at 16 won Hallam Imperial Studies prize with paper on Colonial government, then won exhibition at Somerville College, Oxford; took up nursing; war-work; is now one of first two women Assistant Secretaries in Colonial Government, working in Gambia, W. Africa.

OTHER Assistant Secretary, also in Gambia, is *Miss M. A. Evans* of Morfa Nevin, Caernarvonshire, who was at school in U.S.A., then took B.A. degree at University College of N. Wales, become group leader at Presbyterian Settlement; E. India Dock, London. They live in bungalow staffed by native servants, are keenly interested in their unusual job.

WOMAN with remarkable war service: *Miss Freya Stark*, explorer of Persia, Arabia; has worked for Ministry of Information in Aden, Cairo, Baghdad, Palestine, Syria; speaks seven languages, including French, Italian, Arabic, Persian, Russian.

YOU don't hear much complaint about medical services organized for our men and girls in Europe. *Lady Louis Mountbatten*, very impressed with them, says hospitals with best nurses, surgeons, supplies, equipment in world operate right up to forward areas.

Lady Louis Mountbatten

HAVE you a passion for animals? If so you would envy *Mrs. Florence Nagle*, who runs stud farm, racing stables, kennels, at Westerlands near Petworth, Sussex. She has 10 racehorses training, eight brood mares, three foals. Her first racehorse, Sandsprite, ran second in 1937 Derby.

OXFORD University's first woman professor: *Miss Ida Mann*, 51, Harley Street surgeon, who heads research group of doctors, chemists, physicists, dietitians, psychologists on treatment of eye disease.

WHAT better service can women of safe areas do than help bombed-out women of London, Home Counties, with household goods, furniture, to start new home? Women's organisations in many North-Western boroughs have "adopted" Southern ones to aid them as "godmothers."

SHOULD there be night as well as day nurseries, so that young mothers can leave their babies in safe keeping and enjoy an evening out occasionally? It has been suggested to Royal Commission on Health that many suffer from nervous complaints because they are tied to home night after night with no recreation.

DON'T pretty nurses stimulate patient's recovery? *Miss Rootham*, Matron, North Middlesex Hospital, London, thinks so; advises nurses to do hair and face nicely when going on duty, says it matters more than people think.

Woman's Own

AMBLESIDE BOY'S THEFT

At Ambleside Juvenile Court on Wednesday, a 14-year-old schoolboy was charged with stealing a number of miscellaneous articles, the property of Mrs. S. E. Thring, Merlewood, Ambleside. Mrs. Thring gave evidence that between Nov. and 4 Jan. she missed the following from her house: a toboggan (value 25s.), tricycle saddle, tricycle bell, two tricycle oil lamps, tricycle tool bag, two knives, hamper, tin of pears, billhook, two china vases, knife sharpener, bottle of cider, tin of mackerel, tin of sardines, and bottle of gingerbeer (total value £4 4s. 3d.). The boy had been employed doing odd jobs about the house.

Accused denied taking the billhook and the two vases.

After P.C. Barrass had given evidence, the chairman (Major Porter) said the offence was the more serious because the boy had not taken them all at once under a sudden impulse. As it was his first offence he would be placed on probation for 12 months and fined 10s.

Westmorland Gazette

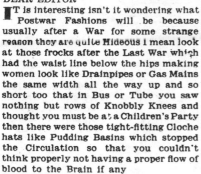

Mrs. Fussbottle
on Postwar Fashions

DEAR EDITOR

IT is interesting isn't it wondering what Postwar Fashions will be because usually after a War for some strange reason they are quite Hideous i mean look at those frocks after the Last War which had the waist line below the hips making women look like Drainpipes or Gas Mains the same width all the way up and so short too that in Bus or Tube you saw nothing but rows of Knobbly Knees and thought you must be at a Children's Party then there were those tight-fitting Cloche hats like Pudding Basins which stopped the Circulation so that you couldn't think properly not having a proper flow of blood to the Brain if any

Well I must say I don't think it's fair to the Dear Boys coming home because Out There feeling so lonely they dote on our letters picturing us as Angels and Visions of Delight quite the Last Word in Feminine Beauty only to step off the Troop Train at Victoria Station shouting *Hooray! home at last!* and see a lot of awful Freaks looking like nothing on earth because it happens to be the New Postwar Fashion Of course they're delighted to see their Womenfolk after so long and full of Love and Romance but they can't help blinking and flinching a bit saying *It's Heaven seeing you again Old Girl but Good Heavens! where on earth did you get that So-and-so ? I've never seen anything like it not even in Cairo*

Well look at what happened after the Boer War tight waspy waists leg-o'-mutton sleeves long trailing skirts and small straw Boaters sometimes adorned with wreaths of flowers and all the brave CID s who marched back singing *The Soldiers of the Queen My Boys Goodbye Dolly Gray It Was Only a Bee-yootiful Picture in a Bee-yootiful Golden Frame* and so on beheld the New Fashions and moaned *Was it for this we Relieved Mafeking and Ladysmith and stormed Spion Kop ?* seeing their Adored Ones even playing Tennis with thick skirts sweeping the ground and sticking out behind with what was called the Grecian Bend meaning *I'm here and the rest is following* Well heroes who've been fighting on the Veldt do expect Womanly Waists to put their fond arms round just to remind them Peace has come but it was just like embracing a Lamp-post and they were afraid to squeeze in case the Beloved snapped in half

Well look what happened after the Crimea and Charge of the Light Brigade huge Crinolines like Army Tents Waterfalls and Bustles that made women look like ships in full sail with Rudders stuck out behind to say nothing of full Puff Sleeves billowing in the breeze like Sails most Victorian houses being so draughty with the Wind whistling through Basements and Attics whenever you opened a door or went to the Coal Hole in the Area looking for Tibbles or the Cook in case she might be sitting there having a quiet talk with Robert on his Beat not wishing to be seen with the Arm of the Law in the Kitchen in case the Between Maids talked

Woman's Own

Snowballing in Derry

Fifteen People Prosecuted

R.M. and Cowardly Conduct

Fifteen people were prosecuted at Londonderry Petty Sessions yesterday for throwing snowballs, and the defendants included young women, who were alleged to have thrown snowballs at sailors and a soldier.

Fines of five shillings were imposed on the following :—John Scott, 4, Benvarden Avenue; Josephine Bridges, 42, Nailor's Row; Sarah McNamee, 7, Nailor's Row; Kathleen Patterson, 14, Lawrence Hill; Joseph McGrory, 27, Ashfield Terrace; William J. Hughes, 11, Aubery Street; James McLaughlin, 15, Thomas Street; Basil Curry, 10, Bond's Place; Bernard J. Nolan, 27, Epworth Street; Kathleen Conaghan, 45, Foyle Street; Charles Gallagher, c/o Melville Hotel; and Ronald Donnell, Edenreagh, Drumahoe.

William Devlin, 19, Sugarhouse Lane, was fined 1s.

A summons against Angus Warke, 60, Duke Street, was dismissed.

Shaun Doherty, 49, Glenbrook Terrace, was fined 10s for sleighing.

The Resident Magistrate (Captain P. S. Bell) said he had seen elderly people snowballed. It was cowardly conduct, and there was nothing funny in snowballing old people. It would have to stop, as snowballing was a grave inconvenience to the public.

Warke's father said his son was attacked with snowballs by other boys and a window was broken. If a policeman had not arrived there might have been more damage.

McGrory was alleged to have been running after girls with a snowball in each hand.

Kathleen Patterson was alleged to have thrown a snowball at a soldier.

Josephine Bridges and Sarah McNamee were alleged to have thrown snowballs at two sailors, who told the police it was not the girls who had thrown the snowballs in order to save them from trouble.

Devlin said he had just cleaned a window when other boys hit it with a snowball and he threw snowballs back at them.

Londonderry Sentinel

MARRIED WHILE ON LEAVE

Chindit Bridegroom at Windermere

The marriage took place on Saturday at St. Mary's Church, Windermere, of C.Q.M.S. John Ralph Laidler, youngest son of Mrs. Cooper and the late Mr. Albert Laidler, "Broadfield," Troutbeck Bridge, and Miss Rose Mabel Burton, third daughter of Mr. and Mrs. T. W. Burton, "Greenriggs," Windermere. The Rev. Lionel du Toit, vicar, officiated. The bridegroom is serving in the Border Regiment. He is one of Wingate's Chindits on leave from Burma, like several more Lakeland soldiers.

He is a fine Soccer player, having in turn played for the renowned Windermere St. Mary's schoolboy team which carried everything before it, and afterwards for the Windermere junior team (specially trained by his father), then for Windermere first, Barrow and Netherfield. He has been assisting the latter club while on leave. He was a member of the Border team which won 59 out of 60 matches in the regimental competition in Burma. Before the war he did a fair amount of track-racing, and he and a brother used to compete in the half-mile at Grasmere and other local sports.

The bride, who was given away by her father, was attired in a gown of white moss crepe, with a coronet of orange blossom, and short tulle veil. She carried a shower bouquet of pink chrysanthemums and maiden hair fern. The bride was attended by her two sisters, Miss Ivy Burton and Miss Olive Burton, who wore gowns of midnight blue crepe, with feather headdresses and silver leaves to tone. They carried shower bouquets of white chrysanthemums and maiden hair fern. The best man was Mr. A. Bosanko, Ormskirk, and the groomsman Sergt. Roy Gudgeon, Kendal. Bridal music had been arranged for, but owing to weather conditions, the organ could not be used. As the bridal procession left the church the bells rang out a merry peal. The reception was held at Elleray's Cafe, and the newly married couple left for Southport for the honeymoon. They were the recipients of many useful and handsome presents.

London To See Paris Designs For Housing

By Alison Settle

THE results of research into housing methods made secretly in France during the German occupation will be shown at the French Housing Exhibition to be opened on Thursday by the French Minister of Information, M. P. H. Tietgen, at the Royal Institute of British Architects in London.

Plans for permanent mass-produced houses based on steel framework is the keynote of the exhibition, and a chief aim is to kill at the outset any mental association between prefabrication and impermanency. The lesson which the exhibition seeks to enforce is that prefabrication is revolutionary only in so far that hitherto houses have been shells providing only one built-in service, that of the hearth with chimney. Now the indispensable services - of heat, light, hot and cold water must be furnished at the outset. If not, they will not be provided for years to come and the "revolution of comfort in living" will have been defeated.

Blend of Materials

The technique used is one of four vertical steel "legs" on to which are hinged all panels and services. Two-skin walls are the most important feature, each made up of small panels and separated by glass-wool and air insulation.

Site mechanics have been closely studied, and it is felt that errors in the Portal bungalow have been avoided. It was realised as soon as the first dummies went up that large panels of steel inevitably buckle on transit and cause grave trouble in erecting on the site. No panel now measures more than two foot across.

The Exhibition shows tall blocks of flats, individual houses singly or in small flatted groups with neighbourhood plans. It does not aim at giving house plans, but instead forms a basic study of new technical methods adaptable to any building. Although steel forms the main framework and often the walls, aluminum, stone, and other available materials are to be used, the architects preferring a blend of materials.

Architects from hard-hit areas of Normandy have just visited England to study the replanning of devastated areas in order to apply our experience to their needs. They are using air photographs to review the needs of their towns. The British Air Ministry has given them permission to use Bomber Command photographs of air-raid damage and of the site previous to bombing to get a bird's-eye view of what must be replanned.

Observer

"This one is to let furnished. Three bedrooms, two reception rooms and four evacuees"

Woman

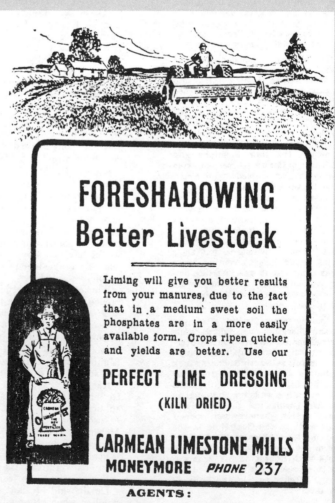

BACON — & EGG!

"You lucky people," as Tommy Trinder would say, and quite a few others, too, in the adjacent island, to whom a shell egg is a luxury.

A new order made by the Lieut.-Governor, amending the Meals in Establishments Order, 1942, permits the service of egg in a main dish containing meat or fish, and its effect is to allow bacon and egg to be served at one meal.

Isle of Man Examiner

Great Increase In University Grants Needed

By A University Correspondent

PROVINCIAL universities hope that the increase in total grants which Sir John Anderson, Chancellor of the Exchequer, is to announce on Tuesday will be a substantial one. The present grants of £2,250,000 are, they say, quite inadequate for post-war development and extension.

Many provincial universities have plans not only for the extension of scientific research but for the development of the Arts Faculties and for the building of residential hostels. These plans will require a considerable capital sum as well as a greatly increased annual income. In general, the income of the provincial universities will need to be at least doubled in the next five years.

Few New Students

With this long-term view, Leeds, for example, will require an extra £300,000 a year and £2,500,000 capital. Capital expenditure will be largely on the building and the expansion of hostels. It is hoped that this increase will be met by the Government and industry.

Birmingham, too, will need an additional £200,000 a year—£100,000 of it immediately. Here, again, post-war development calls for another £2,000,000. At Manchester, "to enable the University to fulfil its various functions properly, allowing only for a small increase in the number of students, its income should be at least doubled in a period of five years."

Universities, without big endowments, can hope for little substantial increase outside the Government and, for scientific work, industry. Thus, post-war university development would involve at least the quadrupling of the present Exchequer grant.

Observer

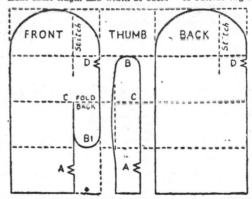

Observer

Franco's Fall Cannot Be Long Delayed

By A Special Correspondent

THE fall of General Franco's régime cannot be long delayed. He is already opposed by the majority of the Spanish people, and now he has lost any hope of foreign support.

Mr. Churchill, in his reply to the letter the Caudillo sent him last November, has, as I forecast a fortnight ago, left Franco in no doubt as to Britain's attitude to Falangist Spain. He has indicated that there is no prospect of a Falangist Spain being represented at the peace conference.

The conversion of Spain to a democratic régime must be the work of Spaniards alone, without any foreign intervention. But it is of the utmost importance to the United Nations that the transition should be a peaceful one. A recurrence of the Civil War must be avoided at any cost. It may also be said that Spain cannot usefully attend any international conference until she has a Government which really represents the freely-expressed will of the people. For that the rights of the opposition parties must be fully guaranteed.

A Manifesto

Expecting an early fall of the Franco régime, various Spanish political groups in exile are becoming even more active. Don Juan, the Pretender, is still working on his manifesto which will call upon Franco to resign; but he is not expected to issue it until Señor López Oliván, his political and diplomatic adviser, goes back to Switzerland, which may be in a few days' time. During his stay here Señor López Oliván will have had an opportunity of meeting not only Spaniards of various sections of opinion but also British friends of Spain who are interested in the peaceful solution of the Spanish problem. Another outstanding politician—Señor Gil Robles, leader of the Catholic Party—is expected in London next Tuesday.

Meanwhile, in France, Dr. Negrín continues to meet and exchange views with numbers of Spaniards of varied political sympathies. His main task, however, will be in America, and especially in Mexico. It is in Mexico that the majority of Spanish political exiles are living, and it is there that Señor Prieto, the Spanish Socialist leader, directs strong opposition to Dr. Negrín. Señor Prieto's absence from the world trade union conference in London is probably due to Dr. Negrín's impending visit to America.

Sense of Urgency

In both of the two main camps opposing the present régime in Spain there is an understandable sense of urgency, due to both internal and international reasons. The monarchists might possibly have the best chance of securing power at the moment. But their chance of making their tenure permanent would depend on very definite conditions. They would have to give acceptable and adequate guarantees that restoration of the monarchy was not proposed from selfish class interests; that the new régime would be one under which all Spaniards could live and work without being persecuted for political opinions; and that it was ready to face the test of genuine public opinion.

The chances of a Republican restoration would be greatly increased if the Republicans could moderate their programme so that the forces of the Right would not be automatically excluded. Paradoxical as it may seem, the ultimate success of any restoration—republican or monarchical—depends less on its supporters than on the treatment and guarantees it offers to its opponents.

WORLD *without* BOOKS

Life is like that for many people today — for those in the Forces, for instance. Knowing how much it means to yourself to have something good to read, it is easy to imagine how much *more* books must mean to Service folk in their brief moments of leisure.

It is so easy to pass on the books you've finished with so that they may bring some comfort to book-starved men and women in the Forces. All you need do is to hand them over the counter at any Post Office—unwrapped, unaddressed and unstamped. Please *don't* take them to a W. H. Smith & Son bookshop or bookstall—the Post Office is the proper place. They have facilities for passing them on, and you may be sure that every book (or periodical for that matter—there's a great demand for magazines in the Services) will be sent without delay direct to where the need is greatest.

Let *your* books go on Active Service again. Send them to the men and women in the Forces.

Issued in support of the Prime Minister's appeal for Books for the Forces by

W. H. SMITH & SON

BOOKSELLERS · NEWSAGENTS · STATIONERS · PRINTERS
BOOKBINDERS · ADVERTISERS' AGENTS · LENDING LIBRARY

1500 BOOKSHOPS AND STATION BOOKSTALLS

Head Office: W. H. Smith & Son, Ltd., Strand House, Portugal Street, London, W.C.2.

Punch

I Grieve for the Hawaiians.

I GRIEVE for the Hawaiians,
  Where blue seas run,
Lying like tawny lions
  Stretched in the sun.

Though tenderly their fingers
  Haunt the guitars,
Though honeyed perfume lingers
  Under the stars,

Though flowers like crimson trumpets
  Hang from the tree;
They have never had crumpets
  For Sunday tea.   V. G.

READERS SAY . . .

You write this feature—we pay 10/6 for each original letter published. Please send your letters to "Readers Say . . ." at the address on page 22

Interval for Smokers

"I am an ardent film-fan, but my visit to the films is spoiled by the thick, cloudy atmosphere created by hundreds of people smoking. Why don't British cinemas have intervals when smokers could retire to a lounge, and smoke to their heart's content? The result would be a purer atmosphere, and a much clearer view of the screen."—*Reader, Edinburgh.*

How a Jitterbug Feels

"Being a keen jitterbug fan myself, I would just like to say a few words on the subject. It makes me feel indignant to hear people saying that it is indecent, disgusting, etc., although I will admit that some couples go too far, and make it appear so. Most likely these critics have no idea of the enjoyment we ourselves get out of jitterbugging. It is not 'showing off' on our part, as some people seem to think. The music gets into you, and you can't help yourself, the faster the music, the faster you go. Have you critics experienced these feelings? Probably not. Then how can you express your opinions? Jitterbugging done properly and decently, as I often see it, is a pleasure to watch."—*Miss W. W., Nelson, (W.L.A.)*

Government for Women

"I've a great admiration for our women Members of Parliament, yet I often wonder if they have accomplished much which could not have been brought about by men. I know it is agreeable to feel that women M.P.'s have equalled—perhaps even outshone—many male Members, but have they truly represented women? Is it sufficient that women should merely carry out Parliamentary work normally accomplished by men? I would like to see a Women's Party formed. As our sex holds numerical superiority in this country, it is possible that women might one day hold a majority in the House. Women in power! As an 'unknown quality' it is impossible to say what a feminine government could achieve. Two wars and the greatest industrial slump in history in a single lifetime does not leave much room for anticipatory criticism from men, anyway. Don't think I'm an extremist. I'm not really. I am just an ordinary housewife who feels that men have not shone so brightly in recent years, and that feminine leaders might bring new ideas."—*L. T., Farnham.*

Wives Who Want Careers

"However desirable it may appear to be to the State that married women should, after the war, smother themselves in domesticity, Local Authorities or public corporations should not interfere in this matter. I do not think it is the State's business to dictate what they should or should not do. All women do not take to domesticity and motherhood as ducks to water, and to my mind it seems better that the exceptions should fulfil themselves as round pegs in round holes rather than in the proverbial square ones, giving no satisfaction or happiness to anyone. We shall want more doctors, more and better lay administration in hospitals, more teachers, etc., if we are to have the promised better world, and if women with careers pay for their homes to be efficiently run, they are giving a job to someone, not doing somebody else out of one, as many objectors declare. Professional women, particularly, should continue their work."—*Mrs. A. S., Netherbridge.*

Children and Chewing-gum

"Is it not a pity that our young people are growing up with the idea that gum-chewing is big, and American, and admirable, instead of being what it is : one of our American friends' less attractive weaknesses? Anybody who has lived over there knows that it is regarded by well-bred Americans as only a much less objectionable than chewing tobacco. I have seen many parents in the U.S.A. doing their best to prevent their children getting the habit, or to break it up if they have. They do so, not only because it is ugly and uncouth in itself, but also because they regard it as a social handicap, like any other unmannerly habit. Is it too much to hope that this country, having escaped so many serious war troubles, may also escape being stuck over with bits of gum?"—*H. S. M., London.*

A Dress for Cinderella

"I would like to tell you how much your excellent magazine is appreciated by the staff and patients of a Casualty Clearing Station somewhere north of Florence. After reading my 'Woman's Own' I post it off to my sister who is serving with the T.A.N.S. She tells me it is very well thumbed indeed by her fellow nurses, medical officers, orderlies and patients. What a wonderful job these women are doing! Everyone knows their selfless care and attention to the wounded, but perhaps you will be surprised to know that this unit has staged a pantomime to amuse the men. As Cinderella, my sister was stumped for a ball-dress, but eventually manufactured one from a mosquito net, using six-inch bandages to make the frills!"—*A Sister's sister, Doncaster.*

Woman's Own

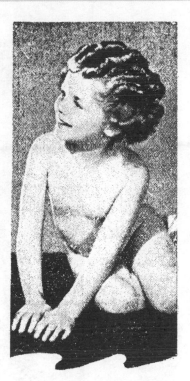

Waste not, want not: salvaging kitchen waste for pig food (Imperial War Museum)

Punch

MARCH
1945

GERMANY FACES WIDESPREAD STARVATION

Immediate Surrender Would Lessen Suffering

WASHINGTON, Monday.—Mr Albert A. Gore, Democrat Representative for Tennessee, who has served with Allied Military Government detachments in Germany, presenting an 8000 words report to the U.S. Congress to-day, said:—

" Political chaos and utter physical destruction prevail in German towns and communities from which our conquering armies have newly driven the German Army.

" All semblances of law and order have vanished with the retreating Nazis. In a few instances the Germans have evacuated entire populations, but in most cases civilians have remained, and many have hidden themselves in the woods, in caves, in holes to escape evacuation and bombardment.

" The physical destruction of German cities, homes, factories, schools, and edifices is appalling.

" The people are generally submissive and servile. People, who perhaps only a few minutes before were shooting at our soldiers from behind barricades, appear hat in hand—the picture of humility.

" Instead of complaining at the lack of justice done in our Military Government Courts, not a few German civilians have said that they provide a more even justice than Germans have been accustomed to

" Food scarcity will become more urgent before another harvest, and if the conflict is prolonged for several months widespread starvation will be inevitable and beyond our power to prevent.

" The German people could greatly lessen their own suffering during the desperate months ahead by thwarting their Nazi masters and surrendering now. If the conflict is prolonged and all Germany's resources are destroyed it will be of no avail for the German people to say that because we have conquered them it is our responsibility to feed them.

" MORTAL FEAR OF RUSSIANS "

" In the approximate one-third of Germany which, by tentative agreement, U.S. is to occupy, I believe we may find at least one-half of the entire German civilian population. My reasons for reaching this conclusion are as follow:—

" (1) The Germans mortally fear the Russians, and are fleeing in untold thousands from that part of Germany which it has been announced Russia will occupy.

" (2) Tactical operations encourage southward evacuations.

" (3) The evacuation of German civilians, industries, and slave labour from west of the Rhine has largely been to the southern regions of Germany.

CHANGES WILL HAVE TO REACH DEEPER THAN THE SCHOOLS

" I have noticed some people speaking and writing as if they imagine re-educating Germany can be done by hanging Hitler and his gang, writing German textbooks, and having the right kind of school teachers to tell German children what a fine thing is democracy

" But we will have to reach much deeper into the German social and political structure than the schools, and over more than one generation.

" The first and most important lesson in the re-education of Germany by utter defeat is being administered, but defeat of the German Army will not be enough. Time will produce the men for another Army. Neither will disarmament alone suffice.

" The only permanent security against aggression lies in, one of the following courses:—

" Permanent occupation of Germany;

" Dissolution of the German nation as a unified political and military entity; or

" The building of a Germany desiring to live in peace with the other civilised nations of the world and willing to seek accomplishment of her aspirations only through peaceful means.

" The latter is the most desired, and, at the same time, the most difficult of attainment."—Reuter.

The Scotsman

THAT PROPHECY OF THE WAR

To the Editor

Sir.—About September, 1940, you published a "Monk's Prophecy," written in 1600, sent you by me. It may interest your readers to note the main points and to see how far they have been fulfilled.

Put briefly he prophesied: (1) It would be a world war; (2) Earth, water and the heavens would be involved; (3) The Black Eagle from the land of Luther would invade half of the land of the Cock (France); (4) The White Eagle (Russia) would surprise the Black Eagle and completely invade it; (5) After a terrible war in which anti-Christ is defeated, an era of peace and prosperity will commence, each nation being governed according to its wish, living in justice.

The four points having been practically fulfilled, it is not difficult to believe that the fifth will soon be realised also.—Yours, etc.,
GEORGE BUCHANAN.
Guildford. March, 1945.

Surrey Advertiser

Controls will be election issue
—LORD RENNELL

Speaking at the annual meeting of the Home Counties Liberal Federation in London on Saturday on the "Removal of Controls, Regulations and Planning," Lord Rennell said the general public was beginning to agitate very seriously about restrictions and the subject would inevitably loom at the General Election.

Rationing was a control made for our good, and prospects of its removal for some time were remote. A particularly mischievous category of orders arose out of a zeal for perfectionism. It was the outcome of a desire by many Ministries and civil servants for everything, and especially everyone, to be tied up in bundles, to achieve uniformity. This was an insidious form of bureaucratic government.

The Marquis of Crewe was re-elected president and Lord Meston treasurer. Chairman was Mr. F. W. Raffety.

News Chronicle

THE NEUTRAL BUSINESS MAN:
Goering.

THE PRIEST:
Goebbels: Black robe covers his club foot.

THE WORLD AND US *by* JOHN GAUNT

They're watching for them!

WILL it be possible to identify Hitler when we catch him? This is the question which is exercising the Allied intelligence departments and the new Allied International C.I.D. recently set up in London to track war criminals.

It is a question which is becoming more urgent as the tide of war gets nearer the "Götterdämmerung redoubt"—the last stronghold of the Nazis in the Bavarian mountains.

Reliable reports reaching London show that a number of Germany's leading plastic surgeons have been brought into the Berchtesgaden fortress during the past few weeks.

Plastic surgery

FANTASTIC as it may seem, the question is being seriously discussed in responsible quarters whether Hitler —under guise of having his bomb injuries seen to—may be undergoing operations to disguise his appearance.

Or is it so fantastic? Remember these men are gangsters, and during the heyday of gangsterism in the United States the gangsters made great use of the plastic surgeon. Tell-tale scars were removed, fingertips changed, faces lifted.

It entailed, of course, fairly long periods of disappearance from public gaze— which was made all the easier if the gangster had a hide-out or a double. Hitler has both.

In any case, Hitler, except when roused by oratory or in a passion, is a dull, colourless little man with lack-lustre eyes. It would need only the smallest alterations, a beard or a clean shave, spectacles, a new type of haircut, and he could easily pass for any little Austrian bourgeois drafted in for forced labour in the fortress area.

Himmler, too, the uninspiring schoolmaster, would be easy enough to disguise, though Goering's size and Goebbels's glowing eyes and club foot would be almost impossible to conceal.

If Hitler does not commit suicide, his likeliest attempted hide-out is now believed in London to be some small Spanish town in the mountains.

It has been suspected that some of his doubles have been in neutral countries for some time, laboriously acquiring new personalities which they can hand over to the Fuehrer if the need arises.

No refuge

THE escape situation has deteriorated for the Nazi leaders recently. The Argentine, for long looked on with favour and the recipient of discreet investments, has declared war. Sweden has declared her intention of not harbouring war criminals and would certainly not receive the more prominent ones.

A year or two more of inglorious life might be open to Hitler and his friends if they took one of the long-distance submarines used for blockade running to and from Japan. These submarines, equipped with the Schnorkel device, could easily make the passage to Japan in comparative safety.

It is pleasant to contemplate Hitler, Himmler, Ribbentrop and Co. leading the sort of despised existence as the guests of the Mikado which Petain and Laval and the French renegades have dragged out recently in Germany.

Daily Express

GEN. SMUTS FOR SAN FRANCISCO

"I Believe This May Be Last World War"

"BIG POWERS MUST AGREE"

GENERAL SMUTS, the Union Premier, announced yesterday that he will lead the South African delegation at the San Francisco Security Conference, and will also attend preliminary discussions in London.

South Africa, he told the Union Assembly at Capetown, is not committing herself in any way until she sees what takes place between the Great Powers.

After outlining the proposals for post-war security drawn up at Yalta, General Smuts continued: "I believe that this may be the last world war. Knowing the methods of destruction already in operation and in contemplation, I feel convinced that this opportunity at San Francisco is a vital moment in the history of the whole human race.

SMALL NATIONS DEFENCELESS

"Small nations cannot defend themselves any more. Even the greatest military Power in the world is succumbing to these new methods of war.

"Unless some way out is found which will render war obsolete—which will eliminate it from the course of human progress—the future is dark beyond measure."

In a review of the Union Government's international policy during the past year, General Smuts said: "A country like South Africa—a great gold-producing country—is immensely interested in the question of stable currencies to some extent linked with gold."

General Smuts, in replying to the debate, said: "The kernel of the whole question is a question of small and great nations. That is a distinction that was never drawn in the old League of Nations, but it is now being used in the proposals for the world organisation."

GREAT POWERS' RESPONSIBILITIES

There were great Powers with great responsibilities, and it was impossible to expect of South Africa what one expected from the U.S.A. If the big Powers made wars, was it not natural and logical that the big Powers should bear the heavy responsibilities? The first obligation which the small Powers would impose on the larger Powers was that they should co-operate, because if the big Powers quarrelled, then there was no use drawing up documents.

The chief responsibility for preserving peace would have to be placed on the big Powers, and the first essential was that they should agree among themselves.

General Smuts said the position of Europe could only be aggravated if the spirit of vengeance were brought to the settlement. "I said that at the Paris Conference, and I say the same to-day. Unless the situation is tackled in a totally different spirit, Europe may go under, and not recover for generations."

"ABOLISH MANDATES"

Replying to a question about South-West Africa, General Smuts said the future of the mandates system was uncertain, and it would no doubt be discussed at San Francisco. The best solution would be to abolish the mandates system, and to include South-West Africa as a province of the Union.—Reuter

---

BILL FOR PROVISION OF U.S. "POLICE FORCE"

WASHINGTON, Monday. — Representative Kepplemann (Democrat, Connecticut), to-day introduced into Congress a Bill providing that the U.S. representatives on "whatever international security organisation is established" shall have the authority, after consulting specific U.S. officials, to pledge the use of "specified numbers and types of military forces."

In introducing his Bill, he said: "Peace is something for which we must prepare and fight as vigorously as we prepare and fight for war."—Reuter

The Scotsman

TOO MANY TOWELS

In a long discussion by the council of the Drapers' Chamber of Trade in London yesterday it was stated that there was an acute shortage of stockings, handkerchiefs, knitting wool, children's coats, sheets, and blankets. But Mr. E. Bates, of Chatham, said there were so many towels that the shops could not get rid of them, and many people would like them taken off the ration. It was stated that taking towels off the ration would cause such a rush that there would probably be an acute shortage, so rationing must stay.

The Times

For Three Years a Prisoner of the Japs

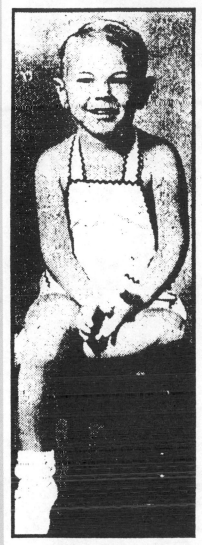

Four - year - old Hugh Cameron, of whom his grandmother, Mrs. M. J. Bartlett, heard the first news to-day since Manila fell three years ago. A baby brother was born in a Jap prison camp on Boxing Day to his parents, Mr. and Mrs. Jack Cameron, who had to give up valuable jewellery for a few ounces of rice. Now they are free.

Evening News

Spies who betrayed British to die

Brussels, Sunday.—A Belgian spy named Jules Renuart and his wife, who lured escaped Allied prisoners of war into the hands of the Germans, have been sentenced to death in Brussels.

News Chronicle

4 MORE NAZI FUGITIVES CAUGHT

THEY HAD MAPS AND RAZOR COMPASSES

"Evening News" Reporter

TWO more of the 70 German prisoners who made a mass escape from a camp near Bridgend by tunnelling their way into a field were recaptured early to-day.

This means that 25 are still at large, and a country-wide search by armed soldiers and police is going on for them. The Metropolitan Police are keeping a close watch on roads leading into London.

The couple—both Army officers—whose liberty ended in the early hours to-day, walked straight into the arms of two police officers at St. Nicholas, a little village six miles west of Cardiff and about 15 miles as the crow flies from their camp.

The two men had compasses made out of a block of wood with a bowl hollowed out in one side. Through the base was a pin and on the point was balanced a magnetised safety razor blade as a needle.

There was a tin lid over the top. Though crude, the compasses worked effectively.

The men also had maps which were well traced on thin paper showing the whole of England and Wales, with parts of the east and south coast of Ireland. Roads, railways, and all big towns were marked on them.

Anti-Climax

Their capture was an anti-climax, for the policemen, hearing the sound of footsteps on the road, drew back into the hedge and waited.

When the two men—who were still wearing their distinctive uniform—came abreast the officers stopped them. They gave themselves up without any struggle.

A big comb-out is going on in the Forest of Dean, where four of the fugitives are believed to be hiding. They got a good start on the first day by stealing a car, and it is almost certain that they reached the forest, which affords ample opportunity for a hide-out.

Small Groups

The net has been thrown over a wide area because it is assumed that when the men planned their escape they agreed to break up into small groups—probably twos and threes—and to make their own ways to the ports.

It is not thought that any master plan was in existence for the men to be picked up by a boat, but that they hoped to be able to stow away on a vessel at either Cardiff or Bristol.

The two German paratroop prisoners who escaped yesterday afternoon while working in fields near Hunsdon, near Ware, Hertfordshire, were recaptured to-day close to the farm on which they had been employed as labourers.

They were found hiding in a hedge by a police superintendent.

Evening News

Two Sons Lost

WITHIN the space of a year Mr. and Mrs. E. T. Bloomer, of 94, Robin Hood Chase, Nottingham, formerly of Victoria Street, Melton, have lost two sons on active service.

Last April, Flt. Sgt. J. E. Bloomer, an old Grammarian, and a keen athlete, lost his life whilst on operations over Germany—he was a Pathfinder—and now the death has been confirmed of O/S Stewart Allan Bloomer, Mr. and Mrs. Bloomer's third son.

He was serving on the corvette, "Vervain", the loss of which was announced a few days ago. He was only eighteen, but had already nearly a year's service in the Navy to his credit, having enlisted as a volunteer on March 14th, 1944.

Stewart Bloomer was educated at the Melton Boys' Senior School and was employed at the Midland Woodworking Company.

Melton Mowbray Times

*Surrey
Advertiser*

HUNTING

CHIDDINGFOLD FARMERS' FOXHOUNDS

Saturday's meet at the Bramley Grange Hotel, where Mrs. Hedges entertained the field with a generous hospitality, ended a week that, as our American cousins would say, "hit the high spots," for with a most successful and enjoyable hunt dance at the Lion Hotel in Guildford, followed the next day with an earthstopper's feast at the Jolly Farmer at Bramley, and then, in spite of a most indifferent scenting day, to kill a brace of foxes and put another to ground, we felt like the mongrel dog who had slipped into the pedigree dog show, who, in boasting to his prize-winning pal, said that he did not want three first prizes and a highly commended, for he had had three fights, and was highly contented.

This little bitch pack really hunted their fox, and worked the line in a hot sun, over dressed tillage and dry ground with a marvellous perseverance; they put up a most notable show under the worst scenting conditions. Finding an unenterprising fox in Birtley Brook, they coursed him to the hills above Gate Street Farm, where he was broken up with great zest. Ridings Brook was drawn blank, but finding again in Homing Copse, a leash of foxes and a deer marched and countermarched all around Grafham Farm coverts, so foiling the ground that it was lucky that the pack eventually settled on one who went away by the Fish Pond, to cross the road into Northbrook, where he fortunately dwelt for a while amidst the scolding screams of jays.

This gave hounds the opportunity to really get on terms with him, and they fairly rattled him out over the ploughland up the hill through Yew Tree Nob, past Holly Barn, due west over the valley to Lodkin, where they turned; then through Kiln Copse to a check.

A timely holloa over the road by Middle Copse put them on again, and they hunted fast through Great Brook over Juniper Hill, to put him down near the Stone Pits south of New Barn, after an exhibition of hound work that could not have been bettered.

Finding again in Leg of Mutton Copse they ran well to just short of Slades, where the shepherd had viewed him back. From here a slow hunt with a very catchy scent took us to Dum Pits, where he was marked in.

The timely arrival and efficient efforts of our terrier party, with Ted Adsett's newly-entered bitch puppy going right up to and baying her fox like the champion she will be, soon gave hounds their reward, and we heard the "Whoop Tally Ho," and the dirgeful note of the death blown on the horn. Over a green carpet of dog's mercury, holding an elusive fragrance of primroses, with the coming winds of night moving gently around us, we jogged home.

EARTHSTOPPER.

BAN ON MAURICE CHEVALIER

NO BRITISH PERMIT

Maurice Chevalier, the French stage and film star, has been refused permission to enter this country by the Aliens Department of the Home Office. He had intended to appear in London at the Victoria Palace for a short season, starting on April 9, under the management of Mr. Jack Hylton.

Before he left yesterday for Blackpool, Mr. Hylton said: "I have just heard from the Home Office that Chevalier will not be granted permission to enter this country. No reason is given, and I am at a loss to understand why the permission has been refused."

Jack Hylton's Press agent stated last night: "Jack Hylton wishes to correct the statement that he was to have paid Maurice Chevalier £1,000 a week. In fact, the arrangements were that he should work on a percentage basis and at a lower one than that which has been paid to some British stars."

Daily Telegraph

'Devil-may-care' PARATROOPS SWEAR by KOLYNOS! of course

. . . for whiter, brighter teeth and a clean, fresh mouth. Cultivate that regular twice-a-day Kolynos habit and you, too, will swear by this cleansing and refreshing tooth paste.

IMPORTANT — USED TUBES ARE REQUIRED FOR MUNITIONS: RETURN THEM TO CHEMIST.

KOLYNOS DENTAL CREAM

The economical tooth paste

"*Have you ever stopped to think that if it wasn't for Hitler we might never have been lance-corporals?*"

Punch

The courtyard at Oflag IVC where there have been no changes in the general layout of the camp since it was last visited in July, 1944.

OFLAG IVC, COLDITZ

Total strength of camp at time of visit was 239 officers and 51 other ranks; the total number of British prisoners of war being 200. There were no changes with regard to the general layout and interior arrangements of the camp since the last visit in July, 1944. The privileges promised by the camp commandant for further recreational facilities had not materialised. It has now been said that the chapel may be reopened.

There is a decided increase in the number of sick personnel, the most common symptoms being nervousness, insomnia and dyspepsia. There is a lack of medical and surgical equipment. British stocks are almost exhausted and the German supplies are inadequate.

(*Visited October*, 1944.)

STALAG IIA, NEUBRANDENBURG

This is a new camp and was visited for the first time. There are 253 American prisoners who were recently captured on the Western Front and 200 British N.C.O.s captured at Arnhem. It is situated in the vicinity of Neubrandenburg, about 70 miles north of Berlin. There are three barracks, of which two are at present partially occupied, and one serves as a reserve for expected new arrivals. There are slit trenches for protection from air raids.

Each barrack contains two sections. The sections are divided into 10 partitions, each partition holding 24 to 30 double-tier bunks, with hessian mat-

tresses filled with wood shavings and two blankets for each man. There are tables and benches, and in each section one oven and one stove; between the sections there is a washroom and a boiler for heating purposes. Hot showers are available once a week. Electric lighting is inadequate.

The cooking is done by French cooks in the camp's central kitchen. The German rations are considered inadequate both in quantity and quality. The commandant agreed to detail American cooks to the kitchen. Red Cross supplies were exhausted at the time of visit.

The camp hospital was excellently equipped; the surgical section is under the care of a Polish doctor.

No Red Cross clothing supplies have arrived so far and many prisoners are badly in need of articles such as socks, shoes, underwear and greatcoats. Prisoners do their own laundry, but it will later be done by the camp laundry when that has been repaired.

There is no American or British chaplain. Prisoners of the Roman Catholic faith may attend Mass in the camp chapel, where a French priest officiates.

Although there is adequate recreational space there is a complete lack of sports equipment and so far the only physical exercise available has been walks. No incoming mail had been received at the time of visit. The visiting delegate was satisfactorily impressed with this camp; the German authorities appeared reasonable.

(*Visited November*, 1944.)

The Prisoner of War

CHILDREN IN PANTOMIME AT KIRKBY LONSDALE

There was a large audience in the Assembly Hall of Queen Elizabeth School, Kirkby Lonsdale on Saturday evening to see two pantomimes performed by children from Bentham, and produced by Mrs. S. Jackson. The first was "The Sleeping Beauty", and the second "Dick Whittington." Many of the children played in both productions. The children in the audience were highly delighted by the many scenes, colourful costumes and delightful dances, while the adults also thoroughly enjoyed both performances, which were enhanced by the lighting effects. Interspersed between the scenes were lively choruses, topical songs and charming dances, while humour, an important part of pantomime, had not been overlooked. With a few exceptions most of the costumes were home-made and were tasteful in design and colour.

The principals took their parts in a praiseworthy manner, and were ably supported by the other members of the cast. The smaller children as "Sunbeams" also played their parts with credit. Miss Thelma N. Lumb was at the piano. Songs were sung during the interval by Miss M. Leeming and monologues given by Miss Lumb. Thanks were expressed to Mrs. Jackson and her party by Miss B. Wilson on behalf of the Return Home Fund Committee, and to Mr. L. G. Defoe, headmaster for loaning the hall and to those who had defrayed the expenses of the evening. Mr. N. Proctor was in charge of the stage lighting.

The proceeds were for the Return Home Fund.

Westmorland Gazette

REMAGEN BRIDGEHEAD NOW 19 MILES LONG

BY RICHARD ROWLAND, REUTER'S CORRESPONDENT

WITH THE U.S. FIRST ARMY, Monday.—The Remagen bridgehead now measures 18 air line miles, or 19 river line miles, with its greatest depth eight miles. Resistance varies from heavy in the north-west sector to light in the northern tip.

Some First Army elements are now almost out of the wickedly hilly and wooded country eastwards from the Rhine in the bridgehead area.

The six lane Ruhr-Frankfurt autobahn is not yet usable.

It was announced at S.H.A.E.F. to-day that traffic is expected to be resumed over the great Ludendorff Bridge very soon.—Reuter.

FRENCH FORCES CROSS THE GERMAN FRONTIER

BY ARTHUR OAKESHOTT, REUTER'S CORRESPONDENT

WITH U.S. SEVENTH ARMY, Monday.—French forces operating on the right flank of the American Seventh Army crossed the frontier into Germany to-day. The crossing is presumed to be somewhere in the Lauterburg area. Around Lauterburg fighting is continuing, with the Americans and the French teamed to take this frontier anchor town.

Elsewhere the Seventh Army front advances methodically.

N.E. FRANCE CLEARED

SIXTH U.S. ARMY GROUP H.Q., Monday.— Except for stragglers, the Germans have been cleared from North-Eastern France, the area of General Dever's Sixth Army Group, it is officially announced. The only German forces remaining in French territory are those in the Wissemburg-Haguenau-Lauterburg triangle. This does not, of course, take into account the German forces still in occupation of some of the French ports.—Reuter.

BRITISH 2nd ARMY READY TO CROSS LOWER RHINE—*Berlin*

Berlin declared last night that the British Second Army is ready for a crossing of the Lower Rhine in the area of Arnhem (Holland.)

"It seems that the British Second Army has finished its preparations," said a war reporter. "Since Sunday there has been intensive and quite unusual aerial reconnaissance over the whole Arnhem and Emmerich area. At the same time the entire area is being shrouded in artificial fog."

The Scotsman

LIVE RAIL RESCUE
Ganger Saved Boy

Sub-Ganger T. Coleman, of Bosham, Sussex, a Southern Railway employee, found a 2½-year-old boy, R. L. Elleker, lying between the live rail and running rail near Bosham Station. He put his cap round his hand and lifted the boy to safety just before a train passed over the spot. He has now been presented with the Carnegie Hero Fund Trust's parchment, a cheque for £10 from the fund, and £10 in savings certificates from the Southern Railway Company.

Evening News

THOUSANDS OF AIRCRAFT WORKERS STAGING BIG UNEMPLOYMENT DEMONSTRATION

Irish News

Protest Against Government's Failure To Provide Alternative Work

SIX thousand aircraft workers in Short and Harland's, Belfast, are expected to down tools to-morrow and march in processional order to the waste ground in High Street to join other colleagues, already out of work, in the first big unemployment demonstration to be held in the city since the war began. This information was given to an "Irish News" reporter by Mr. J. Lowden, organiser of the E.T.U., at a Press conference yesterday.

The route of the workers, he said, had already been planned, and the demonstration would be carried out in an orderly manner. The Short and Harland employees would be joined at various points along the route by workers in Harland and Wolff's aircraft works and by employees in the various dispersal factories. All these workers, he added, expected to be unemployed in the very near future, and they were therefore taking part in the demonstration as a protest against the Government's failure to provide alternative work. Altogether it is expected that 10,000 workers will take part in the demonstration.

TRAGIC POSITION.

Mr. Lowden said this was the only means of drawing public attention to the gravity of the position which had arisen in the aircraft industry. The position, he said, was tragic, and called for immediate solution. The Redundancy and Unemployment Committee, he said, held a four-hour meeting on Sunday to discuss the position, and the information forthcoming at that meeting revealed an alarming position. It had been established definitely that the original contract in respect of Sterling planes had been severely cut, and as a consequence all the dispersal factories were closing and the main factory of Short and Harland would probably cease work in October.

The Aldergrove and Longcash factories had now closed. Altona and Lambeg would close in a week's time, and Largymore (Lisburn), Glen and Regent works (Ards) were closing within a few weeks. Balmoral and Megaberry would close inside three months. The Hallmark factory at Ards was working with a greatly reduced staff. Harland and Wolff's aircraft works would close after the completion of the remaining work in hands, which would be a matter of weeks.

With all these factories closed, Mr. Lowden, as already published in the "Irish News," anticipates the total number of unemployed in the aircraft industry to be 10,000 It is known that in the main factory of Short and Harland there are, excluding staff and supervisory staff, about 6,000 employed.

POST-WAR FEARS.

"No alternative work has been provided for the workers already displaced," added Mr Lowden. "In England, when a worker is declared redundant in one industry he is given employment in another industry, but in Northern Ireland he becomes unemployed."

The workers and union officials were seriously perturbed at the state of unemployment in Northern Ireland at the moment, and had great fears that mass unemployment would face them after the war. They hold the Government responsible for the present state of affairs, as their plans for dealing with the position are totally inadequate. If the Government cannot provide employment for the workers at home, what, they ask, will be the position when the men and women come back from the forces? With the exception of the electrical trade, there were very few unions which could provide work for their members returning from the forces at the moment.

With the object of finding some solution for the alarming position which had arisen in the aircraft industry, four trade union representatives—Messrs. J Lowden, D Madden. R. Thompson and D Gray—are meeting Sir Basil Brooke to-day and would suggest that a joint deputation of the trades unions and the Government should go across and see the Imperial authorities with the object of getting more aircraft contracts or some new industries for Northern Ireland.

Mr Lowden pointed out that if the Prime Minister refused to act on this suggestion the trade unions would take a very strong line of action. The new industries already mentioned as having been set up in the North would to a big extent employ female workers.

Daily Telegraph

S. AFRICA'S DEBT TO EMPIRE

"TRUE SECURITY"

CAPETOWN, Monday.
Col. Stallard, South African Minister of Mines, speaking in the Union Assembly to-day, said that during the war the country had found over and over again that its true security lay in partnership with the rest of the British Empire. The day of the small independent nation was past.

"We are very fortunate in South Africa in being part of the British Empire. I trust that in the discussions which are to take place in London, San Francisco and doubtless elsewhere, we will reaffirm that safe policy which enabled us to play our part in this war," he said.

Speaking on mining, he said that unless those engaged in mining were allowed to obtain a fair profit fresh mines would not be opened.

Ultra-deep mining might call for the investment and risk of £20,000,000. Who would put up that sum unless there were assurances about profit, native labour, taxation and costs?—Reuter.

Daily Telegraph

MIGRATORY BIRDS

"*I THOUGHT you might like to give this prefabricated model the once-over before we started building one of our own.*"—By Gittins.

Evening News

PRISONER TATTOOED HIS DEFIANCE OF HITLER

CAIRO, Monday.

Among the liberated Allied prisoners whose arrival at a Middle East port is reported to-day is Pte. Christopher Conley, aged 25, Fincham Green, Liverpool. He has with him a copy of the charge brought against him at a German court-martial.

The charge alleges that he undermined the discipline of the German Wehrmacht because, on seeing a copy of Hitler's portrait in the doorkeeper's lodge, he used an expression current in the army and made a gesture to tear down the portrait.

"Further," adds the charge, "he showed a tattooing representing Mr. Churchill and Hitler in a boxing match, with Hitler getting a blow on the chin and going on his knees."

For these offences Pte. Conley was given a sentence of imprisonment of which he served nine months.

During his time as a prisoner of war he had himself tattooed with various drawings to annoy the Germans. One shows a British bulldog biting a dachshund; another Mr. Churchill and a bulldog.

Daily Telegraph

Socks, SOCKS, SOCKS!

One and a half cwts. of wool have been knitted up for the Red Cross by Mrs. R. Stevens, of Wartnaby. Mrs. Stevens began knitting socks for the Red Cross in October 1939. Since then she has made 462 pairs. She is aiming at completing 500 pairs.

Melton Mowbray Times

The Real Princess

HANS Andersen wrote a very charming little fairy tale about *The Real Princess* who slept so very badly because there was a pea hidden under her bedding !

Many of us are just as fastidious about our bedding—and for them we are now planning post-war "MODERNA" blankets.

They are to be lovelier even than pre-war. Softest lamb's wool in the newest of pastel shades : unshrinkable and free from that new-blanket smell ! They really will be "The Blanket of your Dreams."

MODERNA
Blankets for Post-War Homes
(Supplied only through Retail Stores)
THOMAS RATCLIFFE & CO. LTD., MYTHOLMROYD, YORKS

ITALIAN FOUND NOT GUILTY

Allegation at a Court-martial

A court-martial at an Italian prisoner of war camp in the North-West on Tuesday dismissed a charge against Soldato Marco Stazi of conduct prejudicial to good order and discipline at Storth on 19 November last in that he improperly associated with a female British subject and engaged in improper relations with her. Stazi was found not guilty and acquitted.

The prosecution was conducted by Capt. J. G. Shorrock (son of the late Mr. W. G. Shorrock, formerly High Sheriff of Westmorland), and Lieut. Harry Allan appeared for the defence, while the president of the Court was Major A. L. O. Owen, Royal Welch Regiment.

The prosecution alleged that the accused had established a certain relationship with the woman, who told the Court that her husband was in the Army serving abroad, that she had a child 2½ years old, and that she first met Stazi after her mother had sent cake to two Italian prisoners outside their house. She talked to the men, and alleged that that evening she met Stazi. She saw him again on 26 November, and did not meet him again until Christmas Day, when the two men were invited in to the house.

On this occasion her mother asked the two men who had been with her daughter. Stazi was alleged to have replied: "I promenade with her." She admitted that she had told her mother she had not been out with either of the men.

Mrs. Denny corroborated the details of the interview.

Lieut. J. Cabassi gave evidence as to the notification on parade to Stazi and others of the regulations affecting their association with women.

The defence was a complete denial by Stazi of any meeting with the woman from the afternoon of 19 November until Christmas Day. When he was taken into the house on that day he did not know what they were talking about, and only learned of the girl's condition on hearing the summary of evidence at the preliminary inquiry.

Westmorland Gazette

GIGLI SINGS IN ROME AGAIN

"NO COLLABORATOR"

From Our Special Correspondent
ROME, Monday.

Gigli sang in Rome to-night for the first time since the City's liberation. The concert hall was heavily guarded by Carabinieri. A tense audience that packed the concert hall expected that there might be some political demonstration against the tenor, who has been violently criticised as an alleged collaborator because he sang to the Germans after Mussolini's fall.

But Gigli made a successful return. Two or three men who whistled disapproval were quickly hustled from the hall. The remainder of the audience shouted again and again for encores.

Gigli, who faced the audience with evident nervousness, had tactfully chosen as his first song an aria by Meyerbeer, whose works were banned under the Fascist régime.

After the concert the singer repeated to me his protestations that he was not a collaborator. "Art has nothing to do with politics," he declared.

Daily Telegraph

64,800 EGGS — AND LORRY — STOLEN

£540 LONDON RAID

"Evening News" Reporter

A LORRY load of 64,800 eggs, worth £540, was stolen by Black Market thieves from St. Thomas-street, Southwark, to-day.

The eggs, in 180 cases, had been brought from the West Country to a Food Ministry egg warehouse for distribution. The lorry was waiting its turn for unloading when it disappeared.

Evening News

Londoners Watch V2 Go Up: 'Like Searchlight'

"Evening News" Reporter

A V2 rocket launched by the Germans recently was seen in many parts of London by early morning workers.

Mr. Branagan, of Darynglon-drive, Greenford, says he was looking towards the east and saw a light travelling almost vertically upwards. On reaching its zenith, it turned towards the north. Another man saw the same thing from Park-lane.

A resident of Addiscombe—Mrs. D. Clayton, of Everton-road—watched the rocket shoot straight up into the air from due east. "I thought at first it was a searchlight," she says, "but after it had gone right up I realised it was a rocket. After it stopped climbing it turned towards the north-west."

Silver Light

"I watched the rocket for more than four minutes," said Mr. W. H Bishop, of Fanton-walk, Shotgate, Wickford, Essex, "and then it disappeared. It seemed to come from the north-east and appeared as a silvery light."

Evening News

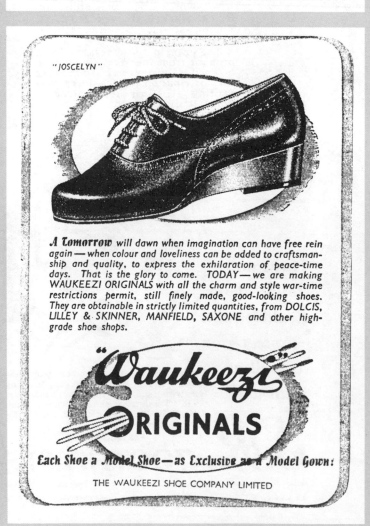
Sporting News

CRICKET

PLANS FOR KNOCK-OUT COMPETITION

Another step towards providing cricket
with a knock-out competition on the lines
of the F.A. Cup is put forward in the
interim report published yesterday by the
sub-committee appointed to investigate
the problem.

The plan embraces the 17 first-class counties
and provides for games of three days' duration
on the basis of one bye round, eight ties in the
first round, four in the second round, two semi-
finals, and a final tie of four days' duration to
be played at Lord's. The winning team would
hold for one year a permanent trophy to be
called " The Cricket Cup."

It is proposed that the bye round and the
first round should begin on the first and third
Saturdays in May, the ties being drawn well in
advance so as not to interfere with other first-
class dates. The second round and semi-finals
would be decided in mid-week because it would
be inconvenient to have the beaten teams and
various grounds idle at week-ends. Apart
from the final, all ties would take place on the
ground of one of the contestants, the team
drawn first in each tie to have choice. Seeding
the draw in the earlier rounds on a regional
basis is not recommended.

The biggest problem the committee faced
was that of drawn matches. A replay is provided for in the bye round, and then if no
decision is reached the team with the superior
record in the last available complete Championship table would go forward.

PROBLEM OF DRAWN GAMES

In the event of a draw in the first, second,
and semi-final rounds the winner would be the
county highest in the current Championship
seven days preceding the start of the next
round. It is felt that the link between the two
competitions would be of mutual benefit providing the rounds are spaced to permit an
alteration in the Championship order between
the date of the drawn match and the next
round. Should the teams be level in the
current table, reference would be made to a
previous season's placings. If the final remained undecided after four days, time lost
through weather would be made up on the
fifth day and then if no conclusion be reached
the cup would not be awarded.

To reduce the number of draws to a minimum
county committees would be asked to direct
their team to enter any match with the intention of winning. Secondly, an extension of
the standard hours of play from 18½ hours to
20¼ would help to bring definite results. Suggested hours are three periods of 2¼ hours:
11 to 1.15, 2 to 4.15, 4.30 to 6.45. (In 1919
the maximum daily period of play was
7 hours 35 minutes, compared with 6¾ hours
now proposed.)

The committee state: " We are very
conscious of the shortcomings of our proposals, but our investigations suggest that no
perfect scheme is attainable. We are agreed
that the competition may be of much potential
long-term value to first-class cricket, and that
even with imperfections a scheme of this kind
should have a trial for a minimum of two
seasons."

In order to make a strong appeal both to
players and the public its inception would be
delayed until the counties are in a position to
field reasonably representative teams. They do
not recommend it being played earlier than the
first normal season.

The Times

APRIL
1945

NEW KING'S FUND TO BE RAISED

HELP FOR WAR DISTRESS

Sir Walter Womersley, the Minister of Pensions, speaking at the Orpington Rotary Club luncheon yesterday, announced that the King had agreed to the formation of a King George VI Fund for similar purposes to that sponsored by King George V after the last war.

The King George V Fund had now been exhausted, the Minister said. The present King, while agreeing to the formation of a new fund, would not allow a public appeal to be made until the present war was over. "I am never short of money," Sir Walter Womersley added. "I have had a gift of £28,000 from the films, although I never make any public appeal."

The King's Fund, formed in 1918 and extended with the approval of his Majesty for the present war, gave assistance in directions which were beyond the province of State liability to war-disabled members of the Navy, Army, Air Force, Auxiliary Services, Home Guard, Mercantile Marine, and Civil Defence organizations, and to widows, children, and other dependents of those who lost their lives through war service.

Observer

Future Of A Ruined Germany
Rural Slum Cannot Help Europe

By GEORGE ORWELL, Observer War Correspondent

AS the advance into Germany continues and more and more of the devastation wrought by the Allied bombing planes is laid bare, there are three comments that almost every observer finds himself making.

The first is, "The people at home have no conception of this." The second is, "It's a miracle that they've gone on fighting." And the third is, "Just think of the work of building this all up again!"

It is quite true that the scale of the Allied blitzing of Germany is even now not realised in this country, and its share in the breaking-down of German resistance is probably much under-rated. It is difficult to give actuality to newspaper or radio reports of air warfare, and the man in the street can be forgiven if he imagines that what we have done to Germany over the past four years is merely the same kind of thing as they did to us in 1940.

But this error, which must be even commoner in the United States, has in it a potential danger, and the many protests against indiscriminate bombing which have been uttered by pacifists and humanitarians have merely confused the issue.

World Impoverished

Bombing is not especially inhumane. War itself is inhumane, and the bombing plane, which is used to paralyse industry and transport rather than to kill human beings, is a relatively civilised weapon. "Normal" or "legitimate" warfare is just as destructive of inanimate objects, and enormously more so of human lives.

Moreover, a bomb kills a casual cross-section of the population, whereas the men killed in battle are exactly the ones that the community can least afford to lose. The people of Britain have never felt easy about the bombing of civilians, and no doubt they will be ready enough to pity the Germans as soon as they have definitely defeated them; but what they have still not grasped—thanks to their own comparative immunity—is the frightful destructiveness of modern war and the long period of impoverishment that now lies ahead of the world as a whole.

To walk through the ruined cities of Germany is to feel an actual doubt about the continuity of civilisation. For one has to remember that it is not only Germany that has been blitzed. The same desolation extends, at any rate in considerable patches, all the way from Brussels to Stalingrad. And where there has been ground fighting, the destruction is even more thorough than where there has merely been bombing. In the 300 miles or so between the Marne and the Rhine there is not, for instance, such a thing as a bridge or a viaduct that has not been blown up.

Esther McCracken's particular genius as a playwright lies in her ability to turn ordinary people into heroines and heroes. Her play "No Medals" at the Vaudeville Theatre, London, with Fay Compton (seen above with Valerie White), in the leading part, pays a witty and charming tribute to the war job done by millions of British housewives

PRESIDENT ROOSEVELT : MEMORIAL SERVICE AT ST. PAUL'S

Four photographs taken outside St. Paul's yesterday when a large and distinguished gathering attended the memorial service for President Franklin D. Roosevelt. They show the King and Queen, accompanied by Princess Elizabeth ; Mr. Winant, the American Ambassador, and Admiral Stark ; Mr. Churchill, with whom were many members of the Government, leaving, and the Lord Mayor receiving Queen Wilhelmina of the Netherlands. Among others present were King Haakon of Norway, King George of the Hellenes, and King Peter of Yugoslavia.

ASSOCIATION FOOTBALL

ENGLAND'S GREAT WIN

England played a great game at Hampden Park, Glasgow, on Saturday when they beat Scotland before 133,000 spectators by six goals to one. It was England's seventh successive win over Scotland and their eleventh win in 15 war-time matches.

England never appeared to be in danger of defeat although Scotland fought every inch of the way in the first half and were level at one goal all at half-time. Incessant rain made the ground treacherous, but in the second half England's forwards juggled and feinted in a manner which bewildered their opponents and in spite of some fine goalkeeping by Brown the score might easily have reached double figures. Matthews, previously held in check by Stephen, began to work more often than not from the inside-left position and, with Carter and Brown scheming, shooting, and controlling nearly every move, England had four attacking forwards in the middle of the field. Lawton, leading the line, beat Harris nearly every time in the air, and on the ground he was yards faster. England's halves and defence could not be faulted, but of the Scottish team only Brown, in goal, Busby, the captain, playing in probably his last international match, and Waddell, the outside-right, emerged with their reputations untouched.

Scotland suffered a great blow in the first minute when Bogan, their inside-right, collided with Swift and had to be carried off the field. Ten minutes later Johnstone (Clyde) came on to deputize, but he did not settle down. Carter gave England a good start with a brilliant goal in half an hour, but Johnstone soon equalized. In the second half Lawton (two), Brown, Matthews, and Smith added goals for England. Smith's goal came from the second penalty of the afternoon, Swift having saved Busby's kick for Scotland.

The teams were :—
SCOTLAND.—R. Brown (Queen's Park); Harley (Liverpool), Stephen (Bradford); Busby (Liverpool) (captain), Harris (J.) (Wolverhampton), Macaulay (West Ham); Waddell (Rangers), Bogan (Hibernian), J. R. Harris (Queen's Park), Black (Heart of Midlothian), Kelly (Morton).
ENGLAND.—Swift (Manchester City); Scott (Arsenal), Hardwick (Middlesbrough); Soo (Stoke City), Franklin (Stoke City), Mercer (Everton) (captain); Matthews (Stoke City), Carter (Sunderland), Lawton (Everton), Brown (R. A. J.) (Charlton), Smith (Brentford).

The Times

LARGE CROWDS AT THE SEASIDE

Most of the coast resorts had more holiday-makers on Saturday on their newly cleared fronts and beaches than at any time since the war began. Skegness had more Easter visitors than ever before in its history.

Accommodation was adequate at most places, and Blackpool even had " plenty of room " because of the reduced travel facilities. But rooms in Brighton were fully booked some time ago, and at Bognor, which had 20,000 visitors, one hotel proprietor was offered £50 for a week's board.

Visitors to Morecambe, who had followed official advice to take rations with them, received a shock, for at some places they were told that they could have " full board or nothing."

The Times

ALLEGED TO HAVE LIVED WITH TWO "HUSBANDS"

Father Said To Have Been Witness At Both "Weddings"

A woman was stated to have had two husbands in the same house at the same time, and who declared that her legal husband allowed the bigamous one to go out with them, because he always paid, was committed for trial at the Central Criminal Court by Stratford Justices on Tuesday, on a charge of bigamy and three charges of obtaining money by false pretences.

The woman, Mrs. Alberta Florence Wells, 31, married, of Hazelwood Road, Walthamstow, was accompanied in the dock by her father, Albert Edward Seipp-Blower, 58, general hand, of Lea Bridge-road, Leyton, who was committed for trial on a charge of aiding, abetting and assisting in the bigamy

The story of the alleged bigamy was told in a long statement made by Mrs. Wells, read by Mr. W. McDonnell, prosecuting.

A VILE TEMPER

In it, Mrs. Wells said she was married to John Henry Wells, at St. John's Church, Leytonstone, on June 8, 1935. They lived together at several addresses including Hazelwood Road, Walthamstow. They were never very happy. Her husband had a vile temper and she left him to live with her father.

While she was evacuated in March, 1941, she met a young soldier, Ashley. She returned home and he (Ashley) met her husband and became friendly.

Sometimes Ashley spent leaves with his people at Brentford, and she spent leave with him there.

"One day Ashley said: 'What about getting married?' I said, 'You know that I am married. It would be bigamy' He replied, 'I know that, but if we got married at least I can keep you, which is more than John is doing.'"

On August 12, 1941, they went through a form of marriage at Brentford Registry Office.

The alleged statement continued: "I must admit that I knew what I was doing. I remember I was very upset and crying. About a week after I married Ashley I told my husband. I expected him to give me a hiding, but he did not. He just said: 'Good, now he can keep you.' We continued to live together, and Ashley still used to come as well."

Witnesses at both weddings gave evidence that Blower was witness at both ceremonies.

Det.-Sergt. Bradshaw said Mrs. Wells made a statement on the false pretences charges, in which she admitted she had drawn a total of £211 15s. between August, 1941, and October, 1944, being separation allowance. At the same time she pointed out that she had not drawn the marriage allowance she would have been entitled to draw from her husband, who therefore she considered she was also in the Forces, and had not defrauded the State of a single penny.

Marylebone Mercury

Sharpers About

HOW PEOPLE ARE BEING GULLED

Householders should be wary of infamous barter merchants who are operating in the island. Their practice usually involves a good exchange — probably a luxury article for something more stable. With stocks at such a low ebb, it is not surprising that some persons have been caught. The deal, arranged and completed in no small manner by the plausible tongue of the thief, is then carried out one-sidedly. The householder, awaiting the return of her "benefactor," has an endless vigil.

Another way of approach, is the well-known "con-man" method. He will probably explain, in rather convincing fashion, the trials and tribulations he has to undergo with regard to his health, and taking the victim into his confidence, will drop a hint of a possible exchange. The exchange, usually a fair one, results partially through the tender-heartedness of those among us who still glory in helping others. The miscreant, promising faithfully to carry out his side of the bargain, and very profuse with his thanks, then departs and is not seen again. Although it is reported that these goods are being placed on the "Black Market," this point has not been substantiated and must therefore be held as just rumour.

The majority of islanders are now taking the abnormal precautions necessary to safeguard commodities, but cases of thefts, through undue care, in some respects, still occur. Stocks should be guarded, not only after dusk but throughout the whole 24 hours, as thieves have recently committed offences in broad daylight.

Make some enquiries before clinching an exchange deal; ascertain whether your dealer is straight or not, and make doubly sure that goods are handed over simultaneously!

Guernsey Evening Press

The way things are

Good hostesses are those who take infinite trouble, those who in their spare time comb the food shops for some unexpected delicacy, who will trudge to Soho, carry parcels and stand in queues. There was never the kick in shopping in days of plenty that there is to-day. That wonderful last bottle of sauce, those red peppers, the prawns, the liver, the kidneys . . .

Good guests are those who arrive with a writing pad and stamps of their own; cigarettes, matches and lighter, their own hot-water bottle, soap and rations, a bottle of drink and an unexpected offering of food—sweets, fruit, a cake—that has cost a little trouble and thought to get. People who take dogs to stay must take said dogs' food with them.

Interest in food increases daily and frail non-eaters are non-existent. Thin women are thin by accident and not by design, and a healthy appetite is no longer something of which to be ashamed. Women are frankly greedy, and surveying a plate of piled-up vegetable *hors d'oeuvres*, will wail " No sardines ?" Recounting a party afterwards, no one asks "Who was there ?" or "What did So-and-So wear ?" but " What did you eat ?" Many women are better looking as the result of hearty meals.

Why not revive the old-fashioned Linkmen to accompany nervous women home at night ? If every hotel signed on half a dozen reliable men as " walkers home " during the hours of darkness (say at 2s. 6d. a time, for short distances only), the men would make a lot of money, and lonely ladies would not have to hire cars at ruinous prices or ring up every taxi rank in London for imaginary taxis.

Private bottle parties are popular, especially in country districts. Guests bring their own drink and a bit more, and the host and hostess have only to provide sandwiches and a gramophone. Some hot soup and possibly a steaming dish of macaroni or spaghetti late in the evening put the seal on the party's success. Service girls cast off their uniforms and don an old evening dress with a thrill; their elders think a bicycle ride in the blackout worth while to meet their neighbours, and gossip about their households.

Never have card games been so popular as now. People who have never played cards in their lives are taking up bridge, poker and gin-rummy. In the country, if you call in somewhere at 6 o'clock for a drink, you'll find yourself embroiled in a game of chance for the hour you are there. . . . All Americans and all Poles seem to play cards well and enjoy them.

Ordinary cotton twill, dyed vividly and bordered with white wool or cotton fringe makes wonderful curtains. John Fowler has done this in *Another Love Story* with great effect. Those old-fashioned bedspreads that we used to see in cottage bedrooms make the most fascinating tablecloths; Mr. Robert Lebus has an interesting collection. He furnishes the bedrooms of his country cottage with bamboo furniture painted white. He grows Knotted Marjoram, Kales, Estragon, all shades of petunia and mauve—lovely to look at, to eat, or to put in bowls.

Piano Practice

"Our son learnt the piano from the age of six. After three years, the daily practice became a bore for him and painful for me, who had to keep him at it. Lest he should hate the thing we loved, we stopped both lessons and practice, but we continued to play our gramophone records and listen to radio performances. We are thankful that the boy is still interested in music, for he picks out on the piano tunes he has heard, tries over in a desultory way any piece he likes, and of his own accord tries to accompany his sister at her violin practice. (We made her wait till she was nine before starting lessons, which she asked to do, but that's another story !)" —*G. D., Leicester.*

Over-Efficient Women ?

"Do not all women over-act in the ordinary course of life? Is not the efficient secretary or shorthand-typist usually over-abrupt and 'efficient' in her mannerisms? I know many highly efficient businessmen who carry lightly their great responsibilities, and who still retain a good measure of personal charm and homeliness in their general attitude. I look amongst my feminine acquaintances for the successful business woman who remains unaltered by being given commercial responsibilities, and I look in vain."—*Mrs. L. T., Farnham.*

Thank You, Pilot

"As I write, my husband is probably approaching the heart of Mandalay, and yet this afternoon, I received a letter from him, in answer to one of mine written less than three weeks ago. Mine took ten days to go—his ten days to come. Nowhere have I seen any written appreciation of the work done by the men (or women) who pilot our mail planes. My letters come remarkably regularly, which means that these pilots must carry on, regardless of weather conditions. I would like to express my most grateful thanks to them. May they be cheered as they fly from one side of the globe to the other, by the thought that they carry as precious a cargo as any. For without letters, it would be hard for the men and their women-folk to carry on."—*Mrs. H. A. B., Scotland.*

Crossing the Road

"To cut down road casualties, especially of children, I'd like to see, on main roads, small footbridges with pavements railed in between each footbridge. Where present crossings are, however, more convenient, such as in towns, a proportion of the Special Constabulary could be on continual duty at these crossings. By such methods, road casualties would be largely cut out, and the present road traffic speed limits could be altered to 'sensible driving'." —*J. E. K., Staffs.*

Letter-Writer's Tip

"When writing to friends in the Forces overseas, I found that before I started the letter I had plenty of news, but when all set to write, I forgot half of it. Now I carry a very small note-book and pencil in my handbag, then anything I see or hear, which my friends would find interesting, amusing, etc., I briefly jot down. When it comes to 'letter-night,' I only have to look at those brief notes and hey presto ! from there on it is plain sailing."—*Scottish reader.*

Woman's Own

NOCTURNE

Shake down the purple dust of
   night,
   And call the soft-fleeced
     wand'rer home,
The lingering gold has taken flight
   And shadows lengthen in my
     room.

Without, the elfin wood-breeze steals
   Between the murm'ring leafy arms ;
Across the moon the mad bat wheels
   To flaunt his stark satanic charms.

Now croaks the moon-faced frog, who
   eyes
   The lapping water's edge. Through
     bars
Of mist and dew a night-bird cries,
   And lo, the pool is filled with stars.

JOHN TRAILL LEITCH

These lovely lines by John Leitch were found among his papers after he was reported missing, and later killed, on a raid over Kiel in September last year He was nineteen.

Woman's Journal

RESCUED MAN FROM BEAR PIT

RECOGNITION OF DUDLEY KEEPER'S HEROISM

An unusual case of heroism was yesterday recognised by the Carnegie Hero Fund Trustees.

John Westwood, a keeper at Dudley Zoo, was awarded an honorary certificate and £10 for rescuing a man mauled by a bear. He saw the bear standing over the man, who was bleeding profusely. Jumping into the pit, he picked up a small ladder and beat the animal on the head and back.

After a struggle he warded off the bear while getting the injured man up another ladder and out of the pit.

Birmingham Post

Mr. Bevin: I Am Not A Traitor To My Party

MR. BEVIN, Minister of Labour, speaking to the Yorkshire Labour Party, at Leeds yesterday, said that victory now appeared to be in sight and the political air was charged with an idea of an election so that the electorate might determine what policy should be followed for the peace and reconstruction, and the kind of a world to follow this war.

"It is suggested that Labour has taken a very responsible step in breaking up the Coalition. Let me say that Labour has done nothing of the kind. The facts are that Parliament was elected ten years ago on a lie—on a self-confessed lie—of Mr. Baldwin. It has run five years over its course. It is right and proper that the electors should have the opportunity to determine their form of Government. The Conservative Party, afraid to face their electors on their own record that led us to this war, resort to other methods and foul suggestions.

"What are the facts? The Cabinet have to face the question that a Bill ought to be submitted to Parliament to extend its life.

Premier Doubtful

"When the Bill was drafted and presented to the House, so doubtful was the Prime Minister about his own party's attitude to it that he introduced it. The Labour Party had to consider what they would advise their followers, and what their attitude would be when the Prime Minister decided to dissolve Parliament. They decided, and rightly, to fight as an independent party and face the electors with their own programme and policy.

"There have been a lot of suggestions about myself. I do not wear 'Loyalty' written on my arm, but I have been loyal to this party for 40 years. I have been through all its vicissitudes. I have witnessed its past and the treachery of some of its leaders. I shall abide by the Party decision whatever that may be.

Serious, Sacred

"I hope the decisions arrived at following the war will be taken calmly and deliberately. Never was there a time when the casting of a vote will be a more serious and sacred obligation. If the people are led away by panic or excitement and do not act with sound judgment they may have condemned future generations to a return to a situation similar to that existing between the wars."

The party which had a majority for over 20 years, with the short exception of two years and six months, completely failed to prepare for defence. It ran a foreign policy which nearly brought us and the whole of civilisation to the dust, he said.

"Now they are hoping that the present generation of young electors will know nothing about it, and that those who are older will have forgotten it. They thought they could buy Hitler and his gang. Big Business was ready to do a deal with them. They preferred to keep millions drawing unemployment pay rather than put them on to useful work. Public opinion was mainly the view of the financiers and speculators, not the masses or nation.

Observer

TYRES FOR RUSSIA STOLEN

Three Men Sentenced At Old Bailey

Three men concerned in stealing or receiving 20 motor tyres and 20 inner tubes belonging to the U.S. Government and intended for shipment to Russia, were all sentenced to terms of imprisonment when they appeared in the dock at the Old Bailey on Thursday.

Albert White (35), a soldier, of no fixed address, who pleaded guilty to stealing the tyres and tubes, and was found guilty of assaulting the police, was sentenced to two years' imprisonment.

William Redhead (27), a lorry driver, of Percy Road, Kilburn, and George William Smith (24), a wood merchant, of Torbay Road, Kilburn, were both found guilty of receiving the tyres and tubes, knowing them to have been stolen.

Smith was sentenced to two years' imprisonment, and Redhead, who was also convicted of assaulting the police, was sentenced to 12 months' imprisonment.

The appearance of Redhead at the Old Bailey recalls to mind his last appearance there.

Three years ago Redhead and a man named James O'Connor were both charged with the murder of Alfred Ambridge (56), a man known in the Kilburn district as "the Horse Doc."

Redhead was acquitted, but O'Connor was found guilty. As sentence of death was being passed O'Connor, to show his contempt of the proceedings, stuck a cigarette in his mouth and gazed round the court. Warders quickly removed it.

Marylebone Mercury

ALUMINIUM HOUSE APPROVED

PREFABRICATION AT AIRCRAFT WORKS

The Ministry of Works announces that the aluminium house designed by the Aircraft Industries Research Organization on Housing has now passed its technical tests.

Modifications in design and construction are being made so that manufacture can start as soon as the Ministry of Aircraft Production can allot the factory capacity. The aluminium house is made in four sections, each complete in itself. Within a few hours of their arrival on the site, these four sections are coupled by interlocking fastenings, and when the services have been joined up the house is ready for occupation.

The house is about the same size as other approved types of temporary houses. It is a single-storey building with front entrance and hall giving direct access to the living room, bathroom, and both bed rooms. There is space in the hall for a pram. The kitchen, which has a side entrance, is separated from the living room by a glazed partition. The bedrooms are on the opposite side of the hall from the living quarters, and between the various rooms are built-in cupboards.

The floor frame is made in aluminium alloy faced with normal timber floorboards. The outside walls are faced with alloy sheet, painted with a rough-cast finish of stone appearance. Inside the walls are faced with plaster board. The wall-filling is a lightweight aerated cement, which has a high insulation value.

The roof is made of aluminium alloy sheet packed with cork, which gives thermal insulation. There is a high standard of thermal and sound insulation throughout, both in the exterior structure and internal partition. In these respects the structure should be better than the standard 9in. brick wall, and the roof better than tiles and roof felt.

The Times

DAY OF VICTORY

"Premature" Talk of Celebration

In the House of Commons to-day Dr. Little (Con., Dow) asked the Prime Minister for an assurance that on the cessation of hostilities a week-day would be set apart for prayer and thanksgiving with a cessation of all work, and the closing of all licensed premises.

Mr. Churchill: I hope and believe that when the time comes we shall celebrate a victorious peace in the manner worthy of the British nation.

Dr. Little: Will he take into account the strong feeling in the country that the day should be a rest from all toil and of sobriety.

Mr. Churchill: I think it is a little premature to go into all the details in advance of the actual moment.

LADY ASTOR'S IDEA

Viscountess Astor (Con., Sutton, Plymouth): If we really celebrate in a proper manner we have got to begin now to prepare, because the drink trade is already making plans to get our men drunk on the one day when we should all be on our knees thanking God for victory.

Mr. Churchill: I really think these misgivings are very much exaggerated.

Mr. Davies (Labour, Westhoughton): Will he not use his great office to discourage this blasphemy that the Almighty has anything to do with war?

Mr. Churchill: That is really raising a point far beyond the scope of the question. (Laughter.)

Mr. Glanvile (Labour, Consett): Is he aware that if he carries out the second part of Dr. Little's suggestion it would be anything but a day of prayer. (Laughter.) Has he ever heard the song: "I am going to get lit up when the lights go up in London"? (Loud laughter.)

Southern Daily Echo

CARE OF THE DISABLED

To the Editor

Sir,—The time is undoubtedly approaching when various bodies will be appealing for subscriptions towards memorials, cenotaphs, etc., in connection with the war. It appears to be generally recognised that these large stone erections are no longer looked upon with favour.

I should like to put forward the suggestion that cities, towns and villages adopt their own Servicemen and Servicewomen who have lost a limb, eyesight or hearing, and provide them with the finest mechanical appliances that science and industry can supply and keep them in good condition.

These men and women are the ones who have sacrificed and suffered and they should have the best. Eventually we shall be meeting them in our streets, hobbling on sticks and crutches or being led about. Shall we pass them by without a nod?—Yours faithfully,

S. H. BEST.

14, Grove House Lane, Leeds, 2, April 24.

Yorkshire Post

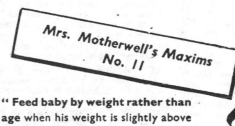

Daily Express

WHAT WOMEN ARE DOING AND SAYING

Photo:
M. W. Elphinstone
H.R.H. PRINCESS
ELIZABETH.

OUR nineteen-year-old *Princess Elizabeth* is delighted to be a member of the A.T.S. at last, for she had long been eager to join. Like everything else she undertakes, the Princess has tackled her new job with great enthusiasm and, in the words of the *Queen*: "She is learning to drive a lorry, and seems to spend most of her time diving underneath one!"

WHAT do Forces men and women want most in a club—parties, outings, or just comfortable home atmosphere? *Lady Freyberg*, wife of famous V.C. general, who runs Fernleaf Club for New Zealanders in London, says they most appreciate simple home atmosphere.

IF you were stricken down with illness, wouldn't you be glad to know that some good neighbour was looking after your home, children, shopping, keeping things going? W.V.S. Housewives Section has rendered splendid help in this way, at request of medical officers. Section has nearly 70,000 members in London area alone.

HOW many well-to-do elderly widows, spinsters, live lonely life in large houses? Councillor *Mrs. Legge*, Mayor of Finchley, London, suggests they could find companionship, relieve grave housing shortage, by letting part to suitable tenants.

AFTER the war U.S. and Canadian girls will be coming to Roedean School with two-year scholarships offered through Kinsmen Trust, of which *Lady Louis Mountbatten* is a trustee. This is Roedean's "Thank you" for kindness, hospitality extended to 50 pupils evacuated to N. America at beginning of war.

WOULDN'T it be a relief to mothers if children could be entertained at school during holidays? Experiment is to be tried at Kensington, London, school, of remaining open three days a week, parents taking turns to supervise children in place of teachers.

EVER thought of specialising on dragon flies? *Miss Cynthia Longfield*, curator of collection at Natural History Museum, London, has done so for years; toured China, Malaya, Africa, S. America, in search of rare varieties; can identify 43 different kinds in Britain.

Woman's Own

Good Housekeeping

TAILORED DRESS in woollen—precision-cut by a master hand and so well made that it could almost be worn inside out ! Every seam is treble-stitched to prevent splitting; shoulder seams have a tape sewn in them to prevent sleeves from slipping over the shoulders; finally, the material is well shrunk to shape in the making. This "Berkertex" dress is one that you can live in—wear it unadorned for every day; dress it up with accessories for special occasions. It has a contrasting collar and pocket flaps and is made in most of the fashionable colour combinations. It needs 11 coupons and costs £3.

TOWN COAT—so termed because it looks superb with smart dark accessories; but we can imagine it equally well worn over a country suit. Its main virtue is its beautiful, clean line from shoulder to hem, allowing for bulky clothes to be worn underneath when necessary; but looking sleek in spite of this. It is a "Dereta" model, and is made in the new oatmeal shade and several soft pastels, as well as brighter fashion colours, such as scarlet. The material is a good quality woollen freize, and the price is £4. The coat is half-lined, and so takes 15 of your coupons. Hat is a "Lystalite" model.

"*P.S. I have grown a beard.*"

Punch

Educating the Nazi

A STORY which reaches me from Italy will appeal to those who, as small boys or girls, have trembled in the tutorial presence. It concerns an English governess of majestic deportment resident in Florence. She was there when the Nazis took over and was in no way disconcerted by the institution of the "new order." From her angle it was merely another foreign eccentricity.

The Nazis took themselves more seriously. They decided that the governess should go to a concentration camp, and one of them went to arrest her. He found an erect and quite composed lady who addressed him as if he were a small boy caught in a misdemeanour.

"My good man," she said coldly, "you can't arrest me. I'm English."

And he didn't. She was still there when the Allies arrived.

Yorkshire Post

"Those fighting chaps are risking all for us. We say 'thank you' by putting all we can into War Savings."

LET'S SAVE AS HARD AS THEY FIGHT

Yorkshire Post

Now—for Freedom
Soon—for the Family

While the lamps o Liberty burned low in Europe, we counted leisure and luxury well lost in Freedom's cause. Then Electricity, source of so many domestic comforts and peacetime pleasures, helped forge the weapons to free the conquered capitals.

We look to the day when Electricity will itself be freed—freed to serve your Family's needs—to warm, to cheer, to cook, to clean, to lighten labour in a hundred ways.

Hasten that day by switching off *now* whenever you can.

Electricity

Sheffield Airman's German Wife

The long-awaited meeting between the 19-years-old German wife of an R.A.F. man and her English relatives took place at a Liverpool hostel yesterday.

Flight Sergeant Donald Meese motored from his home in Sheffield with his mother, Mrs. Sarah Elizabeth Meese, and his 12-years-old niece, Molly, to meet his anxious wife, Ursula Mary.

She is the German girl who befriended him after his escape from a prisoner of war camp in Silesia and helped him to escape from the Gestapo. They married at a Protestant chapel in Cracow, with a wedding ring obtained from a Polish woman in exchange for a pair of shoes.

"Mary is a grand girl. I like her very much, and I feel sure we shall get on splendidly together," said Mrs. Meese, after the meeting.

It was only a matter of minutes after their arrival at the hostel that the happy family, arm-in-arm, left for Sheffield.

SMITH'S CRISPS ON NATIONAL SERVICE

Birthday Gift To Firm's Founder

Founder of the famous firm of Smith's Crisps, Mr. Frank Smith, who attained the age of 70 last Thursday, was signally honoured at a birthday celebration held at the firm's headquarters in the Great West Road.

It had been decided that the most suitable gift to make to Mr. Smith was a portrait of himself. This was painted by Mr. Maurice Codner, well-known portrait painter, and was unveiled in the presence of a large gathering which included representatives of the firm's many branches.

The unveiling ceremony was followed by a luncheon, in the works' canteen presided over by Sir Herbert Morgan.

Among the distinguished visitors was the First Lord of the Admiralty (Mr. A. V. Alexander) and Mrs. Alexander, Mr. Ronald Gilbey, County Councillor A. H. Charlton, Mr. R. F. C. Crowther (president of Brentford Chamber of Commerce) and Mr. Codner, the artist.

COURAGE AND SYMPATHY

The toast of "Long life and prosperity to the founder" was proposed by Sir Herbert Morgan, who said that Mr. Frank Smith possessed both courage and sympathy, which had helped his great undertaking to success.

Mr. Alexander, who added his tribute, said that Mr. Frank Smith had performed a real service to the country in war-time by providing workers with sustenance in a cheap and palatable form. It gave confidence to his colleagues and himself to know that firms like Smith's Crisps were gradually reabsorbing labour.

Replying, Mr. Smith said he would be only too happy to absorb all the labour Mr. Bevin had taken away from them (laughter). He expressed deep gratitude for all the good wishes extended to him.

Middlesex Independent

FAMILIES WITHOUT POTATOES

Scores of families in Wimbledon have no potatoes for dinner to-day. The town yesterday experienced its worst potato shortage. Shops in the High-street area had no supplies in the morning and expected none. Some shops in the Broadway received supplies later in the day and rationed them to 2lb. per customer. During the afternoon women queued outside shops to buy seed potatoes with sprouts two and three inches long.

Daily Express

"MABEL" IS FOUND

CABLE FOLLOWS "NEWS OF THE WORLD" STORY

Following publication in last Sunday's issue of the "News of the World" of the story of a mysterious British woman in Burma, a mother in Cambridge has had the first news of her daughter for four years.

The story, which appeared in "Gossip of the Day," was that troops of the British 36th Division in Burma, while clearing the jungle, were also searching for the British wife of a local Shan chief, known only to them by the name of "Mabel."

Mrs. Edith A. Phillips, of High-street, Old Chesterton, Cambridge, wrote to us that she thought the mysterious "Mabel" might be her daughter.

**The Mahadevi of　The Swahwa of
Mongmit.　　　Mongmit.**

This has proved to be correct, for Mrs. Phillips has since had a cable from her daughter, the Mahadevi of Mongmit, that she has arrived safely and well in Calcutta with her children.

Mrs. Phillips's son-in-law is the local chief of a Shan State in Burma, of which Mongmit, recently taken from the Japanese by the British 36th Division, is the capital. He is known as the Swabwa of Mongmit.

He met his wife, then Mabel Phillips, when he was an undergraduate at Magdalene College, Cambridge, where he studied law. Eleven years ago he married her and took her back to Burma with him.

They made their home at Mongmit, in a house which a correspondent from the 36th British Division describes as "still having the atmosphere of an English country house, though almost burnt out by the Japanese."

British troops, he writes, found Burmese dolls in what must have been a children's nursery, and there was a see-saw in the garden.

Mrs. Phillips last heard from her daughter Mabel four years ago, when she wrote that whatever happened she would stay with her husband. When the Japanese came to Mongmit she kept her word.

In her cable she did not mention her husband. Mrs. Phillips thinks he is probably still with his head-hunters fighting the Japanese.

News of the World

For a Home Coming

Bestway Model Pattern No. 14.

Bestway Model Pattern No. 15.

REUNIONS, meetings, home comings are ahead —have a dress ready, a soft fair frock that speaks of gentle times. There is this silken Model No. 14 with its top draped in graceful gathers—a design both becoming and new. There could be nothing more feminine than Model No. 15 in printed crêpe with its pleated dickey, set in a bodice, which is gathered to outline the figure in a charming princess line above a swinging skirt with clustered centre fullness.

Details of amounts of material and how to obtain these individually cut Bestway Model Patterns are on page 83.

MAY
1945

OBITUARY

THE Daily Express rejoices to announce the report of Adolf Hitler's death. It prints today every line of information about the manner of his death.

It wastes no inch of space upon his career. The evil of his deeds is all too well known.

It gives no picture of the world's most hated face.

It records that Hitler was born Schickelgruber at Braunau, Austria, on April 20, 1889, and that his days upon the earth he sought to conquer were too long.

Daily Express

MORE ON BUCHENWALD

By MAVIS TATE, M.P.

MILLIONS of people will in the last few days have seen films of the German internment camps at Buchenwald and Belsen. They will think they have gained some impression of the conditions under which thousands of people died who had committed no crime and faced no trial. After having studied every available photograph and been to all the films on what are now known as the "horror camps," I can say without any hesitation whatever that they give but a very faint impression of the reality. It is difficult to know why this should be so; probably it is that the films are shown very rapidly and seem almost unreal, and that photographs do not convey the horror of the reality because they are static. Photographs, if they shock one, shock through the eyes; one is not shocked through any other sense. In fact, while it is possible to photograph some of the results of suffering, there are no means by which suffering itself can be photographed.

When I visited Buchenwald, I saw in the first hut I entered—which had been hastily arranged as a temporary hospital by the Americans—human bodies which were reduced to mere skeletons covered with skin. They tried feebly to wave a hand, or perhaps smile (which they could not do because the skin of their faces was so tightly drawn back that a smile was no longer possible), and it was a terrible shock when some of the worst cases tried to tell us what nationality they were. One realised then that, though one had looked at them with pity and dismay, one was still failing to appreciate them as living humanity with feelings and reactions similar to one's own. That was the most appalling and shocking thing.

None of these men had any clothing other than a very short shirt, camp blouse or singlet. Some of them feebly moved aside the quilts that covered them, to show appalling wounds, and one or two were trying to totter around on legs that were literally nothing more than skeleton sticks. There would normally be some embarrassment for a woman in company with several men, or for several men in company with one woman, if suddenly faced with large numbers of semi-nude men. There was no more embarrassment in Buchenwald when faced with these conditions than there would be in passing a heap of dying rabbits, so little did these people give the impression of being ordinary human beings.

The Spectator

HITLER'S DEATH

Mourning in Dublin

The Eire Prime Minister and Minister of External Affairs, Mr. De Valera, accompanied by the Eire Secretary to the Department of External Affairs, Mr. J. P. Walshe, called on Dr. Eduard Hempel, the German Minister, on Wednesday evening to express his condolence on the death of Hitler.

The Swastika at the German Legation was flown at half-mast at 58, Northumberland Road, Dublin.

Londonderry Sentinel

DEATH OF THE FÜHRER

The Fuehrer, Adolf Hitler, has fallen in the Capital of the Reich in the battle against Bolshevism.

His successor is Gross-Admiral Doenitz.

Guernsey Evening Press

Shops To Stay Open

VICTORY FOOD IS ASSURED

SHOPKEEPERS and Ministry of Food officials are to guarantee your Victory food supplies.

Most restaurants and cafés will be open. Food shops will open long enough to hand out essential rations. Bread will be baked on both days. The milkman will call, as usual.

Here are some useful hints given by a food official in case you cannot get to the shops.

"Get what potatoes you can. Keep a few pounds apart. Dried eggs or sardines will make an wholesome emergency breakfast. Spend 17 points on a tin of luncheon meat or sausage meat for dinner and three on a tin of peas. These should see you through as iron rations."

Potato 'Specials'

Bristol and South Wales—two of the potato famine districts—had good week-end food news. The Great Western Railway ran three potato "specials" down to these areas with 1,200 tons of potatoes.

Rhubarb comes down from 7d. to 4½d. per lb. from Monday. A Ministry of Food announcement said that schools with catering or institutional licences can get extra sugar to preserve their own fruit.

A special temporary issue of concentrated orange juice will be available to children from 5 to 10 years of age from May 7 to June 30.

Sunday Graphic

Was 5 Years A Nazi Captive

DENIS CARPENTER WALKED OUT OF HIS PUTNEY HOME IN 1940, A LAD OF 16, AND JOINED THE NAVY.

He walks back this week-end to his widowed and waiting mother, a young man of 21, ripe in experience and suffering.

Nearly five years of captivity in German horror camps and prisons lie behind him. He was recently released, with thousands of others, by the Guards' Armoured Division.

Hardly had he been to sea when he was captured by an armed raider which had 70 British captives. There he stayed for four months, often without exercise.

Transferred in mid-ocean to a German supply ship disguised as British, Denis stayed below for five weeks, fed mostly on maggotty biscuits—"our meat ration," he said—and lost 3 stone.

At a camp near Paris where he stayed for three months, horses' heads were put into water with a few black beans—and that was horsehead soup.

Before getting to Milag Norde, near Bremen, where he stayed for three years, he saw dreadful atrocities at Sandbostel, Bremerhaven.

Worst For Russians

Nearly all the prisoners were seamen, and many were Russians. They were treated with exceptional severity, says Denis.

"We saw exhausted Russian prisoners marched in," he said. "It was January, yet they were taken under ice-cold showers, and afterwards they dropped down dead in the snow. We saw Germans whipping them with sticks and belts, the buckle end. We actually saw the Russians fall down and die."

A Czechoslovakian, Dr. Sperber, a British ship's doctor, who was a prisoner with them, did marvellous work with practically no facilities.

"Red Cross parcels were a blessing," added Denis. "We would have died without them."

Sunday Graphic

21 ARMY   GROUP

PERSONAL MESSAGE
FROM THE C-IN-C

(To be read out to all Troops)

1. On this day of victory in Europe I feel I would like to speak to all who have served and fought with me during the last few years. What I have to say is very simple, and quite short.

2. I would ask you all to remember those of our comrades who fell in the struggle. They gave their lives that others might have freedom, and no man can do more than that. I believe that He would say to each one of them:

   "Well done, thou good and faithful servant."

3. And we who remain have seen the thing through to the end; we all have a feeling of great joy and thankfulness that we have been preserved to see this day.

   We must remember to give the praise and thankfulness where it is due:

   "This is the Lord's doing, and it is marvellous in our eyes."

4. In the early days of this war the British Empire stood alone against the combined might of the axis powers. And during those days we suffered some great disasters; but we stood firm on the defensive, but striking blows where we could. Later we were joined by Russia and America; and from then onwards the end was in no doubt. Let us never forget what we owe to our Russian and American allies; this great allied team has achieved much in war; may it achieve even more in peace.

5. Without doubt, great problems lie ahead; the world will not recover quickly from the upheaval that has taken place; there is much work for each one of us.

   I would say that we must face up to that work with the same fortitude that we faced up to the worst days of this war. It may be that some difficult times lie ahead for our country, and for each one of us personally. If it happens thus, then our discipline will pull us through; but we must remember that the best discipline implies the subordination of self for the benefit of the community.

6. It has been a privilege and an honour to command this great British Empire team in western Europe. Few commanders can have had such loyal service as you have given me. I thank each one of you from the bottom of my heart.

7. And so let us embark on what lies ahead full of joy and optimism. We have won the German war. Let us now win the peace.

8. Good luck to you all, wherever you may be.

B. L. Montgomery

Field-Marshal,
C.-in-C.,
21 Army Group

Germany,
May, 1945.

VE-DAY !

IT'S OVER IN THE WEST

TODAY is VE-Day—the day for which the British people have fought and endured five years, eight months and four days of war.

With unconditional surrender accepted by Germany's last remaining leaders, the war in Europe is over except for the actions of fanatical Nazis in isolated pockets, such as Prague.

The Prime Minister will make an official announcement—in accordance with arrangements between Britain, Russia and the U.S.—at 3 o'clock this afternoon. ALL TODAY AND TO-MORROW ARE PUBLIC HOLIDAYS IN BRITAIN, IN CELEBRATION OF OUR VICTORY.

We also remember and salute with gratitude and pride the men and women who suffered and died to make triumph possible—and the men still battling in the East against another cruel enemy who is still in the field.

Daily Mirror

The Good Old Days

"'When I went out to Papua, New Guinea, I was disappointed because there were no cannibals,' Miss Mary Abel, a missionary of the British and Foreign Bible Society, told a meeting of the Hampstead Auxiliary of the Society at Trinity Church Hall, Finchley Road, last week. 'My uncle went out 16 years ago with James Chalmers, who was clubbed to death and eaten by the cannibals.'"—*Suburban paper.*

Punch

POLICEMAN'S LOT WAS A HAPPY ONE.

At the Tunbridge Wells Magistrates' Court on Monday Sir Robert Gower congratulated Chief Inspector Sly and those serving under him, on the fact that there were no unfortunate incidents in the town during VE Day celebrations.

Chief Inspector Sly replied that the whole town was very temperate.

Kent and Sussex Courier

Crowds gather outside Buckingham Palace to cheer the Royal Family
and the Prime Minister, Winston Churchill

Listening to the King's speech in Trafalgar Square

Dancing in Streets at Guildford

Crowds Join in Borough Rejoicings

Flood Lights Banish War Black-out

Beflagged streets, business premises and private houses; dancing in the main thoroughfares; tea parties for children; the ringing of church bells; thanksgiving services; floodlighting of prominent buildings and bonfires after dark were among V-E Day celebrations at Guildford on Tuesday and the following day, which was also observed as a general holiday.

Crowds assembled in the streets heard by means of loudspeakers at the Guildhall and North Street Police Station a relay of the wireless broadcast of the Prime Minister's statement on Tuesday afternoon, and of the King's speech at 9 p.m.

In the morning the Mayor (Mr. Wykeham Price) had broadcast from the Guildhall the programme for the day, and had invited the public to join in dancing in the streets to music relayed by the loud-speakers. Men and women of the Services—British, Dominion, and American—and civilians responded to the appeal and spirit of the occasion with the utmost good humour.

BURST OF COLOUR

Up to the hours of darkness on Monday night the borough had only a few flags hung in its streets. Overnight, however, buildings became gaily festooned, so that even before nine on V-E Day morning there was hardly a shop, and certainly not a street, which did not boast at least some bunting strung from house to house.

All the main streets of the town were decorated. Flags hung and were draped from the Guildhall balcony, most window displays were confined not to wares, but to large and small flags of the Allied nations, with the red, white and blue predominating. Even private houses displayed Union Jacks, and red, white and blue flowers in vases, and victory slogans.

Most women wore red, white and blue dresses, costumes, jumpers and skirts, blouses and slacks—even shorts. There was hardly one without a festive rosette pinned in her hair or on her lapel. Many wore paper hats, and the children carried flags and streamers as, often led by their fathers in uniform, they gazed at the bunting overhead. For the younger ones it was their first glimpse of nation-wide celebration.

Surrey Advertiser

'It was a few minutes to midnight....At one minute past, all fighting was to cease.... The crowd all faced Big Ben. It was absolutely silent. Big Ben struck. Just before the last stroke it had reached one minute past. A great cry went up and people clapped their hands. Something went off with a bang....The tugs in the river gave the V sign. It was unforgettable.'

How We Lived Then

Leatherhead residents began to prepare for V-E Day the previous evening, and bunting and flags began to put in an appearance, so that when the day dawned the town was gaily decorated.

There was scarcely a house or a cottage in the district from which a flag was not fluttering, while elaborate decorations were carried out at business premises and offices. Children carried small flags, and residents sported the national colours in rosettes and paper hats.

After the announcement the church bells crashed out victory peals, and open-air services were held. At Leatherhead, clergy and ministers, with the combined choirs of Leatherhead Parish Church and All Saints' Church, walked in procession to the terrace of Elm Gardens, where a large crowd waited to take part in the service. This was conducted by the Vicar (the Rev. F. A. Page), and others taking part were the Rev. A. Maby (priest-in-charge of All Saints'), the Rev. Norman G. Cope (Methodist minister), the Rev. P. H. Cooke, and the Rev. H. T. G. Forster (chaplain of Leatherhead Emergency Hospital). Mr. J. S. Carter (headmaster of St. John's College) was present with a number of the boys.

When dusk fell numbers of young people took part in open-air dancing, and revelry was kept up to a late hour. Impromptu bonfires blazed in many parts of the district, and could be seen on the heights around, Epsom, Dorking, and Leith Hill. The explosion of fireworks was heard until a late hour.

Surrey Advertiser

"Here you are—don't lose it again"

Daily Mirror

409 MILK BOTTLES
At One House

When police searched the home of Mrs. Audrey Mold, Albert-street, St. Ebbes, Oxford, they found 409 empty milk bottles To-day she was fined £1 for retaining milk bottles for an unreasonable time.

Evening News

Children in bomb-scarred Battersea celebrate VE Day among the ruins of their homes

CLOTHES: 48 coupons again, but book must last extra month
PETROL: Basic ration begins June 1, you may save it up in cans

More to wear next year—perhaps

Evening Standard·Home Front Reporter JOANNA CHASE

The clothing coupon ration will continue at 48 coupons a year until August 1946. This will be the main clothes news to be officially announced by Mr. Dalton, President of the Board of Trade, next week.

The current issue, originally scheduled to last until August 1, will have to go on to September 1, though children will be allowed to use the new issue on August 1.

The next issue of clothing coupons, to be included in the ration books, will give 24 coupons to last from September 1 until February 1, 1946.

The second 24, to last from February to August, 1946, may be reviewed again next spring, when most of the men and women in the Services will be back in their civilian jobs.

If, by next spring, it has been possible to get production of civilian clothing stepped up 100 per cent above present output, the coupon allocation may be increased for the winter months.

At the moment, however, stocks have fallen so low that there cannot be any increase of coupons.

Evening Standard

What's cooking?

REMEMBER the satisfying sighs and comforting gurgles that came from the saucepan as QUICK QUAKER OATS simmered while the kettle boiled? How welcome that sound will be again—how delicious the first taste of the creamy flavour—how good to experience the tonic effect of Vitamin B_1.

William Joyce's captor feared trick—and shot first
HAW-HAW IS WOUNDED BUT KEEPS ON TALKING

7 hours in ambulance —and never silent

From SELKIRK PANTON: Luneburg, Tuesday

WILLIAM JOYCE—Lord Haw-Haw—who started the anti-British "Germany Calling" broadcasts from the Reich, is tonight a British prisoner in the 74th British General Army Hospital in Luneburg, shot through the thigh by a British officer who caught him yesterday.

As soon as possible he will be brought to England.

Boos and shouts of "Traitor! Traitor!" greeted Joyce as, lying on a stretcher, he drove up in a British ambulance to the Second British Army Intelligence headquarters here, just before eight o'clock tonight.

The shouts came from a crowd of British soldiers, who with officers and war correspondents had waited hours to see this British Fascist arrive after his 150-mile drive from Flensburg, near where he was captured last night.

A British officer opened the door of the ambulance. And Joyce, lying there in striped pyjamas, and looking haggard—but not "critical"—grinned, wrinkling his face with its long scar along the cheek.

As the Tommies crowded round, Haw-Haw, in those sneering tones we know so well, said: "One doesn't look into other peoples' windows."

Daily Express

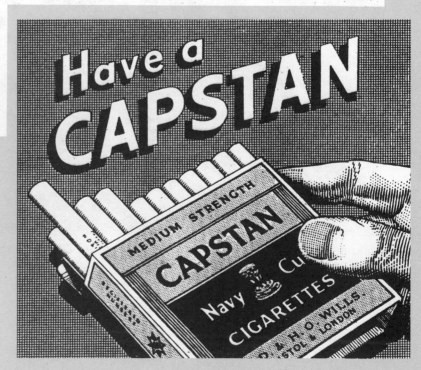

"Bus-Jumping' Ahead of the Queue

First Prosecution at Brighton

PEOPLE who wait patiently for buses only to have someone not in the queue jump on the vehicle before it stops, had their interests protected at Brighton Magistrates' Court this morning, when a 17-years-old youth, Dennis Puddick, of 174 Wiston-road, Whitehawk, who stated he was working as a labourer on bomb damage work in London, was fined 40s. for boarding a moving bus without waiting in the queue on the evening of 25th March.

This was the first prosecution for this type of offence in Brighton, the maximum penalty for which is £100.

Supt. Crouch stated that at the people waiting at the bus stop for people waiting at th bus stop for No. 7 and 7a buses at the top of Queen's-road. A bus came down Terminus-road into Junction-road, and P.C. Dann saw three young men jump on the vehicle. When the bus stopped, he spoke to them and asked them to leave the bus and go to the end of the queue.

Two of them did so, but Puddick refused, and he was warned he would be reported. When the bus left there were still 40 persons left at the bus stop.

"There has been an enormous amount of trouble in the evening, especially when these people on bomb damage work arrive from London. Some of them behave like hooligans," said Supt. Crouch.

The Chairman (Ald. H. W. Aldrich) told the youth that in these days when people's tempers are frayed there was nothing more annoying than this type of behaviour. "As far as this Bench is concerned, they are very glad that this particular offence has been brought to their notice," he said.

Brighton Evening Argus

DEMOCRACY?

We shall avoid a repetition of the blunders committed between the two wars not by public controversy, as "Leader-Writer" suggests, but by having a government of men and women of wisdom and specialised training. I know that it takes 10 years to learn a little about engineering (or farming, or printing, or coal mining). How then can Tom, Dick, and Harriet expect to have opinions worth anything on the government of our complex society?

God protect us from university intellectuals, Tory ignoramuses, and miserable self-seekers bumped together at Westminster and pulled this way and that by *opinion* and the vital necessity of retaining their seats. Let us admit that "government by the people," as we understand it, is sentimental rubbish.—LT. W. M. RUSSELL, 602 Combined Wksp., I.E.M.E., Calcutta, India Command.

The Leader

Montrose Review
and
Angus and Kincardine Shires Advertiser
97 HIGH STREET MONTROSE.
Telephone No. 185.
Montrose, Friday, May 11, 1945.

VICTORY.

Montrose folk were sensibly subdued in their victory celebrations. Hilarity and rejoicing were restrained generally. Remembrance of and reverence for those who had lost loved ones mingled with the welcome which was given to the defeat of Germany and to the declaration of peace. Even in the display of decorations there was restraint. Flags were flown from public buildings and houses. Streamers were stretched across streets. Beyond that practically nothing in the way of gaiety. The jubilation of the populace itself was one of respectful reserve and of quiet satisfaction that the war was over and the enemy's capitulation complete.

Concerning the official declaration of victory there was, unfortunately, muddle, a muddle evidently caused by the number of cooks in the cookhouse, and which created considerable, sharp, and warranted criticism. We certainly expected an official announcement first, but that was not made until twenty-four hours after the truth was known. And had the official announcement been given precedence, which it could have been, the public of this and other towns would have been saved shopping and Post Office inconveniences. However, these are venial affairs, and we here desire to state that as the tattered flags of war in Europe have been furled and the smoke of battle is clearing from the devastated cities and towns, so do we express the hope that a larger percentage of men and women than ever before in history will loathe and curse the fiendish savagery of war.

To-day the whole civilised world breathes more freely now that the arrogant, brutal, and deceitful blood and iron swashbucklers have been smashed, we hope beyond recovery, and that the moral gangrene of German military philosophy has been ruthlessly excised. Only by that can honour and liberty be ours for all time.

We must not trust any German of this or the rising generation. The Allies must occupy Hunland for an indefinite period, and recognise that the friendship of the Huns is as dangerous as it is false. And no more living in a fool's paradise. We must not forget how Britain herself by her negligence, her spirit of appeasement, her belief in Germany's promises, helped in big measure to encourage the Germans to go all out for world domination. Their belief that might is the supreme right, that war is a biological necessity, that war is good for the general health of the people, and that the master-race is in Germany has, we trust, been destroyed, never to menace as it has menaced the whole civilised world on this occasion.

And let's now put "paid" to the Japanese account.

THE OIL RUSH

"Here they come, boys!"

[The basic petrol ration is to be restored.]

'THERE ARE SOME GOOD GERMANS'

Evening Standard

—Says the Primate

The Archbishop of Canterbury, Dr. Fisher, declares in a letter to his diocese: "We must not allow ourselves to think there are no good Germans."

The German people as a whole could not be acquitted of knowledge and of acquiescence in what had been done in concentration camps.

But as long ago as 1936, the Confessional Church in Germany was making official and open protest against the camps; then and since there had been Germans who had resisted Nazism and all its works, and German Christians who in the name of Christ had refused to bow the knee to Nazi doctrine.

Some are ashamed

Some Germans who fled before the war to this country and elsewhere, were and are ashamed of their own people with a bitterness of humiliation such as only a German could feel.

"It is easy, in view of Germany's long record of cruel avarice, it is easy after seeing pictures of these ghastly camps, to condemn the whole race," added the Primate.

"We must not allow ourselves to be unjust in that way to the Germans, even though they be comparatively few in number, who have agonized and suffered, as Jeremiah of old did, for the evils of their people."

West Briton

£500 GIFT LEFT ON ALTAR

The Rev. A. S. Roberts, priest-in-charge of Carbis Bay, on Sunday morning found an envelope on the High Altar which had been left there between the 8 a.m. celebration of Holy Communion and his return for the 10.30 a.m. Mattins. It was addressed "The Priest-in-Charge, Carbis Bay," and when opened contained a type-written note. "To the Glory of God and the endowment of His Parish of St. Anta and All the Saints, Carbis Bay. Non nobis, Domine, sed Nomine Tuo, da gloriam." The envelope also contained one hundred £5 notes (£500). During the service, the Rev. A. S. Roberts announced the gift, there being no indication from whom it came, to the congregation, and the gift was then brought to the altar by the Churchwarden (Mr. W. Polsue), and an appropriate prayer of offering said. As an act of thanksgiving the congregation then joined in the singing of the hymn, "Praise the Lord, ye Heavens Adore Him." On Ascension Day the Rev. A. S. Roberts received through the post an envelope containing £20 in £1 notes, with a note saying this amount was for the bells fund and was a thanksgiving for victory. The donor of this amount is also unknown.

QUEEN GERALDINE. War-ravaged Albania, one of the first European targets of Axis aggression, is recalled by this picture of the exiled Queen of that tiny Adriatic country participating in games at a garden fete which she opened at Cosgrove on Whit-Monday.

Northampton Independent

LEMON HART RUM
The Golden Spirit
With Lemon, Orange or Lime
A *Winner* every time!

LONDON LAUGHS (No 3,311)   *By LEB*

"Five years of Grand Strategy . . . Pincer Movements . . . Infiltration . . . and Bulges, and now, just when things were getting nice and peaceful . . . POLITICS!"

Evening News

Good Housekeeping

THE barbed wire and concrete blocks are gone or going, the proms and piers are being " freed " and tidied up, and once more we may do more than just dream of picnics on the sands, of cliff-top walks and bathing in the sea.

So dazzling is the mental picture that one hesitates to cloud it with the warning that accommodation is unlikely to be much easier than last year, or trains less crowded and difficult.

Such, however, are the facts—yet are we to forgo the breath of sea or mountain air for which we've been pining for what seems an eternity? Even our stern mentor, the Government, tells us that we deserve and need a holiday, merely adding the wise proviso that we should not all attempt to seek it at the same moment.

So, if you're happily not tied down to one or two fixed weeks in the year, won't you consider this flowering month of May or long-eveninged June for your seaside trek ? Surely a little rush in the preparations is a cheap price to pay for easier travelling and better quarters.   Autumn, too, is often more golden and rewarding than mid-July or August.   If at all possible, then you'll leave those dates alone, won't you ?

Whatever your choice, may the sun shine and the news be good, so that this summer may stand out in your memory as the glorious year when you all enjoyed a real summer holiday again.

B.B.C. will switch on July 29

Express Staff Reporter

THE B.B.C. have fixed July 29 for the switch-over from war to peace programmes.

Schedules just issued show that on that date the General Forces programme and the A.E.F. — Expeditionary Forces programme devised for the invasion armies—will disappear.

In their places will be programmes A and B—A, a home service on the long wave, and B, a regional service which will be contributed by eight regional zones.

In months to come, at a date not yet fixed, a third wavelength is to be added, which will be devoted to more serious cultural subjects.

The new long-wave service will be a mixture of light entertainment and serious subjects.

For the British troops in Europe a new service is to be set up and broadcast from Hamburg.

Daily Express

German People Live in Cellars

" When one reads the reports from Allied correspondents about the treatment of the German civilian population in Anglo-American occupied parts of Western Germany, then one's flesh begins to creep," says a London report to the Madrid newspaper, "Ya."

" It is apparently regarded as the most natural thing in the world that the German people are forced to live in cellars and are allowed only one hour daily to carry out the most necessary jobs.

" Children, women, old people, and men all live in the same manner in the occupied territories—a terrible mixup."

Guernsey Evening Press

JUNE
1945

Local M.P. Fetched Surrender Nazis

SALUTES for Lieut.-Colonel Profumo (on right) from two of the Nazi officers accompanying General von Sanger when the party arrived to sign the surrender in the war room indicated on left.

A **Northamptonshire M.P., it is just revealed, was intimately associated with the acceptance of the German surrender in Italy.**

He is Lt.-Colonel John Profumo, M.P. for the Kettering Division, who travelled over the Alps to fetch the German plenipotentiaries to sign the instrument of surrender in Italy and personally escorted the enemy signatory, General von Sanger, to special quarters, where he spent an hour reading and studying the document before signing it.

A graphic description of the events is recorded by Lt.-Colonel Profumo.

30 Miles Over the Alps

He writes: " I was sent by General Clark to get the German Commander-in-Chief.

" The first 80 miles were covered in the General's private aeroplane, and the rest of the journey of about 30 miles was over the Alps across our forward lines. We went in a car, but had to walk part of the way, as the mountain roads were blown.

" After our stretch of walking, German transport was used, as the Nazis were ready and expecting us.

We actually went into the Brenner, before we reached the spot where the Germans were waiting for us.

" We returned with General von Sanger and a representative of General Wolf, German S.S. Commander, and high officers of their staff.

" We travelled back in German transport, did our walk again, and finished off the journey in Allied cars to an aerodrome we occupied in the north, from which we flew to General Clark's headquarters.

" There we were met by staff officers of General Clark, to whose headquarters in a prefabricated hut the German representatives were taken.

The Surrender Instrument

" In the General's private war room, with maps round the walls showing the latest positions of the armies prior to the surrender, were representatives of the Allied Command and General Clark himself.

" Only the German general was received on the first occasion. At that interview

General Clark handed von Sanger the instrument of surrender.

The enemy general took this to special quarters that had been prepared, and I saw him to his quarters and left him for about an hour.

Detailed Discussions

" At the end of this period von Sanger, with his staff, returned to the war room, where detailed discussions took place as to how the surrender should be effected.

" Von Sanger signed for the Germans and General Gunther, Allied Chief of Staff, for the victors. It was all dealt with very speedily and smoothly."

Northampton Independent

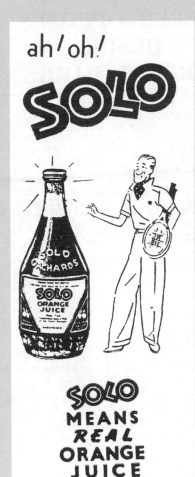
A QUIET RETURN TO THE ROADS

"Basic" Motorists' Driving Commended

Although for the past fortnight the motor-taxation department in Manchester has been besieged by people who are taking out new licences and re-registering their cars, the increase in the traffic on the roads so far has been slight. A motoring week-end is still an ambition which the reintroduction of a very limited petrol ration will do little to satisfy. A monthly mileage of less than 150 reduces "joy-riding" to a minimum and it may be that until the ration is increased most people will prefer to use their cars for short journeys.

There are several good and sufficient reasons why so few of the re-registered cars have reappeared on the roads. Garages in the city and in the suburbs report that they are inundated with demands for repairs. Inquiries about the prospects of obtaining new cars are almost as numerous. "We simply cannot carry out the work as we have not got the labour to do so," said one garage proprietor. He added that few motorists asked that their cars should be tested before they were put back on the roads. In general, people were "not looking for trouble."

TYRES THE MAIN TROUBLE

At another garage it was stated that cars which had been laid up during the war seemed to have "stood up to it" very well. The chief complaint, apparently, is engine trouble, while the difficulty in obtaining batteries and tyres will be the main reason for delay in re-equipping cars for the road. "Tyres are the real trouble," said a garage manager. "At the moment the position is pretty well hopeless. They are almost unobtainable."

In spite of these and other obstacles to free motoring, it is clear that the number of private owner-drivers will be substantially increased within the next few days. And perhaps if summer ever does arrive it will bring with it a revival of the motoring week-end—even if it means the reckless expenditure of one's coupons on a single outing.

Inquiries in Preston and the Lancashire county area yesterday showed that there has been considerably more local traffic, but not an appreciable increase between town and town and to and from the resorts. The official view is that people have been reserving their petrol on account of the bad weather and are saving it for a fine week-end.

"We are very pleased indeed with what we have seen on the roads so far," a "Manchester Guardian" representative was told yesterday. "There have been no accidents. We have had the roads well patrolled and the traffic carefully observed, but we have seen nothing in the way of driving of an unsatisfactory nature."

WIDE ON THE BENDDS

Good driving everywhere was reported by R.A.C. guides in the South of England, their only criticisms being of a tendency to run "wide" on left-hand bends and to disregard "halt" signs.

Breakdowns on the roads were mostly due to tyres.

The return of the basic ration helped to make one of the largest wartime "galleries" on the Purley Downs golf course yesterday, when Henry Cotton and other players engaged in a charity match. The car park was crowded to overflowing for the first time since 1939, and it was estimated that 2,000 people saw the match.

In anticipation of heavy motor traffic, Fleetwood Corporation yesterday opened their car parks for the first time during the war. But owing to weather conditions the "invasion" of motorists was nothing like as large as had been expected. No accidents were reported.

Manchester Guardian

H.M.S. "BELFAST." **At** SCAPA FLOW

DATE
JUNE 16TH 1945.

At about 0900 on the 12th two of the German captains were sent off to King's Pontoon and later the Admiral and the remainder of his staff went off to "Emerald" in one of the picket boats. They were piped over the side, as is customary for all foreign officers, though I will admit I consider that to be carrying etiquette a bit too far.

Journal of J.D.F. Mudford, RN, Imperial War Museum archives

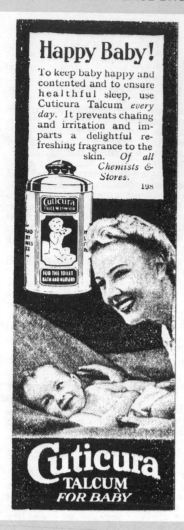

DISCIPLE'S RELICS FOUND

Rome, Thursday.

THE lost relics of St. Paul's disciple, Timothy, to whom St. Paul addressed two New Testament epistles, have been discovered at Termoli, on the Adriatic coast of Italy, due east of Rome, during the restoration of the cathedral there.

Ecclesiastical authorities reported to-day that the bones were found in a small shrine where they were placed in the 13th century.—(Reuter.)

Irish News

Your Vote

THE most important part of a General Election is the part played by the ordinary man and woman—voting. This big job isn't made easier for you and me by the enormous amount of shouting and banging, promising and blarneying done by many of the competing politicians.

Reading and hearing their statements make it look as though they all had the golden key to the brave new world and were all equally desirous of ushering us in along with them. So, we murmur in a daze, what does it matter which I vote for? And if it doesn't matter which, why vote at all?

While it is certain that no party is as clever or as able as each would have us believe (for parliamentary candidates praise their party with the same naïve zest as mothers their first-born) it still behoves us to use our vote. That cross on the ballot paper is our personal contribution to the common good. By using it coolly and carefully we take our part in forming Britain's new life.

That doesn't mean that our vote can be bought by the candidate with the biggest promises. Far from it. Britain has a responsible and heavy job to do—this is no time for promises of easy luxury and soft living—and we most truly need men and women in Parliament of high quality and integrity, fit to lead and sustain us.

Women, less steeped in party politics than men, can more easily listen to speakers of rival parties and vote for the candidate showing the clearest understanding of the common good.

Therefore, those who have no clear-cut party line to follow can use their vote to support the party which they feel will honestly work for the good of the nation.

Woman

PEER OPPOSES HOUSING IN ROYAL PARKS

BY OUR OWN REPRESENTATIVE
WESTMINSTER, Monday.

Disagreement on whether the Royal parks in London should be included among the open spaces on which temporary homes will be erected was expressed in the House of Lords to-day when the Housing (Temporary Accommodation) Bill was given a second reading, moved by Lord WOOLTON, Lord President of the Council.

Lord LATHAM could not see why the Royal parks should be exempt from the bill.

"There is nothing sacrosanct about the Royal parks," he declared, adding that many of them, like Hyde Park, were situated in areas better provided with open spaces than other districts whose open spaces would be used for houses.

Dignity of London

Viscount SAMUEL, disagreeing with Lord Latham, said that it was not only a question of the comparative needs of the inhabitants of the quarters surrounding the Royal parks compared with the inhabitants of the East End or South London.

"There is another consideration which is of very great importance," he remarked, "and that is the dignity and seemliness of London as the capital of Great Britain and the Empire.

"It would be most regrettable if, in Hyde Park, Kensington Gardens, the Green Park and Regent's Park there should be erected for 10 years a number of temporary houses. That would be detrimental to the prestige of London."

Field-Marshal the Earl of CAVAN, Lord BALFOUR of BURLEIGH, Lord HARMSWORTH and Viscount MAUGHAM continued the debate.

Lord WOOLTON, replying, assured Lord Cavan that playing fields would only be used in a case of "dire necessity."

Tributes to Lord Onslow

When the House met tributes were paid to the memory of the late Earl of ONSLOW, who, from 1931 until last year, was Lord Chairman of Committees. References to his long and varied record of public service were made by Lord WOOLTON, Lord ADDISON, for the Socialist peers, Lord SAMUEL, for the Liberals, and Lord STANMORE, who succeeded Lord Onslow as Chairman of Committees.

Daily Telegraph

WHAT WE WANT... to have back

to keep

The National Gallery lunch-time concerts (or their equivalent): oases of beauty in the scurry of working days.... Squares and gardens left free of railings, but with grass respected by the public (perhaps disabled men as garden attendants could help here).... That spirit of neighbourliness which shares the newspaper or anything else.... Informal entertaining.... Short meals.... Airgraphs.... Light-weight books: cheap, easily-come-by editions, like the Penguins.... Queues for buses: first come first served is fairest, at all times.... Decentralization of cultural interests: concerts, London theatre productions, and travelling art exhibitions moving around, not concentrated in the capital. ... The Picture of the Month, at the National Gallery, with all its admirable documentation and data. Clubs for young people, such as some of the Service clubs, or the new Nuffield Centre, where a good time can be had by all, on a shoe-string.... School meals and school milk.... Day nurseries, to let mothers work or shop or simply get a rest.... Some of the present open, bombed-open spaces, in the heart of the city, to let in air, and light, and quiet.... Summer—yes, even double summer time—so that office workers have a chance to sit in the sun like Casper, when their work is done. ... CEMA, or some similar body for the encouragement of the arts—with the backing of the State but the independent taste of a well-chosen few.... The boom in books and pictures.... Bicycles, and some quiet roads on which to ride them. ... The idea of a basic food ration—the right of everyone to the elementary needs of life.... The sense of urgency, the inventiveness that produced Mulberry and a thousand other marvels: it will be needed.... The grooming and neatness of women in uniform, when they return to mufti.... Some Service benefits made available to all of us: D.D.T. to wipe out the moth menace: anti-seasick stuff: the wonderful new drugs and treatments.... A busy and prosperous countryside, and the feeling for the land learnt by some evacuees and land girls.... The blackout, one night a year, a night of full moon, to remind us of its beauty. Perhaps as an institution (like the two minutes silence) to recall the long years of darkness and endeavour, which was this war....

to get rid of

The *c'est la guerre* excuse for every form of inefficiency and discourtesy.... Ersatz flavourings.... Theatres playing at such ridiculous hours: who wants to sit through three acts on an empty stomach, straight from work?... Soya beans and starch lurking in every dish.... Watered-down beer.... Filling up forms.... The necessity of cajoling minor, or major officials; the atmosphere of Civil Servants versus the Rest.... Women who wear trousers when they needn't.... Bullying shop assistants.... Spoiled restaurateurs.... Licensing laws (but what a hope).... Mending, deadliest of occupations, absorbing more woman-hours than is believable.... The chronic discomforts of travelling; every journey like peace-time bank holiday, but without the fun at the other end.... The time-wasting necessity of turning up hours before trains are due to leave.... The need to book restaurant tables hours or even days beforehand, making social life boringly rigid.... The string bag which has never left our hands since wrappings were banned.... Queues.... Identity Cards—Britons never, never, never shall be slaves, like the poor be-*papiered* continentals.... Petty thieves and amateur burglars who pinch the irreplaceables of our homes and wardrobes; the pre-war professionals at least kept to the big stuff, and those who owned such could take proper precautions and be handsomely insured.... Words like SEAC and UNIO which pepper the newspapers.... The shortage and shattering price of drink, so cramping to hospitable instincts.... The dirt and squalor of our homes, with peeling paint outside and shabby furnishing within.... Military critics.... Crowds—too many people in a given space, trying to eat, drink, shop, get about or see a show.... Austerity—in its limited meaning of cramping dress restrictions, and in its larger meaning of a whole, thin-lipped attitude to life....

Our men.... Our children—evacuated for safety; put in nursery schools or left at boarding school for the holidays because we were too busy with our war jobs to look after them.... Sheer stockings, lots of them.... Wine—cheese—fruit. Fruit and more fruit.... A rebuilt Queen's Hall.... Evening décolletage. ... Lovely colours in fabrics, cosmetics, house paint, and all else.... Scarlet buses; scarlet fire engines.... Real, slap-up wedding cakes.... Easy, inexpensive world travel facilities.... Ice-cream sundaes: quantity and quality on the American scale.... Taxis, in plenty—and then high heels, long evening dresses, silly hats, and all the gay nonsense that such a plenitude permits.... Working jewellers, clockmakers and shoemakers who will undertake repairs quickly and efficiently.... Perfume.... Fountain pens.... Alarm clocks.... Elastic.... Jersey fabrics.... Four posts a day.... Restaurant cars on the trains—but *not* those awful pretentious four-course meals with dabs of pink sauce on the pallid fish: let's have first-rate snack-bar and drink-bar cars instead.... Lingerie with lace and frills and fine hand-work: austerity is particularly hard worn next the skin.... Easy telephoning—but was it ever?... Shoes plentiful, beautiful and sized so that everyone can be well and easily fitted.... Corsets ditto ditto.... Household furnishings: no matter, at first, how cheap, so long as they are gay, pretty and unrationed, to brighten our war-worn homes.... Purchases tied up in paper and string—actually delivered if we wish, and delivered with some regard to our domestic arrangements.... Sausages, the real thing.... Loaded bookstalls, with every magazine stacked in full view.... Flowers in our flower-beds and cabbage banished to its proper place out of sight and out of smell.... Cars and petrol and some nice new tyres, not re-treaded either.... Late-running buses and trains.... The pictures and all the other precious things from the National Collections, banished for safety nearly six years ago.... The commons and open spaces which Service and other Ministries have borrowed from us, the public, for war purposes.... A sea view, uninterrupted by concrete blocks, barbed-wire entanglements or grandstand scaffolding: and a free run of the cliffs and beaches without the danger of being blown up by a mine.... Nail varnish, combs, nourishing face creams for our dry skins—in fact, the whole battery of beauty.... Those forgotten phrases—music in our ears—"How many would you like?" "I'll keep one for you," "Shall I send it on approval?" "How soon can you manage a fitting?" ... Anyone whose peacetime plans centre on being a domestic worker. Oh yes! Oh YES....

ONE THING WE ALL WANT—TO LIE IN THE SUN WITH OUR FEET UP

• RHYME AND REASON •

GO ON
SPEND
IT !

Hey diddle diddle,
Don't finger or fiddle,
Those notes are a full week's pay.
The Squander Bug wants you to
                    fritter the lot,
Keep on saving and drive him away.

BUY
3% DEFENCE
BONDS

BECAUSE:

The interest is paid regularly half-yearly.

The Bonds are repayable at par ten years after date of purchase plus premium of £1 per cent.

Defence Bonds can be bought in multiples of £5 for cash or with 6d., 2 6 or 5/- Savings Stamps collected in easy stages.

They are on sale at Banks and at most Post Offices.

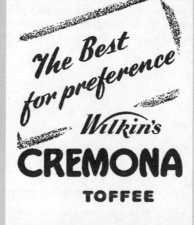
FASCISTS BUSY IN BETHNAL GREEN

Back to "Smear and Run" Tactics

There are signs that the Fascists of Bethnal Green, never entirely silenced, have renewed their activities for the election campaign. The Borough is divided into two constituencies, North-East Bethnal Green and South-West, in each of which there is a three-cornered fight. In the North-East part, Dan Chater, the Labour candidate, has his committee rooms in Cambridge Road. His agent, Mr. H. E. Tate, arrived there on Saturday morning to find in white paint across the window in very large letters, "Vote for Bill Buckhurst" (who is the Conservative candidate). The same slogan was on the newly decorated shutters of a Jewish shop a few doors away and on the window of the Communist Party rooms a few doors still further up. Mr. Tate wrote to Mr. Buckhurst's agent, and in the course of his letter said: "The last time this was done was when there were Fascist disturbances in the East End," and added that if this was how the election was going to be conducted the sooner the workers of Bethnal Green were acquainted the better. On Monday morning when he arrived at the committee rooms he found the Fascist sign—P.J. and a flash—painted on the window in red. It was cleaned off, but by the afternoon there was another one.

Mr. W. Johnson, who described himself as a Communist, who is helping to canvass for Dan Chater, said that on the windows of the Communist Party's rooms there was painted up "Vote for Bill Buckhurst" in front of a photo of Stalin, and the Fascist sign in front of "Monty's" photo. The windows have now been covered with posters to prevent any more signs being painted there. Mr. Johnson told a JEWISH CHRONICLE representative that some of the people working for the Conservative candidate are known to have been Jew-baiters in the past and hangers-on of the B.U.F.

Jewish Chronicle

Backwater for P.M.

IN Socialist-ruled Glasgow, I hear, there is widespread protest against a refusal to allow Mr. Churchill to speak in George-square, the main square of the city, when he visits there on Thursday. The application asked for the use of George-square for a three-minute speech.

As a result of this decision it is likely that the Prime Minister will make his speech in Blythswood-square, which is off the beaten track and only about half the size of George-square.

Reason for refusal

Mrs. Jean Roberts, convener of Glasgow Corporation Parks Committee, explains that she had been called on at very short notice to decide whether or not Mr. Churchill could be allowed the use of George-square. She says the application was refused in view of the damage that might be caused to the flowers and grass in the square.

"I would have come to the same decision," says Mrs. Roberts, "had it been any other party leader."

Evening Standard

The coming of peace is as challenging as the coming of war. GRETA LAMB tells you how she believes our young women will meet it

SOME people are afraid it is going to happen all over again "this time" : that youth, especially the feminine youth, of the country will spend the immediate post-war years in a riot of mad parties and general lawlessness.

They remember how, soon after the shackles of the last war were thrown off in the early twenties, lots of girls bobbed their hair, bobbed their frocks to above the knee—and their morals followed suit.

The ones who could afford it, the Bright Young People of the West End, spent most of their time organizing treasure and scavenging hunts over half London. Parties were given with live horses or some other animal as the guest of honour, and young girls came home with the milk. Gate-crashing was thought, not vulgar, but extremely funny.

The new freedom went to their heads. They had the vote but did not trouble to use it.

But I, for one, have enough faith in this generation to be pretty sure that it isn't going to happen again. When you have always known social freedom, as girls of to-day have known it, there is not anything to kick against. There is no windmill they need to fling their bonnets over—now.

Never before has the youth of Britain been so

serious-minded; not "pi," but seeing with a straight eye things as they really are. They have had plenty to think about in the last five years and they have not wasted their time. In 1938 it was considered fashionable to be hard-boiled. To be adult you had to be a cynic; you saw through everything. Most things were a bore and what was the use of worrying, anyway?

But when war swept away most of their fun, leaving them with only the bare bones of existence, they began to value all the things they had accepted so lightly before; a roaring coal fire became a luxury, half a pound of chocolates a thrill. Their eyes were opened to all they had lost and they began to appreciate in retrospect their world as it used to be.

The new hard-living brought out the best in them. They learned to live in a crowd (never an easy thing for women), to keep their tempers when tried almost beyond endurance, to stifle irritation. Can you imagine Bright Young People doing that?

You have only to watch the Service girls in trains and teashops to sense the new comradeship between them. There is something very fine about it. This is bound to be when they have faced death together on gun sites, or have known their particular aerodrome to be the enemy target. It wouldn't be possible for these girls to have the small minds that, if not exactly expected of them, were at least tolerated as being typically feminine before the War. It is not thought modern and the last word to be hard-boiled now. To-day, loyalty, integrity and honest thinking

have come back, and it would be an insult to these girls to imagine they are going to throw them away with their uniform.

Ask any girl what she wants from the future. You won't hear many saying, "a good time." What they want is their men back and homes of their own. And the ones who have not this to look forward to will want to go on with a useful job in peacetime. Women have learnt, not the dignity of work, but the interest it can be. Many of those who did not have jobs before have told me that they cannot imagine how they tolerated their pre-war lives. They don't want to go back to just shopping with the car and playing bridge.

But there is one danger I see.

At first, just the novelty of a kitchen of their own and a home to manage, will be enough. If there are babies to mind and bring up their hands will be full.

But there will not be babies for everyone, and I think the girls without them will be the ones who will ask more of life than they used to. I do not mean more fun, but something to get their mental teeth into.

More girls than ever before have known, in diverse ways, what it is to really use their brains. They cannot, and we should not expect them to, let them go rusty when their war jobs are finished.

Having got them thinking, after generations of inertia, for heaven's sake let us give them something to go on thinking about. Let the politicians hold meetings addressed wholly to women, where they can air views and put forward their own interests. Let us have clubs where young mothers can meet, for it can be a lonely life being a young mother, especially if she is in a strange town. Her husband is probably away all day, and conversation with a baby, however charming, is apt to be one-sided !

It would be good to have more debating clubs in small towns. The city-dweller is often provided with them, but there are not enough clubs in small places. In theory debating may sound dull, but in practice it can prove most exhilarating. Where else, in so short a time, can you rub shoulders with so many points of view? For only with lots of human contacts can life be lived to the full.

Evacuation had some drawbacks—as many people found. But surely there is something in the idea ! Could we not start a scheme where families who live in cities and crave for the country could change houses with those, say, by the seaside, who would love a spell of town life?

I am no ardent "feminist" but I do think the future well-being of our country lies in the hands of the women. Given the right lead and the least encouragement, surely the girls who have so abundantly proved their worth, will turn into, not Bright Young People, but worthwhile citizens of the country they have helped to save.

Woman's Own

Custody of the Elephant

There have not been a great many marriages of English soldiers in Italy, but there was, I hear, a good deal of excitement among Italian parents when they realized that a British or an American soldier would not expect any dowry, so that they would be able to keep the 25,000 *lire*, or whatever the sum might be, which they had been saving through the years in order to get their daughter settled.

The Anglo-Saxon countries, to use the convenient if pretty loose term, are less dowry-minded at the beginning of a marriage, but they pay a good deal of attention to the division of property at divorce. I have just been reading of a couple in America in the circus business where the wife has demanded the custody of the elephant. If it were this country that would raise an issue of Magna Carta, that no man shall be deprived by law of his wainage, or the tools of his trade.

The Tablet

Somebody's coming to tea . . . will there be muffins with lots of butter? The silver service is on duty, sparkling with pride and lovelier than ever. Nora's so proud and careful of her silver. She always cleans it with **SILVO**

A CHILD TO LOVE !

The children you love are safe, we hope. But what if love and happiness were suddenly taken from them? Would you not wish that they might come to safe and loving hands?

We have over 6,000 children—somebody's children—to help and love. Will you, in thankfulness for the luckier ones who do not need us, remember our family with your gift?

Your vocation may be looking after children! If you think so, please write to us—of course, only those with a genuine love of children need apply.

All gifts gratefully received by the Secretary, W. R. Vaughan, O.B.E.

THE CHURCH OF ENGLAND

WAIFS & STRAYS

SOCIETY

JOEL STREET - PINNER - MIDDX.

Bankers : Barclays Ltd., Kennington, S.E.11.

CHARGED £32 FOR £7 10s. PERAMBULATOR

Trader and Wife Fined £103

Fines of £103 with fifteen guineas costs were imposed on Samuel Allen and Clara Allen, trading as Browns, in Victoria Street, Manchester, by the Manchester City Stipendiary Magistrate, Mr. J. Wellesley Orr, yesterday for selling a perambulator over the controlled price. Samuel Allen was summoned by the Board of Trade under the Second Hand Cost (Maximum Prices) Order for not exhibiting a price ticket order, for making false statements, and for selling over the maximum price. Clara Allen was summoned for making a false statement to a Board of Trade inspector, and for aiding and abetting.

Mr. C. O. Hockin, prosecuting for the Board of Trade, stated that the defendants sold a perambulator for £32, when the regulation price should have been £7 10s. The customer presented a cheque, which was refused, and to secure the perambulator left £3 deposit. A few days later she visited the shop and gave a further £29 in one-pound notes. A receipt for the money was refused, and she reported the matter to the Prices Regulation Committee. Mr. Hockin added that the stock-book showed a sale of £8, but even on that the maximum price was £6 17s. 6d., and with a basket attached the excess profit was £24 10s.

In a statement Samuel Allen said he sold the perambulator for £8 and the balance of £24 was for reconditioning. He said he gave two receipts for these amounts.

Samuel Allen was fined £50 for exceeding the maximum price, £40 for making false statements, and £3 for failing to exhibit a price ticket. His wife was fined £10 for making a false statement. The prosecution were allowed fifteen guineas costs.

Manchester Guardian

RUGELEY INFANT WELFARE CENTRE

First Outing For Six Years

More than 50 mothers and their babies, with the health visitor and the voluntary workers from the Infant Welfare Centre, spent a most enjoyable afternoon at Tamworth on Monday.

Leaving Rugeley at 1.30 in two specially chartered buses, they journeyed via Lichfield. It was originally intended to have an hour's break in the city, but time was short so they went straight to Tamworth. Here, for an hour, strolling round the shops and visiting the castle occupied the time pleasantly, and early in the afternoon all met for tea at the pavilion in the grounds near the castle. This was excellently arranged and served, and left plenty of time for walking or sitting in the park while the toddlers played before boarding the buses for home about 5.15.

Rugeley was reached about 6 p.m., and all agreed that the first outing from the centre for six years had been a real treat.

Lichfield Times

FOOD SHORTAGES

Controls Must Continue
—Col. Llewellin
From our London Staff

Colonel Llewellin, Minister of Food, told the National Association of Multiple Grocers at a luncheon yesterday that while shortages persisted in many essential foods it would clearly be impossible to abolish food controls and restrictions, of which many people were getting so tired. "They would get more tired," he said, "if we took them off while there is great shortage of supplies."

He was not asking people, he added, to make sacrifices to provide the Germans with food. "These people must reap what they have sown. In regard to German prisoners of war, who, of course, we cannot let die on our hands, their rations have now been cut to a level far below that of our civilians. Those who do not work are to receive only two-thirds of the calories that the people of this country, on an average have, and they will only get very small quantities of rationed foods at present short—mainly meats, fats, sugar, and dairy produce."

The Minister said that although he had been well aware that a general improvement in food could not be expected for some time after the end of the war, he and his Ministry had made a plan for concessions and small easements after victory which it was a disappointment to have to abandon through circumstances beyond their control.

Mr. Alan Sainsbury, the chairman, said that the traders he represented, whatever their difficulties, accepted the reductions in rationed goods and other supplies as an inevitable necessity for the time being. "Looking farther ahead we, as traders, realise that as long as there are shortages of essential foods, shipping priorities, and difficulties of international payment, in the interest of 'fair shares,' both national and international, rationing and price controls will have to continue."

Manchester Guardian

NOTTINGHAM ANTIQUITY TO BE DESTROYED

"To-day—for historical records let the day and date be set down—Monday, June 25th, 1945, the demolition commences of the picturesque black-and-white timbered building, for long in use as two shops, in Bridlesmith-gate," writes "S.R." "This is the oldest building of domestic use left in Nottingham. Again our Corporation is responsible for the destruction of a building of historic interest which belonged to a Nottingham of long years past."

Mr. J. T. Edlin, chairman of the Works and Ways Committee, invited to comment on the matter, said the building had been condemned as unsafe. The matter first came before the Works and Ways Committee in October and the owners were notified of the condition of the property and were given time to put it in order. That apparently was not done and contracts for the demolition of the building were then obtained and the owners again notified.

Mr. Edlin added that the city engineer was of the opinion that the property could not be made safe and as it was likely to be a danger to the public the local authority had to take some action. The cost of repairs would probably have been more than the building would have been worth.

Nottingham Guardian

DRIED EGGS'

NOTES AND RECIPES

Mixed Diced Vegetables—As many varieties of vegetables as available, well drained and just heated in a little margarine. Add to the egg mixture when it is semi-cooked.

Creamed Leek—Thinly sliced leeks stewed in enough milk and water to cover, with pepper and salt to taste. Liquor thickened with flour. Two tablespoonfuls of mixture to be added to each portion of egg. Add when the egg is almost cooked.

Cauliflower with Cheese—Toss small cauliflower sprigs in grated cheese before adding to partly cooked egg mixture. In season, green peas or diced tomato can be used. The last two mixtures are excellent served cold on lettuce leaves, dressed with salad cream and sprinkled with a mixture of finely chopped fresh mint and chives.

Jersey Evening Post

Liberal Candidate

Major Joseph Grimond, the Liberal candidate for Orkney and Zetland.

The Orcadian

they're coming out

Joan Lambert has news for N.F.S. and would-be teachers looking for jobs in civvy street

THE war job of girls in the National Fire Service is over —what is worrying many of them is whether there is a place for them in the peacetime organization. Unlike other jobs in what we know as Civil Defence, the N.F.S. still has a job to do—fires still need to be put out!

The decision to retain girls in the Service is yet unmade; and, unfortunately, hundreds of girls are having to leave the N.F.S. although they would like to make it their peacetime career.

For those who have written to ask why this is, I shall go into a little of the background story. First there is the problem whether the N.F.S. will remain a national undertaking or revert back to the control of the local authorities. Until this is settled, the position of the women will also remain unsettled.

Some local authorities do not want women in the Fire Service—I cannot imagine why not in view of their excellent war record—but that is one point to be remembered. In the early days of the war, firemen under twenty-five were called up for military service; their jobs must be kept open for them until they are demobilized, so it is difficult to gauge the peacetime staff needs in local areas.

Qualified for the Job

One thing, however, is certain. Girls can do an excellent job in the control room, on the telephones and in the canteens, and it seems to me only right that those who have qualified in these jobs and want to keep them should be encouraged to do so.

In the meantime, however, many girls of the N.F.S. are looking for work. The Fire Brigade Union and the League of Firemen are doing what they can to sift out suitable local vacancies.

How many N.F.S. girls realize that they have two months—and in some cases three—to find themselves a job before they need to be "directed" by the Ministry of Labour—this doesn't mean that the Ministry of Labour doesn't help in this interim period. Of course it does, but these fire girls deserve a breathing space to fit themselves into the community in a job they like.

Naturally, the girls in the N.F.S. are eligible for all the training schemes for ex-Service girls, and for those who have been on national work during the war years.

Shadow Colleges

In the early days of the war there were shadow factories to increase war production; now there are shadow colleges to increase the number of women teachers, who are urgently needed in our new school programme. These colleges are carrying out the one-year emergency training scheme.

It is not necessary to have a School Certificate in order to qualify for this emergency training, but applicants without such qualifications will be asked to write an essay as a test in the use of English.

The age limits are between 19 and 35—older candidates must provide evidence of exceptional ability, and younger girls will be advised to take longer courses.

If you wish to apply, write to the Ministry of Education, 23 Belgrave Square, S.W.1, for a form, marking your envelope RE (Training). Suitable applicants will be interviewed near their homes.

I was interested to discover that a special emergency training is also being arranged for girls with knowledge of domestic science.

Whenever I visited Service depots during the last five years, I was struck by the excellent work of the cooks and caterers—now these girls, if they wish to become teachers, can specialize in domestic science. They take the year's emergency training first, and then are recommended for an extra two terms at a domestic science college.

Full information of these training schemes, and any others being arranged by the Government for ex-Service girls, can be obtained from the local offices of the Ministry of Labour.

"French Himmler" Arrested

Young Jerseyman Largely Responsible for Capture

A JERSEYMAN, SERGEANT ANDRE LABBE, SON OF M. AND MME. A. M. LABBE, OF HALKETT STREET, WAS LARGELY RESPONSIBLE FOR THE CAPTURE IN MILAN OF JOSEPH DARNAND, THE HATED HEAD OF THE VICHY MILITIA.

SERGEANT LABBE, CABLES EDWARD MURRAY, BRITISH UNITED PRESS CORRESPONDENT, WAS WAITING IN A GARAGE WHEN HE HEARD SOMEONE WHISTLING A FRENCH TUNE. HE FOUND THE WHISTLER — A MECHANIC WORKING UNDER A CAR. THE MAN BROKE DOWN WHEN SGT. LABBE SHOT QUESTIONS AT HIM, AND ADMITTED HE WAS A MEMBER OF DARNAND'S NOTORIOUS MILITIA.

On the basis of information from this man, Sergeant Labbé, Sergeant William Hepburn, from Scotland, and Sergeant Harry Gorfunkle, from Northern Ireland, searched the Edolo area. After searching several houses near the small town they reached one where they had reason to believe an important enemy subject was hiding. Sergt. Hepburn knocked at the door, told the occupants he was hungry, and asked if they could give him food. Once inside he called on them to surrender. Then Darnand, smoking a pipe and looking more like a local official, told him who he was.

He has already been turned over to the French authorities and is on his way to Paris.

Regarded as second only to Laval as a collaborationist, Darnand believes that he will be shot in France since several of his militia lieutenants have already met the same fate.

Darnand had arranged to meet his secretary, Zusaane Charasse, in Milan on the morning of June 27th. It is learned she was taken into custody at the exact time the meeting was to have taken place.

Jersey Evening Post

"Isn't it grand to be getting back to normal!"

Punch

Lichfield Times

OLD-AGE PENSIONERS ENTERTAINED

Some 80 old age pensioners of Rugeley were treated to a social evening and supper on Monday at Rugeley Town Hall.

The effort was provided by the Rugeley Old Boys' Club under Mr. F. P. Venables, who acted as M.C. The pensioners partook of an excellent repast, followed by a concert.

The toast of the King was proposed by Mr. Bennett, president of the club, and the toast of "The Old Boys' Club" by Captain Steventon, the response being given by Mr. Venables.

Mr. L. Toye proposed the toast of the visitors, and Mr. K. Baker replied.

The oldest woman in the company, Mrs. Maddox, of 17 Horse Fair, who is 84, was awarded 5s.

READERS SAY . . .

You write this feature—we pay 10/6 for each original letter published.   Please send your letters to " Readers Say " at the address on page 18.   Don't forget to include your own name and address and keep your letters brief.

Back to the Old Home

"With the war in Europe over, I have heard many people with relations in the Forces, give a detailed description of the preparations they are making for the homecoming of their loved ones. One person told me the other day that she meant to have Andy's room freshly painted in a different shade, and the furniture changed about for his return. But I couldn't help feeling that she was wrong. After all, won't that room have been one of Andy's most vital links with home? He probably recollects the exact position of every object in the room; the old wicker chair, the china dog, etc. Why not let him have it that way a little while longer? It will be hard enough for him to adjust himself to a new life."—*E. C. J., Glasgow.*

Civilians' rights

"I wonder how many people agree with the Government's idea of allowing the demobbed men and women of the Forces to have first claim to jobs? I think it unfair. Many are still in civilian jobs, not through choice, but because of their health, or because the Government said they were of more value in their present jobs, or because they were still too young to be called up. Therefore, I think everyone should be given the same advantages to enable them to find jobs now that the European war is over."—*Miss M. O., Near Oswestry.*

Spinsters . . . A Stale Joke

"I wonder if, now the war in Europe is over, people will take a different view of spinsters? Most people seem to have the most erroneous views about them. A well-known writer in a Sunday paper the other week asked quite plaintively, 'Why are all spinsters so sour?' He must have been singularly unfortunate in those he had met. Most people think spinsters must of necessity be dowdy, minus the least sense of humour, looks or sex appeal; otherwise why are they single? That any woman remains single by choice is, of course, fantastic! Looking at the large number of unmarried women of any uncertain age, people must know that the above is simply not true, but the idea still persists. With the mother-in-law joke, the spinster, or 'old maid,' one has still the power to make most audiences rock with laughter. The married still look on the unmarried with some kindly patronage. This may possibly be because she will, (even if her marriage has not turned out quite as expected) at least be able to have 'Dearly Beloved wife of . .' on her tombstone, whereas the lonely spinster will be just plain Jane Smith.' "—*M. B., Middlesex.*

History Up to Date

"It was with much interest that I read Edgar Granville's article 'Will Our Children Forget?' I would like to say that I think that if our history lessons at school had been a little more up to date, and we had learned more of recent history, we would not have forgotten what the Germans have been like during the past fifty years. I sincerely hope that our children have an opportunity of learning about World Wars Nos. 1 and 2, and that the events of May, 1944—May, 1945, will be made as familiar to them as those of 1066. I think that the more the German atrocities of this war are brought home to them through schools, the less likely they are to forget, and the less probable will be World War No. 3."—*Mrs. D. C., Romford.*

Books for Hospitals

"I wonder would everyone who has any spare books (providing they are clean) parcel them up and send them or hand them, to their nearest hospital? I am in hospital at present and I do enjoy a book.—*N. K., Liverpool.*

Woman's Own

An Overheard Conversation

"I'm going to vote Socialist," she said, "because Mr. Churchill is a Socialist."
"Oh no, he isn't," they said.
"Oh yes, he is ; I've heard him on the wireless."
"Well, whether he is or not, you can only vote for him in Essex."
"I don't care ; I shall go to Essex and vote for him there."

The Tablet

Teach children
KERB DRILL

See that they always do it and set a good example by doing it yourself.

▲

1. *At the kerb* HALT
2. EYES RIGHT
3. EYES LEFT
4. EYES RIGHT AGAIN
    then if the road is clear
5. QUICK MARCH
    Don't rush
Cross in an orderly manner

JULY
1945

Tory Offer: 'Television in Every Rural Home'

Daily Worker Reporter
BANBURY, Monday.

THE Conservative candidate here, Colonel Dodds Parker, is going about suggesting that "a television set in every cottage" will be one result of a Tory win.

This—in a constituency where thousands of cottages are without light, water or drainage—has caused a great deal of amusement among the electors.

There are whole villages—for example Taston which is owned by Ronald Tree, Tory candidate for Market Harborough—which share one tap.

People here who have kept their Labour views to themselves for years are now openly canvassing, and heckling the Tory meetings.

Indignation

If this is a safe Tory seat, what must the doubtful ones be like! There is a confidence, a determination, a class feeling in the villages that I have not met in the country before.

The Tories are behaving as if they owned the place, as, of course, they do.

They have aroused deep indignation in Woodstock by plastering W.V.S. mobile canteens with electioneering posters, and in Charlbury by setting up their committee rooms in a house in the town centre which was presented to the town for a social centre some months ago by a leading local Tory.

True, the transfer of the property has not yet been legally completed, but as several people put it to me: "After all, we were clapping Mr. Morris's generosity back in February."

Not only are farm workers and the men and girls who since the war have been drawn into the factories of Oxford, Banbury and Witney, alive to the issues, but many shop-keepers too have made up their minds that it's time for a change.

Though many are still nervous of saying how they will vote, there is no doubt where their sympathies lie.

Mr. Harold Earleigh, son of the old Liberal M.P. for this division, has issued an appeal to Liberals to vote Labour this time.

Seeing how many people in these parts begin by saying: "Well, I've always been a Liberal," this should add weight to Labour's drive.

Brian Roach, the Labour candidate — an International Brigader, by the way—is confident that he will win the seat.

After what I have seen, I would say there is only one thing that can lose it for him: over-confidence, and lack of an organised drive on the doorsteps during the last few days.

Oxfordshire people don't want the Tories.

Daily Worker

"KIWI does more than give the finest shine. It penetrates right down into the pores of the leather, keeps it smooth and soft—makes shoes wear twice as long for every sprat you paid for 'em."

"Dinkum?"

"Sure. That's why all Anzacs use KIWI—wouldn't use any other. Same goes for the Canadians and the Poles, the Dutch and the French. To say nothing of the entire British army and people!"

KIWI DARK TAN

KIWI BLACK

4d. and **8**d.

Also Tan, Brown, Ox Blood, and Mahogany Stain Polishes.

K.469
THE KIWI POLISH CO. PTY., LTD., BRUMWILL RD., EALING, LONDON, W.5

£400 p.a. from wagering

AT Boston, Lincs, Mr. Malcolm Hall told the Grantham Rotary Club of a man who makes £400 a year by wagering with his friends and acquaintances a level £1 that their cigarette lighters do not work the first time. Sometimes he wins and sometimes the lighter-owners collect, but in the aggregate it is a wager worth £8 a week to him—free of income tax!

Sunday Express

ONE FROCK £112

British girls may be having a hard time as far as clothes are concerned, but how would they like to pay these prices:

Printed rayon summer frock, £112; tailor-made ensemble (ersatz material), £150; hat, £25; shoes, £37; handbag, £50; slip, £20.

Fantastic, but it is fair sample of the prices in Paris fashion houses these days.

Sunday Pictorial

AMUSING INTERLUDE AT CONSERVATIVE MEETING

There was an amusing interlude during the Conservative meeting at Llandudno Town Hall on Saturday evening, when a man at the rear of the hall who claimed to be a dock labourer from Scotland-road, Liverpool, and a soldier on reserve, shouted out, "I am going to speak"

After several people had told him to sit down and he protested, another voice said: "I don't know who you represent, but you are doing a lot of harm."

Another man got up and said: "I have been away for 5½ years myself and I want to hear the Conservative candidate."

Lt.-Col. Price White, the candidate: "I will have my say and then you can have five minutes up here."

The dock worker agreed to this course and walked to the front of the hall and solemnly saluted Col. Price White as he stood up.

Half-way through Col. Price White's address he got up and said: "I have to go now, Colonel, but I think you will be last in the election."

Col. Price White: Will you have 5s on it?

The man: Yes.

With that both handed over their stakes to the chairman, Mr R. Vincent Johnson.

As the man was leaving the hall the candidate declared: "That's the sort of bloke who wins wars for us."

A Voice: And the peace, too.

Col. Price White: Good luck to him, and I will help him to do it

North Wales Pioneer

PRINCESS ELIZABETH VISITS MARYLEBONE

Opens Library For Nurses

Princess Elizabeth, attended by the Hon. Mrs. Vicary Gibbs, opened the new library at the Royal College of Nursing, Cavendish Square, Marylebone. She was handed a bouquet by an Indian student nurse.

The Princess said: "Your college is laying the foundation of a wonderful educational future for the nurse, but not only that I think it is every one's ambition to serve their country, and you are in a position to do it."

After tea the Princess saw the film "Student Nurse," illustrating the life and training of a nurse.

Marylebone Mercury

GUERNSEY GRAPES DUE SOON

Will cut price

GRAPES from Guernsey, where the vines are yielding good crops, are expected in two months' time. This should reduce the price to about 6s. 6d. a lb., though it is not known yet how much fruit the growers will be allowed to send.

Beans from Guernsey are already in the London markets in small quantities.

A few plums will be on sale this week at 6d. a lb., but until apples arrive there will not be much fruit as the cherry crop is now practically finished.

Oranges diverted

London would have had 100,000 cases of oranges at the week-end if the "go-slow" at the London Docks had not diverted them to another port.

Broad beans are plentiful and should be obtainable at 3d. a lb. Peas should retail at 3½d. and 4d. a lb. New potatoes are in good supply.

Imported rabbits from Australia should be on sale this week. Supplies of fish are stable; 379 tons arrived in Billingsgate over the week-end.

Supplies of canned meat and fish on points are very low in most shops. Many grocers have been without tins of Spam for some weeks.

Sunday Express

Battle of the Boyne

— ooo —

Celebrations in the North-West

Derry Demonstration At Fountain Hill

20,000 at Tyrone Rally

Thousands of members of the Orange Order from many parts of County Londonderry, County Tyrone and East Donegal took part in the City of Derry Grand Orange Lodge's demonstration in Londonderry on Thursday in celebration of the 255th Anniversary of the Battle of the Boyne.

The celebration was the first since 1939, and, although there were not so many brethren taking part as in the pre-war years because of the number in the Forces, there was ample evidence that during the intervening six years since the last demonstration enthusiasm and interest in Orangeism has grown to a very considerable extent and that the Order is on the threshold of a big expansion.

The procession formed up on Mall Wall and Bishop Street, and, after halting in The Diamond, where a wreath was laid on the War Memorial, the brethren marched to a field at Fountain Hill, where the celebration took the form of a service of thanksgiving for victory.

The address was delivered by Br. Rev. S. Chadwick, M.A., rector of Donagheady and Deputy City Grand Chaplain.

Londonderry Sentinel

MARKETS AND POLITICS

Confidence is notoriously a tender plant, peculiarly susceptible to the chilling effects of uncertainty. This characteristic must figure largely in any explanation of the course of Stock Exchange prices in abnormal times. Its influence has been reflected repeatedly not only during the European war but amid the political unsettlement which has culminated in the General Election whose outcome is to be decided by to-day's polling. Markets were cock-a-hoop as the day of victory over Germany approached, as well they might be, but even before VE-day could be announced reaction in prices had set in. During April interest tended to switch from gilt-edged stocks to Industrials. The latter reached their peak at that period on 30th April, when THE FINANCIAL TIMES index stood at 146.83, but within a few days signs of restiveness among the Socialists brought into the foreground the possibility of an election. Investors therefore tended to avoid the Stock Markets until the outlook should appear clearer.

The Labour Party Conference decision of 21st May made an election virtually certain, and so cleared the air to some extent. By the time the Prime Minister had formed his new Government with a view to a dissolution of Parliament, Industrials had declined to 136.71, a fall of nearly 7 per cent. in less than a month. Home Rails reached their lowest of 61.92 on the same day, gilt-edged and Gold-mining shares touched bottom a day or two later. Gradual revival since has testified to underlying confidence in the ability of a victorious Britain to survive the tests which will be imposed by the combination of Far Eastern war with transition in part to peaceful pursuits at home.

The Stock Exchange as a whole has become more and more convinced that Mr. Churchill will be put in power again, and takes a cheerful view accordingly. That investors share it is evident from the accession of business indicated by 7,400 markings yesterday, a rise of 50 per cent. over those of the previous Wednesday. In bringing about a recovery in gilt-edged from 114.67 to 115.07 the recent help of reinvestment of Conversion Loan and Australian funds has been a factor, but expectation of a strong and stable Government is a more lasting one. Home Rails, at 65.18, against 61.92 in late May, are adjudged to have the perils of nationalisation further removed from them. They have still some time to run under their war-time agreement. With the flow of materials and labour still adjusted to conditions of greater or less scarcity, production of civilian goods cannot get into full swing all at once, but freedom for enterprise is another benefit to be associated with defeat of Socialism. There are hopes of tax remissions of some kind, too, before long, and altogether the outlook is deemed so promising that the Industrial index is up again to 144.04. Gold shares are a class apart. They have not retained the whole of the improvement due to the raising of the price to be paid for gold (out of which they have higher expenses to meet), but they stand at 158.85, against 153.67 on 30th April. Declines over the same period remain in the other sections as a reminder that the election has still to be decided and that uncertainty is much more easily created than allayed.

Financial Times

'VOTE AS RED AS YOU CAN'

Pollitt, Cripps, Morrison Give Rousing Eve-of-Poll Calls

"VOTE AS RED AS YOU CAN," WROTE THE SOLDIER TO HIS WIFE. IN THAT SINGLE INSTRUCTION ON HOW TO USE HIS PROXY VOTE, ONE FIGHTING MAN HAS SUMMED UP THE DEMANDS OF SCORES OF THOUSANDS OF THEM " OVER THERE."

Quoting that simple and splendid letter last night, Mr. Harry Pollitt, Communist candidate for Rhondda East, gave a great eve-of-poll call to the nation (printed in full on Page 2).

The call of the soldiers, the call of all who understand the issues at this election is to vote for the Communist candidates where they are standing, and the Labour candidates everywhere else.

With one day to go before polling day, and the fight everywhere reaching its hottest point, **Sir Stafford Cripps,** Labour candidate for Bristol East, gave this message to the Daily Worker:—

"The workers of Great Britain have at last the chance to prove their strength and determination in an election which will decide their future.

"We must get rid of the old policies that gave us so many miseries and injustices in the years between the wars. This is D-Day for the assault on private enterprise.

"If the workers put their backs into the job then we shall celebrate V-L—Victory for Labour—Day in three weeks' time.

"Forward to the assault. See that no vote is wasted and win the victory that alone can give our men and women in the fighting Services a fair chance when they come home."

Speaking at East Lewisham, **Mr. Herbert Morrison** said that the Tories and their leader were continuing to the last minute their strenuous efforts to prevent the electorate voting on the real issues—the post-war economic and industrial problems.

Daily Worker

HAPPY FEET for Happy Holidays

Soothing & Healing

Zam-Buk

For All-Day FOOT COMFORT

Manchester Guardian

GIRLS' CHOICE OF A CAREER

Medicine or Teaching

At Broughton High School for Girls speech day yesterday the head mistress, Dr. Margaret C. Wicks, said that while medicine seemed to have a great attraction for girls as a career it was pleasing to find that quite a number of pupils were now showing an interest in teaching as a life-work. "Teaching is a fine and rewarding career and no work can be more important to the nation," she said.

The school had the record number of 481 pupils this session and there was every prospect of the number being even greater in September.

The Mayor of Salford (Alderman J. Binns) presided and the address was given, and the prizes distributed, by Dr. Katharine H. Coward, a Salford scientist on the Ministry of Food research staff.

Manchester Guardian

MAURI REMANDED ON MURDER CHARGE

Ronald Bertram Mauri (32), motorlorry driver, of no fixed home, was at Uxbridge yesterday remanded until next Thursday charged with the murder of Vera Guest, aged 18, of Nottingham, who was found strangled in a house at Hillingdon on July 11. Mauri, who had wound marks on the right side of his forehead, was closely guarded as he entered the court.

Divisional Detective Inspector Harold Cripps, of X Division, said that when he told Mauri at Monmouth Hospital on Tuesday that he would be charged with the wilful murder of Vera Guest, Mauri made no reply. At Uxbridge the charge was read over to him, and on being cautioned he said "Yes."

Asked if he had anything to say, Mauri said, "No, sir. I just ask for legal aid." This was granted and he left the court.

HEAVY POLL IN ELECTION: OVER 70 PER CENT. VOTED

Dundee Courier

Three Weeks' Wait For Result

MANY SCOTTISH INCIDENTS

Mother And Daughter Made Air Dash From Holiday Resort

Polling yesterday in the first General Election for ten years was heavy. Most of the estimates were that between 70 and 80 per cent. of the electors recorded their votes.

There will be a wait of three weeks before the result is known, the delay being imposed to enable the votes of men and women in the services to be counted and added to those recorded at home.

In most constituencies the poll opened quietly, but it became brisker in the towns during the morning, when the majority of women interrupted their shopping to vote.

In some working-class divisions both men and women marked their ballot papers on the way to their jobs, but the rush was expected in the evening after working hours.

Because of local circumstances polling in 23 divisions will take place later, and in Central Hull the election is deferred because of the death during the campaign of the Socialist candidate. In three other constituencies there is no contest, so that, including the universities, 613 seats contested by some 1600 candidates, were at stake yesterday.

PRINCE MICHAEL OPERATED ON

Three-year-old Prince Michael of Kent was operated on successfully yesterday for tonsilitis and adenoids at the Great Ormond-street Hospital for Children.

The Duchess of Kent was at the hospital ail day. Reports on the Prince's condition last night were satisfactory.

News of the World

NEW RULE STARTS DIVORCE RUSH

BIRTH CONTROL CASE MAKES LEGAL HISTORY

"News of the World" Special

SCORES of wives intend seeking divorces on the grounds decided in the Court of Appeal "childless couple" case, which, while making legal history, is arousing violent controversy among lawyers and Churchmen.

The Court ruling, which, three days later, was supported by a similar decision in Montreal, was that a nullity decree can be granted where, as a result of a husband's persistent and habitual use of birth-control methods, a wife is unable to bear children.

News of the World

THE FOLLOWING ARTICLE, WITH THESE HEADLINES APPEARED IN "THE DAILY WORKER" OF JULY 12th:

Carried Out Nazis' Orders, Still Rule Jersey

Daily Worker Reporter

ST. HELIER, Wednesday.

If a Commission of Inquiry were to come here from Britain, the Bailiff, the Attorney-General and other officials would be deprived of their posts as the result of their activities during the German occupation.

This is the conviction of leading Jersey lawyers with whom I spoke to-day.

They also consider that the whole States of Jersey, and particularly the Superior Council, would have to face the very gravest charges.

I understand that the Jersey Bar Council, at a meeting last year, expressed the opinion that the members of the Superior Council, presided over by the Bailiff—which was the main instrument carrying out German orders—had usurped powers which had never been conferred upon them.

'Secret' Order

I have a copy of one Order dated May 24, 1941, in my possession. It is an Order restricting the import and export of goods from the Island except under licence.

This Order, however, excepted "the importation of goods which are proved to be intended for the personal use of the importer or of the members of his family."

Members of the States have told me that they themselves did not know of this Order, and that knowledge of it was restricted to members of the Superior Council. If this is so it would appear that they were able to obtain supplies for themselves when the rest of the Island was going short.

"The Superior Council," the Order begins, "in compliance with the directions of the Field Commandant, hereby orders as follows." And this is the way every Order begins.

And it is signed by the Field Commandant, Johannes, and the Bailiff.

Same Statute Book

Every law made at the order of the Germans was entered on the same Statute Book as had been the laws approved by the King of England. They went through the same procedure and were read by the Attorney-General with the mace in its usual position.

This was in accordance with the German Order of July, 1940.

"Such legislation," this Order declared, "as in the past required the sanction of his Brittannic Majesty in Council for its validity, shall hereafter be valid on being approved by the German commandant and thereafter sanctioned by the Bailiff of Jersey."

The Germans ordered, the States agreed, and the Bailiff sanctioned.

The lawyers also told me of innumerable cases in which officials of the States of Jersey had taken action against their own citizens on the basis of anonymous letters.

Jailed by Nazis

Most of these letters informed on people who were keeping illegal radio sets. But instead of keeping the information to themselves, and thus protecting the Islanders, police officers have told me that they were instructed by higher authorities to inform the Germans.

In one case, for instance, after a radio set had been taken by the local policeman to the parish hall and the owner had been told that nothing more would be heard of it, the policeman received instructions to take the set to German headquarters.

As a result, numbers of people were sentenced to long terms of imprisonment by German courts-martial, many were deported, and a number had died in concentration camps. -

London Visit

The Bailiff of Jersey, Mr. A. M. Coutanche, accompanied by the Attorney-General, Mr. C. W. Duret Aubin, are due to arrive in London to-day. They are to be accompanied by the State Treasurer and the State Auditor, together with members of the Department of Finance and Economics.

The mission is ostensibly to discuss financial matters with Government experts, but I understand that a number of other matters are due to be discussed.

A representative of the Public Prosecutor has been in the Island in the past few days and is now reporting back to London. He has caused surprise by stating to various people that he did not see how anything could be done to rectify the injustices about which the population of the Island are clamouring.

OUR COMMENT

It is a striking commentary on this article and all its foul implications that the so-called secret Order, the Import and Export of Goods (Control) (Jersey) Order, 1941, was registered by the Royal Court on May 24th, 1941, and was reproduced in extenso as an official announcement in *The Evening Post* of that day.

In addition, the Order provided for the setting up of the "Imports and Exports Advisory Committee" to advise the Superior Council in the exercise of its functions under the Order, and that committee, composed of Mr. S. B. Hankinson as President, Dr. R. N. McKinstry, Medical Officer of Health, and Messrs. E. W. Hettich, N. A. Allport, J. M. Norman and G. D. Smith, with Mr. W. J. White as secretary, met regularly to consider applications for licences under the Order throughout the period from May, 1941, to June, 1944.

This is clearly, therefore, yet another fabrication of the malicious minds and lying tongues which were so busy throughout the Occupation seeking to encompass, in the face of the enemy, the downfall of His Majesty's lawful Government in this Island.

We are satisfied that no decent-minded person would for one moment give credence to an article such as this, and it seems almost inconceivable, in face of the irrefutable evidence to the contrary, that any Jersey lawyer or member of the States should have a mind so distorted or so base as to make himself responsible for the publication of such abominable lies.

Jersey Evening Post

Mr. Palmer and his family enter their new home.

Vigilantes Give Family of 13 New Home

MR. JOHN PREEN, Paddington builder and Vigilante leader, who, in nine days, has put twenty-three families into unoccupied houses in the borough, yesterday "installed" thirteen members of a family in an eight-roomed house at Denholme-road, Maida Hill, W.

They were: George Palmer and his wife, who lived with two of their children, a baby girl of 11 weeks and a boy of 3½ in one room in Herries-street, Paddington.

Mr. Palmer's sailor brother, badly wounded, who refused to leave hospital because he had nowhere to go.

Mr. Palmer's mother-in-law and his four sisters, one a cripple.

A sister-in-law and her husband and an orphaned niece.

The house into which the family moved has been empty for three years except for one part used for firewatching.

"The house is in fair condition with only four panes of glass broken," Mr. Preen said last night. "and it is in far better condition than many round here.

"Many unoccupied houses in Paddington have gone to rack and ruin," he added. "Lead piping has been cut away, cisterns and sinks stolen and anything of value removed. One house had eight doors stolen.

"If most of the houses had been repaired six months ago, the repairs to each would have cost only about £50 instead of £200 or £300 today.

Each of the twenty-three families put into houses by Mr. Preen have signed an agreement to do no damage to the premises and to pay rent when demanded at the controlled rate. They have also agreed to accept suitable alternative accommodation if offered by a responsible authority.

A warning against a gas leak was chalked on a wall inside the house, but Mr. Preen said it was only a blind that did not fool him.

● Men on board the battleship Vindictive at a meeting last week to decide what to do with their canteen funds voted £50 to Brighton Vigilantes in appreciation of their work in helping homeless families.

Sunday Pictorial

Q & A

—or what people SAY they want

Average post-war expectations and demands of housewives answered by

An Electrical Expert

with comments where required by Good Housekeeping Institute

Q *" After the war, shall I be able to buy a vacuum cleaner that picks up the ' bits '—crumbs, ends of cotton and so on—as well as the dust ? The plain dark carpets over most of my house seem to need at least two operations, with carpet-sweeper and vacuum cleaner, to keep them perfect. Would £15 buy such a cleaner ? "*

A Efficient vacuum cleaners well able to pick up everything will undoubtedly be on the market again after the war, and some models should be available for less than £15.

Comments : The Institute tested many vacuum cleaners before the war with brush attachment or other device, which were quite as effective as a carpet-sweeper for picking up pieces.

Q *" American papers are beginning to show pictures of wonderful new post-war refrigerators. Will there be anything of the same sort here ? Can a middle-class family of four hope to get a refrigerator big enough for everyday needs for, say, £25 in the spring of 1946 ? "*

A Plans have been announced for the production of a new standard 4 c. ft. electric refrigerator large enough for a family of four, and probably costing less than £25, but the date when it will be available depends on the progress of the war in the Far East, which absorbs all our manufacturing capacity.

Comments : We hope to publish shortly an article on household refrigeration, in which various aspects of the matter will be discussed more fully.

Q *" Will there be reasonably priced kitchen mixers —such as they have in America—which do everything from mixing cakes to grinding coffee ? "*

A Several British manufacturers are reported to be working on plans for better-than-ever kitchen mixers at reasonable prices.

Comments : Small mixers could be bought in this country before the war for from 5–6 gns., and the Institute carried out tests on several good machines of this type.

Q *"Will the new strip lighting be easy to instal, and what will it cost, compared with ordinary electric light bulbs ? "*

A New fittings are being developed to simplify the installation of fluorescent tube lamps. At present one 5-ft. 80-watt tube costs 24s., but lasts twice as long and takes less than half the current of the 200-watt filament lamp (costing 6s. 11d. for a clear lamp and 7s. 6½d. for pearl giving the same amount of light).

Q *"Will gas and electric meters be less unsightly and take up much less space after the war ? "*

A Compact designs of " electricity supply controls," containing not only the meter but all the switches and fuses in one unit, have already been developed either for mounting on the surface or to be sunk in the wall.

Q *" Will ex-Service men be encouraged to work in small parties owning their own equipment, to call and do particular housework such as vacuum cleaning and electric polishing every week or every day, so the housewife doesn't have to buy and store any equipment at all ? "*

A Such a scheme is no doubt possible, but let's hope there is more productive employment for ex-Service men. Anyway, would there not be practical difficulties in arranging convenient appointments ?

INTRODUCING "OPERA IN ENGLISH"

War-Time Achievements of Sadler's Wells

When the London "blitz" began in September, 1940, opera and ballet performances at Sadler's Wells Theatre had to stop, and the building was taken over as a rest centre; but Tyrone Guthrie was anxious to keep a nucleus of the opera company together for an experiment he had in mind.

And the story of that experiment and its growth and success, already known to some in Cambridge, is sketched in some detail in the first of a series of Sadler's Wells Opera Books, just published for the governors of Sadler's Wells Foundation by John Lane, The Bodley Head.

"Opera in English," a collection of essays written by such experts as Mr. Guthrie himself, Prof. Edward J. Dent, Edwin Evans, Joan Cross and Ninette de Valois, is an attractive introductory volume, putting very persuasively the case for the playing of opera in English, and, incidentally, tilting effectively at the old cult which pandered to foreign productions and the worship of big voices and conductors. Against this a plea is made for a presentation that pays due regard to the music, the drama, and the general production; and Professor Dent argues soundly for, first, a careful revision of the translations of foreign works now presented, and, secondly, the creation of a national opera that shall be based on a large repertory of our own native works.

THE EXPERIMENT, AND CAMBRIDGE'S HELP.

The story of the experiment mentioned above—a tour of small industrial towns lying outside the normal circuits by a tiny cast of singers and an orchestra of four—is related by Miss Cross, who reveals some of the difficulties, and tells how it developed until, with the aid of "a generous grant from the Trustees of the Cambridge Arts Theatre, Kurt Jooss undertook a full-length production of 'The Marriage of Figaro,' with designs by William Chappell."

Each of the other three books of the series deals with one opera—Mozart's "Cosi Fan Tutte," Benjamin Britten's newly-produced "Peter Grimes," and Puccini's "Madame Butterfly"—with particular reference to its current production in English by the Sadler's Wells Company, but also with more general reference to the work itself, its history, and the ideas which it suggests or with which it is associated. Each volume has a synopsis-story, an analysis of its musical construction, and a series of full-page illustrations of its latest production.

These books will prove invaluable to all opera lovers, and should help to inculcate in others a liking for an art whose appeal has been greatly widened by the modern and courageous approach of all associated with Sadler's Wells Company's brave endeavours.

Each book is published at the modest price of 2s. 6d.

Cambridge Daily News

VENERABLE CHEESE

Modern science is amazing in its contrasting forms of enlightenment.

For the last decade or two it has been enlarging public knowledge of the health value of vitamins in our food, and the great proviso in that doctrine was that the food must be fresh. The far-travelled lettuce, the limp boiled cabbage lose much of their vitaminous virtue the further removed they are from their earthy origin.

Now comes discovery winging its way from the opposite tack. An Ottawa health official has found penicillin in certain kinds of cheese, and we all know what penicillin means nowadays — "the magic mould," the wonderful life-saver.

Mould is, however, the operative word. Not freshness this time, but ripeness is all. In fact, over-ripeness.

The Ottawa claim applies "particularly if the cheese is very smelly and very mouldy." Not that it is entirely novel to find virtue in this form of decay and putrescence. Gorgonzola has been a music-hall joke for generations, but some epicures find the supreme delicacy of cheese in one that is distinctly "high."

These connoisseurs may now claim the preferences of their palate reinforced by the testimony of medical value. During the war they have lamented our limitation to a standardised cheese devoid of all flavoursome character. Can it be expected, even in age, to evolve a mould potent with penicillin?

It is time for our Food and Health Ministries to take counsel with the Milk Marketing Board.

Dundee Courier

A GREAT DAY HAS DAWNED. With our hearts filled with thankfulness for victory, let us make this great resolve! Let us continue in our striving for a land free from anxiety and want—that the sacrifices of war may not have been in vain.

GIVE THANKS BY SAVING

HARVEST HOLIDAY

Although the European war is over, farmers need all the help they can get to gather in the harvest again this year, for the food situation is as vital and as grave as ever. Besides helping the farmer, a working holiday on the land provides a heavenly change for all jaded city dwellers. The surroundings are pleasant, the life healthy, and the company varied and stimulating. If you're interested, write to the Regional Secretary, South East Regional Office, Flat 73, Block 4, Bickenhall Mansions, London, W.I.

Woman's Journal

THE ELECTION AND AFTER

The City, with the nation, was shocked by the political landslide revealed yesterday. A substantial marking down of Stock Exchange prices was traditionally precautionary rather than due to selling pressure. Significant of the importance attached by the world to stable Government in Britain was the unsettlement spread abroad as the certainty of a Socialist Government became plain. While the country's affairs may be in the hands of a different set of people for the next few years the problems to be solved are unchanged and as urgent as before. The war with Japan remains to be prosecuted with the utmost vigour to the end. The tasks of resettlement and economic reconstruction call for prompt and vigorous delineation and application of appropriate measures.

The initial need is for clear formulation of the policy of the new Government, which Mr. Attlee undertook to form after Mr. Churchill's resignation last night. This is the first Labour Government to command a clear majority. It must be hoped the victors will not allow their great majority to persuade them to extremist courses such as would aggravate world anxiety. In point of fact, much in the manifesto of Mr. Attlee was designed to appeal to the moderate man. The practical difficulties of some of the more visionary aims are likely to become quickly apparent, but in a number of respects the gulf between the Conservative and Socialist programmes is not wide. Mr. Attlee favours the removal of irksome controls as soon as the need for them is ended. He wants planned location of industry and the elimination of depressed areas. It is the Socialist policy, he declared, to stimulate an efficient industry, and especially to help our export trade. One way of doing that would be by a reduction of taxation, and that is among the points on which the nation, virtually assured of favourable action if the Conservatives had been returned, will require speedy enlightenment.

No one supposes, Mr. Attlee has said, that all industries can or should be socialised forthwith. Light, fuel, power and the iron and steel industries were cited as being ripe for transformation into public services, although there was no indication of the way in which the consumer might be protected against a monopoly worked by the State.

Financial Times

July 26th Thurs. Election Results. Lots of extra Staff on Copying Table to get out & rush results as they come in. The 1st lot came before 11 am! Got a shock as so far, Labour is leading – it's terrible to think of Winston being put out, after all he has done. Even Norwood has gone over for the first time & poor Duncan Sandys is out! It's a very strange affair as I've seen such a few Labour Posters about in our windows.

July 27th Fri. Shock & consternation at final Result. large Labour Majority. Think it must be the forces vote as cannot hear all around, who has voted Labour! Very depressing, anyway. Fancy Mr Attlee as Prime Minister. am simply furious at the unthinking ingratitude of the Public. Don't think this Party has had enough experience & will get us into muddles soon – am sure. Felt so strongly about this, that I wrote a letter of thanks to Mr Churchill – it's the least one can do. I expect he will have thousands.

Diary of Miss N.V. Carver, Imperial War Museum archives

Labour win the 1945 General Election: Prime Minister elect Clement Attlee and his wife, Violet, arriving at Transport House, Smith Square, on 26 July 1945

Now it can be told . . .

Many of the Heinz Varieties that you could not get for so long have been on Service with the Forces. Here is a list of what they have had, and, knowing Heinz quality, you can judge what has been done to keep them 'fighting fit':

SELF-HEATING CANS

of Kidney Soup, Cream of Green Pea Soup, Mock Turtle Soup, Cream of Celery Soup, Oxtail Soup, Cream of Chicken Soup, Cocoa Milk, Malt Milk.

DEHYDRATED VEGETABLES

Potato, Carrot, Cabbage.

OTHER VARIETIES

Baked Beans — Tomato Soup — Celery Soup — Minced Beef and Vegetables — Savoury Rice and Sausages — Corned Beef Hash — Stewed Steak — Canned Mutton — Pork and Vegetables — Beef Stew — Boiled Beef, Carrots and Dumplings — Meat and Vegetable Ration — Steak and Kidney Pudding — Mutton Broth — Treacle Pudding — Mixed Fruit Pudding — Marmalade Pudding — Rice Pudding — Sultana Pudding — Date Pudding — Vegetable Salad — Sausages —Chicken and Ham Paste—Spaghetti—Coffee.

HEINZ
57

Always ready to serve..

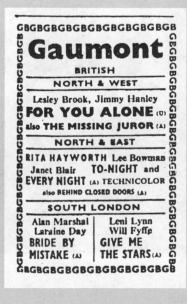

AUGUST
1945

Utility Size for Handkerchiefs

A special utility-size handkerchief for boys will soon be in the shops.

An official of the Board of Trade stated to-day that to make the best use of surplus material supplied by the Admiralty, 19-inch square handkerchiefs for men and 15-inch square ones for boys were being made, instead of the present 18-inch square for men. They would need half a coupon each.

The handkerchief-buyer of a large London shop commented: "The public won't give half a coupon for the smaller sized handkerchief. They are liable to remain frozen until rationing is suspended."

Oxford Mail

To keep your stockings ladder-free

You should wash them frequently.

For gentle rinsing, there's no doubt,

Will long prevent them wearing out.

Now that there's no Lux, you need to take more care when washing stockings. But rinsing through after wearing, even in water alone if you can't spare soap, restores elasticity—helps to prevent ladders.

ISSUED BY THE **LUX** WASHABILITY BUREAU

War Bus Service Recognised

Clippie Never Late Or Absent

Miss Ivy Basford, of Colwyn Street, Birkenhead, was never late, never absent, and had not a single day's sickness throughout her service of over five years as a bus conductress with Birkenhead Corporation.

She is to be presented with a gift by the Transport Committee in recognition of her loyal and unbroken service.

The third of four daughters of a widow, Miss Basford became a bus conductress in June, 1940. The blitzes on Merseyside began soon afterwards and members of the Transport Department had a most arduous winter to face.

Miss Basford makes light of her achievement, but told the *Echo* the

Miss Ivy Basford

winter of 1940-41 was certainly the most exacting of her career. When on late turn it was often early morning, owing to air raids, when she and her driver got back to the depot.

"Many times, in fact," she said, "I have only just had time to slip home and have a wash, and get back to take out one of the early morning buses.

HOME WRECKED

"My worst time was after the blitz on the night of March 12-13. Several mines fell near our house in Laird Street, which was wrecked, and we had to go and live at Pensby.

"I had to cycle the six miles to and from work, but I managed it all right. When I was due to take out the first bus from the Laird Street depot at 4.40 a.m., I had to get up at 2.45 a.m. in order to be in time. On the other hand, on a late turn, I did not get home until after midnight.

"I recall one night when I had a very narrow escape. It was just about midnight, and there was a raid on. I decided to cycle home through it, and all went well until I reached Arrowe Park. An enemy plane dropped his stick of bombs about 100 yards from me, and one piece of shrapnel pierced my steel helmet."

Miss Basford has an elder sister who has also been a conductress for five years. The only time she has been off was for a period of three weeks through food poisoning.

OUR BABY SERVICE *conducted by* NURSE HALE, S.C.M., G.L.I.H. & H.V.

He's a handful!

THE absence of fathers during the long years of war has made it very difficult for mothers to bring up their little boys just as they would like. Those who were quite small when father went away, are now between eight and twelve years old, and they may have got rather out of hand. Naturally, Mother is anxious that Father should not be disappointed in his little son—when he comes home.

If your husband will not be demobbed until some time next year you have ample time to get your unruly youngster into line. It may not be easy, but it can be done, and the best way, as I see it, is neither to grumble at, scold, nor punish him because, after all, if he is badly behaved it is really your fault to a large extent, isn't it? If "fault" sounds a little severe, please remember that I realize only too well the difficulties you have had to face while Father was away. Instead, try explaining how he can help you, and how tremendously important it is that when Father comes back he finds a son that he can be proud of. I feel sure that if you appeal to his better feelings he will respond.

Children appreciate it if we take them into our confidence and bitterly resent being told to do something which seems to them to be unreasonable for no better reason than because you tell them to. Talk to your son as man to man; explain that war has been pretty hard upon you all, and you know that it has brought certain hardships to him, but point out how much more it has meant to Father to be far away from his family for so long.

Show him he can make Father's homecoming happy by doing his share of the daily tasks. If you take it all with a light hand, work together and share and share alike he won't resent it, and will develop a sense of responsibility. If, on the other hand, perhaps because you are tired and feel you've had too much to cope with, you nag at or argue with your small son, trying to drive him to do what you want because you think it is his duty, you will never get his co-operation. Avoid threats because once made they must be kept and if unreasonable, because made in a flash of temper, he will lose faith in you. Prove to him that you mean what you say.

PROBLEM OF THE COLOUR BAR

A.R.C. "Chief" at Rotary

NEGROES AND THE WAR

A PLEA for education so that white and coloured people may learn more about one another, was made by Mr. J. L. Rodgers, Director of the Burleigh House American Red Cross Club at Cambridge, when he addressed members of the Cambridge Rotary Club on Tuesday on the colour bar.

His address, given at the club's weekly luncheon meeting at the Dorothy Cafe, was followed by a short discussion, in the course of which the speaker suggested that the atomic bomb has changed the basic relationships of mankind.

The President of the Club, Rotarian A. K. Dewey, welcomed Rotarian L. F. Jackson back, after nearly six years on war service.

In introducing the speaker, he mentioned that after nearly three years in this country with the American Red Cross, Mr. Rodgers is leaving at the end of this week.

VARIED CONCEPTIONS.

Mr. Rodgers began by pointing out that the colour bar question varied with the locale; in Britain, for instance, the problem was different from that in South America, and it varied again between East and West America.

"Personally, I think the time has gone when we should indulge in recriminations," he remarked, "because what little I know of history tells me that all people have sinned against one another. To begin to list the faults of one race, as against another, is a waste of time."

Exeter Express and Echo

FOUR generations were present when little Sheila Victoria Mary Diaper was dedicated at Burnt House Lane Mission Hall, Exeter. The service was performed by Mr. Harry Pankhurst, the missioner. Sheila is the only child of Mr. and Mrs. Diaper, of 29, Coronation-road, Wonford, and her father is on service with the B.L.A. In addition to the little girl and her mother, there are in the picture Mrs. Paltridge (grandmother), who also lives at 29, Coronation-road, and Mrs. Short (great-grandmother), of 6, New Houses, Bridford.

Liverpool Echo

FIVE DIE IN BOMBER

Crash At Prees To-Day

A Wellington bomber from Tilstock R.A.F. station, Salop, crashed into a field at Ivy farm, Prees Lower Heath, near Whitchurch, early to-day, and all five members of the crew were killed.

Their bodies were found amongst the wreckage of the plane by men of the N.F.S. belonging to Whitchurch and Hodnet.

No buildings were involved, but there was an enormous explosion as the machine hit the ground, shaking houses and waking people over two miles away.

Clothes Ration Warning

Coupons May Have To Last Longer

Two important announcements were made by Sir Stafford Cripps, President of the Board of Trade, yesterday during his week-end visit to Lancashire.

Addressing a gathering of 2000 employers and operatives in the cotton trade at Oldham yesterday, he appealed for more workers in the spinning section.

We had reached a point in our supply of cotton cloth, he said, where it was doubtful whether we could maintain the ration of clothing even at its present rate. Even if production were to be increased now as the result of the ending of the Japanese war, it could not affect the supplies of clothing in the shops for another eight months.

"I shall have to consider very closely whether for the next rationing period of clothes, which begins next month, I shall not have to ask the public to make the new issue of coupons last for a longer period than before.

"Further than that, the supply of cloth is so extremely short that I do not see how it would be possible to relax the restrictions on the sale of clothing or of extras which have been cut out by the austerity demands. Nor is it possible to foresee any substantial improvement of supplies of bed linen, curtains, and all those textiles so essential for furnishing the homes."

COTTON INDUSTRY.

Sir Stafford told a press conference in Manchester yesterday that it was not part of the Government's policy to nationalise the cotton industry. The cotton leaders—employers and unions—had agreed to the setting up of a commission which would frame definite proposals to give general confidence in an early and satisfactory implementation of the intention to revise wage agreements and reform the staffing of the machinery to benefit employers and employees.

The Government were prepared to assist the cotton industry to the best of their ability, provided it was clear that the national interest of producing as great a volume of goods as possible at reasonable prices and with good working conditions for operatives took precedence of all other considerations.

Dundee Courier

Not the least of all that you will prize among the blessings of peace — will be your Kayser-Bondor stockings. Perfectly sheer ... beautifully full-fashioned to fit immaculately ... in an array of fashionable shades... *these* are the promise of Kayser-Bondor !

KAYSER-BONDOR

Punch

"Yes, we ought to have been back home days ago, only that the trains always seem to draw up so that we're opposite a luggage-van."

RUBBER TYRES NEXT SPRING

Race To Meet Car Production

From A Special Correspondent

Had the Japanese war lasted a few weeks longer there would have been no natural rubber available in this country after next March. Even as matters stand, the position will not be easy for some time, although the synthetic bridge will avoid any serious shortage or outrageous price situation.

News from the Far East is that the Malayan plantations have not suffered unduly from the Japanese occupation.

One of the most urgent obstacles to overcome is the shortage of tapping equipment. This consists of porcelain or light metal cups that are held by bands to the tree trunks to collect the latex fluid. Some months ago permission was sought to have the necessary tens of millions of cups put into production, but the authorities decided that the situation, as it was then, did not warrant high priority being given to the request.

VJ-Day has altered that decision, and now a race is on to produce and ship the gear at the earliest date so that the expected acceleration in car output next spring can be matched with tyres of natural instead of part-synthetic rubber.

Sunday Times

Oxford Mail

MEN GET 5½D. MORE AN HOUR

Inquiry Told of Women French Polishers

Men and women did identical work — french polishing — but the men received 1s. 8½d. and the women 1s. 3d., said Mr. G. Woodcock, of the research department of the T.U.C., giving evidence before the Royal Commission on Equal Pay in London to-day.

Another instance of men and women receiving different payment for identical work was given by Miss Florence Hancock, of the Transport and General Workers Union, who said that in Manchester she saw teams in which there was complete interchangeability between men and women engaged on making bulkheads.

But at the end of the week the women had pay packets based on women's rates and the men had earnings based on men's rates.

Miss B. Anne Godwin, of the Clerical Administrative Workers Union, criticising those who regarded women as a "reservoir of cheap labour," said if equal rates were paid for the job the best person would emerge regardless of sex.

VICTORY brings nearer the day when I'll return, meanwhile—

use my STORK COOKERY SERVICE

VICTORY CAKE
and how to ice it

THIS is a cake worthy of Victory. How to make it and how to ice it with your own home-made icing bag is clearly explained and illustrated in Leaflet No. 66.

STORK MARGARINE
COOKERY SERVICE

COUPON—CUT THIS OUT NOW

Send this coupon in an unsealed ½d-stamped envelope to The Stork Margarine Cookery Service, Unilever House, London, E.C.4, for Cookery Notes No. 66 "Victory in Europe — Cakes and Icings."

Name..

Street...

Town..

★ Until Stork Margarine is again available let The Stork Margarine Cookery Service solve your war-time cooking problems.

JSC 90-137

HONEST PERCY PRAWN

No Pretence about Prawn.

WHAT'S NAMED on a Shippam's label can be tasted in the paste. In the past our labels have promised prawn, lobster, pheasant and other good things. One day they will promise these favourites again.

Meanwhile our customers know that Shippam's meat and fish pastes are made of the best ingredients released to us by the Ministry of Food.

Shippam's
MEAT and FISH PASTES

C. SHIPPAM LIMITED CHICHESTER SUSSEX

Oxford Mail

Hitler's Brother Released

Alois Hitler, the Fuehrer's half-brother, has been released by British police after six weeks of questioning since his capture in the Hamburg area.

"It is clear to us," says a British Military Government statement, quoted by the Associated Press, "that he has led a perfectly blameless existence, and has been scared stiff of being associated in any way with the Fuehrer's activities. He was released yesterday."

Alois was the proprietor of a beer tavern in Berlin during most of the war

FOR GOOD OR EVIL

Punch

'I find it difficult to describe my own feelings: it obviously is a relief to know that the killing has ended. It would be even better to know that this relief was not premature, as many people, myself included, believe . . . But – this is a fairly new thing, I think – very many people have realised the previous "they" must be replaced by the post-war "we".'

Mass Observation archive, University of Sussex

10 August 1945: Paper showers from windows in Lower Regent Street as office workers hear rumours that Japan is negotiating for peace

an electrifying statement that America has dropped the first Atomic Bomb on Hiroshima in Japan. It sounds terrible — the destruction caused there. Then on 5th. Russia declared War on Japs + by the end of the week they had surrendered! Another lot of hurried preparations for VJ Days.

August 15th — This day has been declared VJ — at last — the real end of the War — got up to be on at 8 — but heard on Radio that today was a Hol! Rushed round to get some bread — 9 am were long queues. It was raining but felt I must go up to Town as the King was opening Parliament (by a lucky chance). Put on old clothes + thick shoes + buzzed off. Met Hilda Brading at Tulse Hill + together we climbed on top of 33 Tram bound for Westminster. There was "some" crowd when we alighted, but we edged our way nearer to the front. It was a damp, but such a jolly + excited crowd. We couldn't see much of the Procession but the tops of heads, but we joined in the cheers, however, + after it was over got out on to the Embankment + along Whitehall to Trafalgar Square. There was another large concourse here but we stood in the Mall + had the luck to see the King + Queen very well on their way back to the Palace. More rain came on but we lingered about, watching a Guards Regiment being dismissed + enjoying the fun. When we arrived in front of the Palace hundreds of thousands of people were waiting, hoping that the Royal Family would come out on the Balcony. I went towards Victoria eventually, but just as I passed the Gates they did come out, so I ran back to the front again. It was grand — they looked so fine + the cheers were deafening. It was now 1 pm so I hurried off hoping to catch a number 2, which I was lucky enough to do + got home by 1.45. Had dinner + a quiet afternoon. Put out all the flags again.

Diary of Miss N.V. Carver, Imperial War Museum archives

Girls draped with the stars and stripes celebrate VJ Day by marching and singing in Trafalgar Square

Crowds try to break the police cordon at the State Opening of Parliament on VJ Day

"Be funny if the siren went now, wouldn't it?"

Sunday Express

I thought Tommy's suit was clean . . . until I saw Mary's **Persil-bright** one

DANCING BAN IN VIENNA
"Wasted Energy"

From Our Special Correspondent

VIENNA, Saturday.

There will be no dancing in Vienna during September and October. This was decreed to-day by the Government, for sanitary and aesthetic reasons. Instead, the city is to be cleared of all the piles of rubble and refuse, and as much property as possible made habitable before winter.

The ban on dancing is to remove any possible cause for the useless dissipation of energy.

All men between 15 and 50 and all women between 16 and 40 are, when not otherwise employed, to do 60 hours work a month for the city. For former Nazis the hours are doubled. Children and students will work 40 hours.

Sunday Times

THIS ENGLAND

A 5/- prize for the first entry in this column goes to James Kirkup.

Paste entries on postcard or slip of paper and give details of origin. Address to THIS ENGLAND, 10 Great Turnstile, W.C.1.

Grand Victory Atomic Dances will be held at the Heaton Assembly Rooms.—Advert. in *Newcastle Evening Chronicle*.

New Statesman

OFFICIAL COPY

Crown Copyright Reserved

SPECIAL ARMY ORDER

THE WAR OFFICE,
18th August, 1945

1/GENERAL/5085   **A.O. 133/1945**

MESSAGE FROM HIS MAJESTY THE KING TO THE NAVIES, ARMIES AND AIR FORCES OF THE BRITISH COMMON-WEALTH AND EMPIRE

The surrender of Japan has brought to a victorious end the war which has engaged our full fighting strength all over the world. I send my heartfelt congratulations to the men and women of my Navies, Armies and Air Forces throughout the British Commonwealth and Empire.

Through the long years of the grim struggle with our enemies in the West and in the East, your unflinching resolution and indomitable courage in the face of manifold adversity have earned you the eternal gratitude of your countrymen.

Many of your comrades have fallen in the fight. With you, I grieve for their loss, for the sufferings of the wounded and for the sorrows of the bereaved. With you, I look forward to the safe homecoming of those who have had to endure captivity.

By God's mercy, the forces of evil have been overthrown. But many tasks remain to be accomplished if the full blessings of peace are to be restored to a suffering world.

It is the duty of each one of us to ensure that your comrades have not died in vain, and that your own hard-won achievements are not lost to the cause of Freedom, in which you undertook them.

On behalf of all my peoples, I thank you. God bless you all.

GEORGE R.I.

Sunday Times

More lamentable mismanagement than the VJ holidays produced it would be difficult to imagine. To fix Wednesday as a holiday was calamitous even if there were certain superficial reasons—the fact that people would take Wednesday off anyhow, or the desire to synchronise festivity with America (which is only approximately possible anyhow). At nine o'clock on Tuesday evening the public were officially urged to go on with their work as usual. At midnight that night, when four-fifths of them were presumably in bed, and again at seven the next morning, when half or two-thirds of them were presumably still dressing or still asleep, the news that Wednesday was to be a holiday was given. Whether the information gratified anyone I have not discovered. Everyone I have heard of roundly cursed the whole business ; some wished they were working normally ; some wished the war was still going on (not quite seriously, I trust). Housewives in search of emergency provisions formed vast queues at bakers and butchers ; van-loads of goods drove up to factories where there was no one to receive them ; many business men living outside London heard nothing of the holiday till they got to their local stations ; finally, in the Gower Street district of London, at any rate, the eight o'clock post arrived at after half-past twelve—and Wednesday happens to be Press day for the weekly reviews. Some people no doubt enjoyed it all. But a sudden holiday creates a disastrous dislocation in national life, and if the Ministry of Labour issued a statement of the loss of production measured in man-hours the result would be staggering. However, it no doubt had to be, so the only thing was to get it over and then on with the job.

Spectator

SURRENDER ACT AT MANILA

Allied Missions Join Gen. MacArthur

It was announced at the headquarters of Gen. MacArthur, Allied Supreme Commander, at Manila yesterday that the conference with the Japanese surrender emissaries will begin there to-morrow morning. Missions from Adm. Lord Louis Mountbatten, C.-in-C., South-East Asia Command, and Marshal Chiang Kai-shek, Chinese generalissimo, have arrived at Manila, and Russian envoys are hourly expected.

The first surrender steps are meanwhile announced in South China. The Chinese First Army will receive the capitulation of large Japanese forces at Canton shortly, it is announced in Chungking.

This formal act of submission, which has no connection with that of Gen. Okamura, in the Hunan province of Central China, will be made, it is expected, to one-legged Vice-Adm. Chan Chak, the new Mayor of Canton, who on Christmas Day, 1941, led a party of British officers from Hong Kong into Free China.

While Japanese peace emissaries were preparing to leave Tokyo at dawn to-day (Japanese time) on the first hop of their 2,000-miles flight to Manila, news agency reports were telling of isolated instances of active opposition to the Allies.

KILLED OVER TOKYO

A photographer was killed and two members of the crew wounded in one American plane when 14 Japanese fighters attacked two B-32s on reconnaissance over Tokyo yesterday. Both the American planes were badly damaged. Two of the Japanese aircraft were shot down.

Last night's Moscow communiqué states that resistance is being met on several sectors. But the number of surrenders has increased. In the Khailar region, north-west of Hsinking, the Manchurian capital, an encircled garrison of 5,000, led by a major-general, laid down their arms.

This followed a broadcast from Khabarovsk stating that Gen. Hata, Japanese Chief of Staff in Manchuria, had been ordered to Soviet H.Q. in Manchuria by this morning (Japanese time). Red Army planes have flown to Harbin to fetch Hata.

LANDINGS IN KOREA

Another Khabarovsk broadcast said that more Russian troops have landed behind the Japanese lines along the Korean coast. Russian warships and planes are attacking Japanese positions along the coast night and day, the Radio added, and will continue to do so until complete surrender.

Stories of Japanese treachery are reaching Moscow from Sakhalin island, the northern half of which is Russian and the southern Japanese. Japanese troops wearing Red Army uniforms are reported to be attempting to penetrate the Soviet lines, making surprise attacks, sniping and laying ambushes. Japanese wounded are said to be shooting and knifing Soviet Red Cross workers. A correspondent of the newspaper " Izvestia " commented : " Hatred of our troops for the Japanese is growing hourly."

AND NOW TO WORK

Evening Standard

A Reply To Marguerite Steen

Has The War Really Changed Our Women?

To the Editor of the 'Sunday Graphic'

SIR,—Marguerite Steen, in her article in last week's *Sunday Graphic*, suggests that the blame for the present spate of domestic difficulties rests on the men of Britain.

Let me offer the views of three young infantry officers who have just returned and are now facing the difficulties of rehabilitation.

Firstly I must say that we admire heartily the women of Britain, of whom we have heard so much, who have worked throughout the war to give us the weapons to win. But since we have returned, we have yet to meet one.

We disembarked, not expecting any particular acclamation, but at least we hoped to find the work of the fighting forces overseas had been realised and appreciated by our womenfolk.

What did we find? That any expectations we had of picking up the threads of our domestic life were lost in a wild fandango of pleasure-mad, sensation-seeking civilians. And somewhere in this chaos were our womenfolk.

Enemy Propaganda

While in our slit-trenches our troops were bombarded with Nazi propaganda by leaflet and wireless suggesting that our home life was being broken up by Service and civilian men alike. Invariably such efforts were greeted with laughter and jeers—until the first leave parties returned from home. The facts they brought were more disturbing to our morale than any enemy propaganda had ever been. But we still believed such stories must be isolated cases up to the time that the outcry arose at home against fraternisation.

Did our womenfolk believe that all our men were being unfaithful on the slightest excuse? Or were the circumstances at home the foundation on which these fallacies were built?

Well, we have come back, and now we are making our own observations. Miss Steen tells us that the reason our womenfolk are "putting us on the side-walk" is that we do not know the subtle technique of flattery nor loudly voice our appreciation of them. We think most of us have been trying to show some appreciation for the last six years. And if our tongues have forgotten easy

phrases, have not these women forgotten how to value sincerity and true regard and are lost in the banal vocalisms culled from the cinema and the news articles on "How to Win Your Woman Easily."

We suggest that the womenfolk of Britain are captivated not by these easy phrases, so beloved by this novelist, nor even, to be just, by the "wads" of Allied soldiers, but by the unsettling action of war which has given new freedom to Woman and the vast influx of strange and foreign uniforms, bringing new customs and new techniques.

Social Independence

With this new freedom, enhanced by a greater feminine income than ever before, women have given themselves over completely to experimenting with these new sensations so near at hand. That is why Marguerite Steen's questioner remarked on the failure of women to unite or co-operate.

The feminine companionship that Miss Steen remarks on was forced on them willy-nilly, either by circumstances of work or a mutual desire for safety. But now that the inequality of the sexes is gradually being adjusted, can these women extend this companionship to their returning menfolk?

From what we have seen, we must say "No." For we can only see two classes—those who have achieved social and economic independence and are resolved to hold on to it at all costs; and those who have found the answer in vicarious plea-

sures. We realise that domestic readjustment must require mutual effort. Who is in the best position to lay a secure foundation? Those who have been divorced completely from home life or those who have maintained at least some semblance of domestic comfort?

We are accused by Miss Steen of riding roughshod over women's sensitivities. May we inform her that these social refinements do not flourish at their best in slit-trenches.

Free To Decide

Perhaps during the last few years girls have forgotten how their menfolk used to behave; perhaps, seeing new examples, they have come to prefer the new. That must be for them to decide. We also are free to decide if we are to change our inbred characteristics and alter our whole individual outlook. On that decision depends not only our domestic readjustment, but also the future of the family life of Britain.

According to Miss Steen the women of Britain have shown a preference for the new style of personal relationships. Perhaps this is momentary. If their attitude has changed in the last few years, perhaps it will again.

We condemn the fact that it has changed at all, and we challenge Miss Steen and the women she has championed to prove that our condemnation is unjustified and that the returning soldier will not find his wife or sweetheart wrapped up in these minor details of deportment and careless of the underlying fundamentals at issue.

THREE INFANTRY PLATOON
COMMANDERS
(Ex-Overseas).

SEPTEMBER
1945

MR T. JOHNSTON ON MODERN SPEECH IN SCOTLAND

Influence of Hollywood Slang

Hollywood with its American slang is, in the opinion of Mr Thomas Johnston, late Secretary of State for Scotland, one of the adverse influences with which those who have been striving to preserve the Scots tongue have had to contend.

Speaking at the diamond jubilee dinner of the Burns Federation, held in Glasgow on Saturday evening, Mr Johnston, in an appreciation of the work of the Federation, said it had helped to preserve the dialect and speech forms of our ancestors Before it was inaugurated the torch had been carried on by Burns Clubs at their annual suppers and dinners, where there were various ascriptions to Burns of poetry he never wrote. (Laughter.)

WORK OF BURNS FEDERATION

They need not, however, unduly look down their noses at these old Burns clubs, for they carried on Scottish traditions and speech forms when more responsible organisations were busily engaged in selling the pass. They had to thank the Burns Federation for the great change that had come over the Scots tongue, the Scots dialect, and Scots literature in the past half-century. It had exercised a very happy influence on the Committee for the Training of Teachers, where there was now a much greater emphasis on the study of Scots in the curricula for the teaching profession.

The Federation first proposed and to a very large extent promoted and built up the necessary funds and enthusiasm for the Chair of Scottish History at Glasgow University. But, above all, it was to the credit of the Federation that it stepped in at a critical moment and saved the great effort of Dr Grant, in building up the Scottish National Dictionary, from possible financial defeat.

PRESERVATION OF SCOTS DIALECT

It had been a struggle to ensure the preservation of the Scots dialect. There had been in recent years many influences driving it from the scene. The cinema and Hollywood, with its American slang, were rapidly affecting the speech form of our generation, but he believed that the advocates of the Scots dialect would win. Mr H. G. Wells said he found he could not understand that dialect. To that he (Mr Johnston) replied—" No more can I understand Chaucer."

" We believe," Mr Johnston added, " we have something to contribute to the world as an organised entity, and that the world will lose something if Scotland becomes a region or a postal district. We are happy to know that we have in our land an organisation built up, nourished, and firmly fixed, which is determined to preserve our language and our literature,

and to preserve the Burns tradition and the glories of his song, so that we can hand on to those who come after us the Scots tongue, Scots language, and Scots literature."

Mr Johnston proposed the toast of " The Burns Federation," and this was replied to by Mr John S. Clarke, the president who presided at the dinner.

Mr W. D. Cocker, who gave the toast of " Scottish Literature," said that our literature did not begin and end with Robert Burns. Burns was a star in our literary firmament, but he was one of a constellation—a particularly bright constellation that had shone for many centuries, and would shine for many centuries to come. In proportion to its population Scotland had produced more poets, authors, and men of letters than any other part of the English-speaking world.

Looking back across the centuries, they could take justifiable pride in Scotland's literary achievements and look forward with hope and confidence to the future.

ABLE SCOTTISH WRITERS

Scotland had as good a modern literature as she deserved, said Mr J. M. Reid, responding to the toast. Perhaps, indeed, our literature was better than we deserved.

People whose attention was fixed on literary geniuses of the past—such a genius as Burns—were perhaps apt to set too high a standard when they came to consider modern writing. Scotland to-day had a large number of able writers. For the first time for several generations most of these authors had their attention fixed on Scotland and a Scottish audience rather than on London and a wider English-speaking one.

But a literature could not exist without readers. Writers must live and must be able to feel that they had an interested public.

Mr Reid appealed to members of the Burns Federation and those whom they represented to buy and read modern Scottish books, and to talk about them, even if what they had to say was critical.

ATTITUDE TO BURNS FEDERATION

Sir Patrick Dollan, in proposing thanks to all who had taken part in the proceedings, referred to Mr Reid's remarks, and said that if Scottish writers would not look down their noses so much at the Burns Federation they would get more appreciation than they did at present.

He would suggest that the first thing they should do was to join the membership of the Burns Club in the district in which they lived. So long as Scottish writers were thinking of London publishing houses and not of the Scottish public they would never get the circulation and the appreciation they expected.

Glasgow Herald

MEN OF "HEROIC 77TH"
AFTER THREE YEARS IN JAP PRISON CAMPS
Officers Kept Records Under Noses of the Enemy

IN THIS, THE FIRST OF A SERIES OF THREE DISPATCHES, IS TOLD THE HISTORY OF A BRITISH REGIMENT FROM THE DAY IT SAILED FROM THE HOME COUNTRY FOR THE GREEN HELL OF JAVA UNTIL LIBERATION CAME TO THE SURVIVORS A FEW DAYS AGO. OFFICERS WHILE IN CAPTIVITY AND AT THE RISK OF THEIR LIVES COMPILED THE STORY OF THE REGIMENT'S ORDEAL IN BATTLE AND IN PRISONER OF WAR CAMPS.

LIEUT. WOOLER.   LIEUT. REARDON-SMITH.   MAJOR GASKELL.   E. CURTIS.   R.S.M. SPENCE.

From VICTOR LEWIS, "Western Mail" War Correspondent
SINGAPORE, Tuesday.

WAITING patiently and cheerfully in the notorious Changi P.O.W. Camp here are 200 men and 11 officers who, in a matter of days, will be sailing for Britain—Cardiff and home.

They will bring with them scores of tales of horror, heroism, and tragedy—and a saga of undying courage and unfailing morale in the face of a greater battle against disease, ill-treatment, and starvation than was probably fought by any other units which fell into Japanese hands.

They are the survivors of the 77th Heavy "Ack-Ack" Regiment, R.A., raised and trained in Cardiff and district.

Their epic story is written on six sheets of rice paper. It is a story which will thrill and horrify South Wales, for it runs the whole gamut of war's worst experiences.

Even the ingenious rice paper recording of it is a drama in itself.

"Spirit Has Not Died"

Sitting in his prison quarters last night monocled LIEUT.-COL. H. R. HUMPHRIES, Commanding Officer of the 77th and pre-war Post Office telephone official in Cardiff, told me with justifiable pride the full story of his men, and after an hour's talking said:

"Tell South Wales that I and the men of the 77th send their greetings on liberation. We are all well. Our spirit has not died."

Western Mail

V2 on Show

A V2 is to be shown to the public for the first time during London's Thanksgiving Savings Week, which begins next Saturday. The rocket, which was captured in France, has been at an R.A.F. secret research station since its arrival in Britain.

Western Mail

Western Mail

Woman Hairdresser Fined £40

For refusing to sell a comb at the controlled price of 5d. to two different customers Isabelle Violet Jones, who carries on a hairdressing establishment under the name of "Norma's" at 12, Lambpit-street, Wrexham, was fined £40 with £23 4s. costs by the Bromfield justices at Wrexham on Tuesday.

When two women entered the defendant's shop on different dates and asked for a comb they were told that a comb would be presented if the customer bought a bottle of brilliantine for 2s. 6d. In the first instance the customer paid 2s. 6d. and received a comb but only a voucher for the brilliantine, of which there was presumably none in stock.

The Bench characterised the offence as a deliberate design to evade the Act in order to obtain an extortionate profit.

Kensington Post

DRUNK ON HORSEBACK
Done "In Spirit Of Bravado"

Confessing that it was "just a bit of swank," Ronald Sunnucks, 48, for 25 years an estate agent, with addresses at Granville Place, Oxford Street, and Kendal Street, Edgware Road, was fined £2 with £1 16s. 9d. costs at Marylebone for being drunk while in charge of a horse, and a further £4 for ill-using the animal by riding it while it was in an unfit condition. John Keefe, a stableman, of Garbutt Place, W.1, who let the horse out on hire, was fined £5 with 30s. costs, for allowing the horse to be ridden in that condition.

It appeared that Sunnucks hired the horse, a broken winded animal, in the presence of a number of people, and rode it up and down Granville Place, hitting it continuously with a crop, until it was tired out and exhausted. A veterinary surgeon who examined it said it was suffering from a very severe chill, approximating to pneumonia and ought never to have left the stables.

At the police station it was said Sunnucks claimed very friendly relationships with members of the nobility and asked the police to phone to the House of Lords.

Sunnucks told the magistrate he did it in a spirit of bravado.

23,500,000 Oranges for London: Bananas in New Year

Sir Ben Smith, Minister of Food, had some cheerful news to give his press conference yesterday. A boatload of oranges from South Africa is due to dock in London next Thursday. It will bring about 23,500,000 oranges, and they will all be for Londoners.

The first cargo of bananas will arrive from Jamaica early in the New Year. They will be brought by three ships of the pre-war fleet of special banana boats, which are being reconditioned.

The largest contract for canned fish ever made with Portugal has been agreed to and will involve approximately 2,000,000 cases.

The United Kingdom will also be the first country to conclude a contract with Norway for canned fish since the country was occupied by the Germans. An agreement has been reached for the purchase of 180,000 cases of brislings. These supplies will probably be available at the end of this year or the beginning of next.

Sir Ben Smith said he hoped to raise the present standards, but warned them that he is "fighting a hard battle to prevent our rations from being further reduced."

He explained that three boats of bananas could bring only a small proportion of the pre-war imports, and probably sales would be restricted to children and juniors.

Considerable quantities of sardines would be available for distribution in December.

The soap ration would be unchanged, but cutting out coupons would make sure people were not getting more soap than they were entitled to and would improve distribution.

Sir Ben said that the figures of our export trade during the first six months of this year were a remarkable tribute to the aid which this country had given to liberated Europe. The limited stocks of foods which we now held were only sufficient, with the expected imported supplies, to maintain our present standards.

He hoped to raise those standards, but during this period of world shortages he must ask the public to be satisfied with any small improvement that he could introduce.

Country's Weekly Needs

He gave figures showing Britain's weekly housekeeping requirements—over 30,000 tons of carcase meat, about 7000 tons of bacon, 10,000 tons of margarine and lard, 3000 tons of butter, 4000 tons of cheese, 6000 tons of jam and marmalade, 3000 tons of tea, and 30,000 tons of sugar.

Of the 30,000 tons of sugar needed less than half was accounted for by the domestic ration of 8oz. a week. The rest went into cakes, biscuits, chocolates, sweets, and to canteens and restaurants.

That weekly quantity represented a year's production of some 20,000 to 30,000 acres of sugar beet or 10,000 acres of sugar cane.

The 4000 tons of cheese required each week had to be produced from 9,000,000 gallons of milk—the yearly output of 20,000 cows.

The 3000 tons of butter took the yearly milk yield of some 45,000 cows, and the 30,000 tons of carcase meat meant 120,000 beef cattle or 1,500,000 sheep.

Glasgow Herald

STALIN TO RETIRE

Paris Report of Ill Health

The independent French newspaper, "Paris-Presse," stated yesterday that Stalin was likely to relinquish the Presidency of the Council of People's Commissars this winter and retire from all political activity because of ill health.

The newspaper's copyright article—which the Associated Press was authorised to quote—described Stalin as suffering from a liver ailment in conjunction with general fatigue.

The ailment developed into a serious state as far back as 1942. This, it was said, was the explanation for Stalin's delay in arriving at the Potsdam Conference.

The article did not specify the source of the report, but private information said that it came from foreign sources close to the Kremlin.

Glasgow Herald

Meat, Bacon Rations to Be Increased

THE meat ration for Great Britain is likely to be increased by fourpenny worth before Christmas. The Government had hoped to be able to make the increase on October 1, but shortage of shipping has prevented them from doing so.

"More than two-thirds of the pre-war fleet of vessels used to transport meat have been stripped during the war of their refrigerating plant and the work of re-equipping them has now been given top priority.

It was learnt in trade circles yesterday that the Argentine have 240,000 tons of beef against the normal 20,000 tons waiting to be shipped here and as soon as the ships have been refitted they will be put into immediate commission and will start bringing the bulk of this amount over.

Mild-Cured

During the past week the meat ration for Britain has been made up of seven per cent. veal, 12 per cent. pork, 15 per cent. mutton, and the remainder home-grown Scotch beef.

London has received from Denmark in the last five weeks 7,500 tons of Danish bacon which was specially salted for the German market.

From Monday of next week this is to be replaced with a special mild-cured bacon more suitable to the English palate. The bacon ration is expected to be increased by one ounce before the end of this month.

Western Mail

Black Marketeers Meet the 'Demobbed.'

By Our Own Reporter

THE Army Demobilisation Centre for South Wales situated at Hereford, has attracted one of the biggest black markets in the country. Soldiers coming from the depot carrying their new civilian suits are accosted by men who offer them up to £15 for their complete outfit.

So serious has the matter become that the military authorities warn the men before they are demobilised that they will probably receive offers for their new outfits. The men are also warned of the high ruling prices of clothing in civilian life, but there the matter ends as far as the Services are concerned.

Many soldiers who have just been demobilised like to celebrate the occasion with a glass of beer in one of the local public houses. Those who have evaded the racketeers on the street often find members of the same gang eager to buy them a drink immediately on their entering the house. The bargaining then becomes easier.

Private's Ruse

I was told an interesting story of how one Army private beat the "clothing-snatchers" at their own game. He obtained one of the boxes in which the new outfit is packed—if the men do not want to change at the centre—and filled it with oily rags.

The box was then neatly wrapped in brown paper. He was duly accosted by a wheedling buyer who offered him £15 for the box complete as it was.

The soldier murmured that it was "hardly worth that," but the buyer was so persistent that he would "take a chance."

Fifteen pound notes changed hands on the street and the soldier went gaily on his way to start his seven weeks' leave.

Western Mail

Nylon Stockings

Hopes that a limited number of British - made nylon stockings would be available in the shops early next spring are not likely to be realised. Factories engaged during the war in spinning nylon for parachutes and tow ropes for gliders have not yet had time to switch over production to the different type of fine yarn used in stocking manufacture.

"It is wishful thinking if the public expect to buy nylon stockings made in this country for at least a year," a hosiery manufacturer told the *Western Mail* yesterday, "unless it is possible to import the yarn from America. We are experimenting now, but are finding the yarn very different to handle from rayon or silk and have men over in the United States studying the new technique."

Western Mail

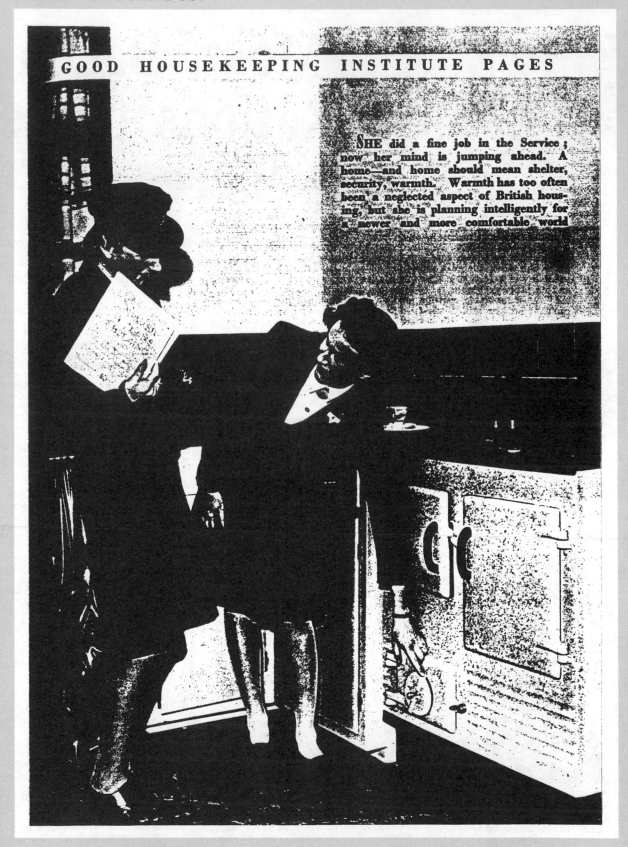

Some Post-War Uses For Those Helmets

ROSE BOWL.   BIRD BATH.   SOUP.   PUNCH BOWL.

Liverpool Echo

Glasgow Herald

GLASGOW'S ORCHESTRAL SEASON

Sir Thomas Beecham Guest Conductor of "Scottish" for Two Weeks

BY OUR MUSIC CRITIC

The orchestral season in Glasgow opens on October 6 and closes on April 6—our third season of six months. Warwick Braithwaite is once more conductor of the "Scottish," Wilfrid Senior conducts the Glasgow Choral Union, and Reginald Whitehouse is leader of the orchestra.

There is one important addition to the scheme this winter. Sir Thomas Beecham comes as guest conductor for the fortnight beginning November 24, which means that he will be on the rostrum at three Saturday and three Sunday concerts.

All the Saturday evening concerts are, of course, in St Andrew's Hall at 7.0, and the Sunday concerts are again in Green's Playhouse at 3 p.m.

Appeal for Guarantors

On the financial side the scheme will again enjoy the support of the Corporation of Glasgow and other municipal Corporations, "and it is confidently anticipated that the Union will benefit to a not less extent than hitherto under the guarantee scheme of C.E.M.A. But the season will be more expensive than before, and the committee make a strong appeal for a large guarantee fund."

It will be remembered that there was no call on the guarantors last season, and we may have the same happy result this time—a possibility that should encourage patrons to come forward in great numbers. The more guarantors there are, the less they will have to pay in the event of a call being necessary.

The committee suggest that any one not wishing to risk the minimum guarantee of £5 may be willing to give a donation to the cause. Any such contribution, however small the amount, will be welcome.

There will be an increase in the price of single tickets for the Beecham concerts, but this will not affect the subscription rates. Prices all through are as reasonable as ever, and the public will be glad to know that "the request for an extension of the privilege of seat reservation has been met by making it possible to reserve seats in any portion of the area as well as in the balconies."

Saturday patrons who are not subscribers should note the scheme for group ticket vouchers. These can be had in books of 12, and can be used in any number for any concert except the Beecham events and the Plebiscite.

Sketch Programmes

The programmes are interesting and attractive, and can be fully studied in the prospectus. There is appropriately a big choice from the great standard works, but newer music has not been forgotten. Bliss's "Checkmate" Suite, the Walton symphony, his suite "Henry V.," and his "Scapino" overture, Delius's "Brigg Fair" (Beecham includes in his first programme "The Walk to the Paradise Garden"), the Fantasia on a Theme by Tallis of Vaughan Williams, also his symphony No. 4 in F minor, Sinfonietta of Moeran, Elgar's second symphony, and an example of Scottish music—an overture, "Springtime on Tweed," of Moonie, are the chief numbers in native music.

These, with symphonies of Haydn, Mozart (it is good to see the lovely "Prague" symphony remembered), Beethoven, Brahms, Tchaikovsky, and Sibelius are prominent features of the Saturday programmes. The prospectus does not give the Sunday programmes.

Solo pianists include Lamond, Pouishnoff, Kentner, Clifford Curzon, Moiseiwitsch, Colin Horsley, Julius Isserlis, Wight Henderson, Moura Lympany; and there are two violinists, Ida Haendel and Yfrah Neaman. The majority of these appear also at the Sunday concerts.

Besides their annual performance of "Messiah," the Glasgow Choral Union are presenting Berlioz's "Faust," Vaughan William's "Sea Symphony," Brahms's "Song of Destiny," and "These things shall be" of John Ireland. The prospectus may be had from the principal music-sellers or from the manager's office, 53 Bothwell Street, Glasgow, C.2

U.S. SOLDIER DIVORCED

Wife Releases Him to Marry English Girl

A Chicago message on Saturday stated that Mrs. Eunice Coffman (34), had obtained a divorce on a charge of desertion, asserting that she wished to permit her soldier husband to marry an English girl who is expected to become the mother of twins. The suit was undefended.

Her husband, Private Frank Coffman, is now back in the United States on leave after serving with the U.S. 135th General Hospital Unit at Leominster, Herefordshire. He is 35.

Mrs. Coffman told the Court that she had received a letter from the Red Cross informing her that her husband was the father of twins which X-rays showed would be born to an unmarried English girl soon. The girl's name was not disclosed.

Mrs. Coffman's lawyer, William J. Terrell, recalled to the Court the case of Sergt. William Red Thompson, jun., of Pittsburgh, Pennsylvania, who acknowledged that he was the father of quadruplets born to Norah Carpenter, an English girl and whose wife refused to divorce him.

HOT-WATER BOTTLES ON SALE SOON

On account of an increase in production and a reduction in hospital demands, rubber hot-water bottles will soon be once more on sale to the general public.

Hereford Times

Glasgow Herald

Bringing Home Our Prisoners

Writing of the task of rescuing and bringing home our men, Major Wilfred Martin, of S.E.A. Command, states:

You may be wondering why the organisation of rescuing and despatching and notifying relatives in this country of the 100,000 Allied prisoners of war and civilian internees in S.E.A.C. is taking such a time. Every day without news is causing more anxiety to relatives and this is fully realised by the R.A.P.W.I. (Recovery of Allied Prisoners of War and Internees) working in S.E.A.C.

Here are new facts which go to explain some of the causes for the apparent delay.

There were 150 camps in Malaya, French Indo-China, Siam and Hong Kong. How to get at these camps was one of the most complicated planning problems of this war.

UNRELIABLE MAPS

Apart from Hong Kong and Siam, little was known when the Japanese surrendered of the various allocations of the camps, the numbers, or of the condition of the P.o.W.s A marked map claiming to show allocations of the camps with figures was brought by the Japanese delegates to Rangoon for the first peace negotiating meeting. Markings on the map have since proved to be very wide of the mark. Prisoners have been found in camps reported unoccupied by the Japanese.

Now take a look at the tremendous distances both for taking in supplies and bringing out the liberated prisoners. It is 1,600 miles from Ceylon to Singapore; another 1,400 to Hong Kong. Rangoon is nearly a thousand miles from Saigon by air. Sourabaya is 800 miles from Singapore. Aircraft engaged on these various flights have had to carry extra petrol. Their human cargo, therefore, had to be reduced. The mercy ships had to sail long distances along communications closed for more than three years, through newly swept waters. You all know that most of the available shipping, when war ended in the Far East was already manned and loaded for the assault on the west coast of Malaya. This re-allocation all took time.

MONTY'S UNCLE MARRIED

79-Year-Old Lincs. Rector's Bride

More than 25 years ago the Rev. E. M. Farrar, uncle of Field Marshal Montgomery, met Miss C. H. Fitzmeyer while on holiday at the seaside.

This afternoon, six weeks after Mr. Farrar's retirement as Rector of Bolingbroke, near Spilsby, Lincs., at the age of 79, they were married at St. Mark's, Kennington, London.

Field Marshal Montgomery's 80-years-old mother, who had travelled from Ireland for the purpose, was there to give the bride away.

Miss Fitzmeyer had a distinguished nursing career in the war.

To the men of the forces we lift our hearts, hats and voices; yes, and our glasses, though they cannot yet be charged with

KIA-ORA

Kia-Ora fruit squashes were and will again be the world's best.

Cambridge Daily News

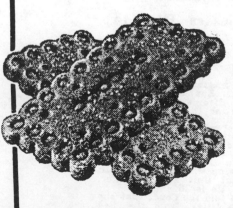

For something extra *nice to eat*, try

"LEMON FINGER"... *it's a treat!*

M&D BISCUITS

Brighter and better biscuits! That's the policy behind the latest biscuit novelty by Meredith & Drew — "Lemon Finger".

This deliciously sweet, crisp, sugar-sprinkled golden biscuit is refreshingly flavoured with real lemon juice.

Biscuit makers of distinction for 114 years, Meredith & Drew use the finest ingredients available and no substitute flavourings.

That's why "Lemon Finger" tastes so good.

MEREDITH & DREW

Governor's Wife Tells Of Tortures

Japs Tried To Degrade British Women In Singapore

Lady Shenton Thomas, wife of the Governor of Singapore, to-day told of forced marches in the tropical sun, swoops by the secret police who committed their atrocities in the Y.W.C.A. building, and letters thrown away by bored Jap sorters.

A TOTAL of 4,507 internees are to-day being cared for in Singapore Gaol, where Lady Shenton Thomas, wife of Sir Shenton Thomas, Governor of the Straits Settlements at the time of the capitulation, saw Japanese atrocities during her imprisonment there.

In peace-time the gaol accommodated 700 criminals, but 3,157 men, 1,021 women, and 329 children of many nationalities were crushed into it.

The Japanese swept many Singapore Jews into the camps. It appears that the Jews controlled the black market and this was the Japanese way of taking over the business, says a Reuter correspondent.

Lady Shenton Thomas told me of forced marches of several miles under the hot tropical sun, many of the people being without hats, some even without shoes, when the civilians were first interned.

Every now and then the Kempei (secret police) took away men who almost without exception came back dying. On one occasion the victim was brought back dead.

"It was dreadful to see men who had gone away big and burly come back weighing only five stones," she said.

In what may have been a grim jest the Japanese had taken the Y.W.C.A. building in Singapore as the secret police headquarters, and it was here that the atrocities were committed.

1,000 LETTERS KEPT 6 MONTHS

"Once the Japanese told us 1,000 letters had arrived, then they kept us waiting six months for them. They often threw mail away when they got tired of sorting it. We didn't receive one-third of the letters."

In addition to the small quantity of rice, one of the chief dishes was slimy "duckpond soup," made from the green tops of sweet potatoes.

"I once measured the bread ration. It was four inches square and half an inch thick. That had to last two people for 24 hours. Tea was always without milk or sugar."

The internees kept a piggery, intended to provide some meat—they had none for a year—but found they had created a rod for their own backs.

"Frequently the Japanese insisted that the pigs should get the first of any extra food. Once a quantity of soya beans became available. The pigs got it all.

"Then the Japanese took the rest of the pigs for themselves."

"Chinese girls got things to me in Changi Gaol. I know the Japanese tortured one and her husband in front of each other."

LIVED ON RUMOURS

"We lived on rumours," added Lady Thomas, "though we got to know of big events in due course."

News of the Japanese surrender was given to the camp by a daring Eurasian boy who twice cycled past the wire fence singing a song into which he introduced the news.

There was a total lack of privacy in the camp, even for bathing. On the whole, the women managed magnificently. Although they had only what they had been able to take with them, they kept up appearances.

One of them was reduced to a pair of khaki shorts which had a large bright blue patch on one side, and a red and white check patch on the other.

FLOOR TORTURE

A report drawn up by three doctors of the civilian internees' camp said:—

"From eight o'clock in the morning until ten o'clock at night, inmates had to sit up straight on the bare floors with their knees up, and they were not allowed to relax or put their hands on the floor, or talk or move except to go to the toilet. Any infraction involved a beating.

"Nearly all the inmates suffered enteritis or dysentery. No soap, towel, toilet articles, or handkerchiefs were permitted.

"Three women taken from Changi Prison were detained in exactly the same conditions as the men, and shared the cells with male prisoners of all races.

"The women were afforded no privacy, and any attempt on the part of the European men to screen them was broken down by the guards.

"They were subjected to obscene gestures by Japanese prisoners in the same cell, who tried to compel them to perform the most sordid tasks.

"The buildings occupied by the Japanese military police resounded all day and night with blows, the bellowing of the inquisitors, and the shrieks of the tortured.

TORTURE CHAMBERS

"From time to time victims from the torture chambers would stagger back, or if unconscious would be dragged back to their cells.

"In this atmosphere of terror these men and women waited sometimes for months for their summons to interrogation, which might come at any hour of the day or night.

"Usually interrogation started quietly, and would so continue as long as the inquisitors got the expected answers.

"If for any reason such answers were not forthcoming, physical violence was immediately employed."

Among the methods used was beating all over the body with iron bars, brass rods, sticks, bamboos, wet knotted ropes, belts or revolver butts.

The victims were sometimes suspended by the wrists from a rope.

Allied prisoners rescued from a Japanese "hell hole" in Kowloon to-day had their first drink of beer in 44 months, but their starved stomachs could not tackle beefsteak.

Major K. N. B. Crawford, of Winnipeg, saved many lives by perform-

LABOUR IN WOOLLEN MILLS

Women To Be Trained

A party of girls, ex-munition workers from various parts of Lanarkshire, displayed great interest when they were shown the various processes in the manufacture of Border tweeds.

The girls were visiting woollen mills in Galashiels and Selkirk in the course of a programme arranged by the Ministry of Labour who, in conjunction with the Scottish Woollen Trade Employers' Association and the Scottish Woollen Technical College, are endeavouring to attract female labour to the Borders, where there is a great shortage of certain types of workers, particularly weavers and menders.

At Galashiels they were also shown over the Technical College, where the first part of their training would be carried out. After three weeks in the college they would then transfer to the mills to operate modern high-speed power looms. The first of these girl trainees begin their course of instruction next week.

OUR BABY SERVICE conducted by **NURSE HALE,** S.C.M., G.L.I.H. & H.V.

Happy returns

Part of his childhood is bound up in that other home— he'll need understanding to help him settle down in his real one again

SOME mothers whose children were evacuated during the war years may be faced with difficulties now that they are back. The children are probably very different beings from those who went away from home four or five years ago. Maybe complications will arise with the older children of twelve or thirteen, for they may criticize their homes and make hurtful comparisons between their own and their temporary homes. Those who have lived in and loved the country will miss it terribly and will, for a time, feel cooped up in towns.

Do try to understand the children's point of view, and don't feel resentful of the late foster-mother. Don't brush these criticisms aside, but think about them carefully to see whether, after all, there are some things which need improvement. We are so apt to go on in the same old groove without questioning whether there is a better way.

Remember that children are very conservative little creatures who dislike changes, and that it was very upsetting for them to be suddenly torn from home and sent to a strange place. No doubt it took them a long time to settle down and now they have to start again. So it is not surprising if they are difficult, but if you are patient and understanding they will soon find their feet again. Don't let them see that you are hurt or resentful when they criticize you or their home otherwise you will lose their confidence. Good temper and understanding will win them back to you.

Nice children are loyal children and if you want yours to be loyal to you you must encourage their affection for the foster-mother who came forward to help you through a difficult time. Remember that it was not easy for her, and I know you do not want to spoil for your children one happy memory, do you?

You may notice signs of nail-biting, thumb-sucking and bed-wetting. The latter is particularly trying, but if it happens, don't put it down to mismanagement on the part of the foster-mother, but remember that it is caused by a nervous reaction owing to changed conditions. Just now the children feel a little insecure but this will pass if you make no comment on wet beds, and never punish or scold, for a feeling of guilt will only make matters worse.

You can best help the children by restoring their confidence, not by spoiling them in order to win their affection, for children see deeper than this, and will certainly take advantage of you, but by your watchfulness and understanding. This will make them feel that they can bring their problems, their joys and their sorrows to you knowing that you will help them.

I do hope that mothers will do all they possibly can to help the children to settle down and so re-establish a happy, secure home life once again.

Trains to be warmed up

For night travel

FROM tomorrow steam heating will be provided by the Southern Railway on all passenger trains running at night and on special troop trains during the day.

All the railway companies are ready to warm their trains if the weather should become colder. A few long-distance night trains on the G.W.R. are already heated.

Unless the weather becomes exceptionally mild, the ban on the central heating of buildings in the South of England will be lifted during the second week in October, on a date to be finally decided according to the forecasts.

In Scotland and Northern England the ban will be lifted a week earlier.

Sunday Express

ARGENTINE TO SEND GRAF SPEE CREW HOME

BUENOS AIRES, Tuesday.

DR. JUAN COOKE, Argentine's new Foreign Minister, said at a Press conference here that members of the crew of the scuttled German battleship Admiral Graf Spee, interned in Argentina, would be repatriated, and that Great Britain and the U.S. would be asked to afford the necessary facilities for this.

He also announced that all German or Japanese associations in the Argentine would be closed down, and that a decree had been issued banning publication of all Axis journals. Another decree compelled all Axis companies to make a sworn declaration of their assets.

Dr. Cooke said that Poland had requested the establishment of diplomatic relations between their two countries.

Instructions would be cabled at once to take necessary steps to this end.

Asked whether this would lead to prompt recognition of the Soviet Union by Argentina, he replied with a smile, " I would not like to venture on this point."

Well-informed circles stated last night that one of the conditions of Dr. Cooke's acceptance of the portfolio of Foreign Minister was a free hand in Argentina's foreign policy.

Ministers may be replaced by men of proven democratic ideals. Reuter.

Grimsby Evening Telegraph

MOZART DRAWS CROWD
War-time Concert at Guildhall

"WAR-TIME concerts, 1945," formerly the "Thursday War-Time Concerts," had an enthusiastic send-off last evening at the Guildhall, Cambridge, when the programme was devoted to Mozart, and the occasion drew one of the largest audiences in recent years.

With the New London Orchestra, under the conductorship of Alec Sherman, with Max Salpeter as leader, and with several newcomers amongst the instrumentalists, were Elizabeth Schumann, who has been in America for some years, and Pauline Juler, who is well known to Cambridge audiences.

A TREMENDOUS WELCOME.

Elizabeth Schumann revealed that she has lost none of her great mastery of technique and she gave two groups of songs: three arias, including the Wiegenlied, from Figaro, and two from Don Giovanni. The latter included the Batti-Batti, sung with a delightful touch of intimacy. Elizabeth Schumann received a tremendous welcome and her appearance marks a noteworthy event in local musical history.

Pauline Juler's playing of the clarinet concerto (K622) provided another fine example of virtuosity, this time by an artiste whose reputation is enhanced by every fresh performance and whose career is destined to be one of brilliant achievement.

The orchestra played the Overture to "Figaro," but it was the crowning Symphony in E flat (K543) which revealed its best qualities. The two opening movements were taken with great confidence and treated with breadth and colour, thus providing the full effect of contrast for the menuetto : allegro and, in turn, for the finale. If the orchestra had been a little over-assertive in its accompaniment of some of the songs, this was amply atoned for by the discriminating treatment of the symphony. Max Salpeter led very discerningly, and Alec Sherman's direction was alert and inspiring.

Cambridge Daily News

GOOD HOUSEKEEPING INSTITUTE
COOKERY DEMONSTRATIONS

Tuesday Lunchtime : 1.5 *to* 1.55 *p.m.*, 3s. 6d. *each, including light luncheon.*
October 2nd, Eking out the Meat Ration.
October 9th, Simple Soups—use of stock pot.

Wednesday Afternoon : 3 *to* 4.15 *p.m.*, 3s. 6d. *each.*
October 3rd, Yeast Cookery—bread, buns, etc.
October 10th, The Sweet Course—hot or cold.

Thursday Lunchtime : 1.5 *to* 1.55 *p.m.*, 3s. 6d. *each, including light luncheon.*
October 4th, Breakfast Dishes—including omelets.
October 11th, Soups and their Garnishes—including melba toast, croûtons and vegetable balls.

Thursday Evening : 6 *to* 7.15 *p.m.*, 3s. 6d. *each.*
October 4th, Cake and Pudding-making—rubbed-in and creamed mixtures.
October 11th, Stewing and Casserole Cookery.

What Was in Refrigerator?

CAFE OWNER ACQUITTED

WHETHER or not defendant should have entered on his records some corned beef which the police said they saw in his refrigerator, but which he denied ever having had, was a question that had to be decided by the Borough magistrates on Wednesday.

Defendant was Douglas Fletcher (25), of Jim's Cafe, Newmarket Road, Cambridge, who was summoned for failing to keep an accurate record of rationed food obtained by the cafe, at Cambridge, on June 28th. He pleaded not guilty through Mr. Stuart Horner (instructed by Mr. V. O. D. Cade).

WHAT POLICE FOUND.

Mr. C. H. Parker, for the Food Control, said defendant kept a shop at Histon Road and a cafe at Newmarket Road. At the Histon Road shop there was a refrigerator, and on June 19th, when the shop was visited by the police, nine large unopened tins of corned beef were found in the refrigerator.

When the police returned on a second occasion there were only four tins, three of which were empty. Defendant, when questioned, denied that the tins had been moved or altered since the first visit by the police.

Det.-Constable Douglas confirmed the statement, and said he called the first time in connection with a burglary at the premises. Defendant had told him the beef was for use in the restaurant.

Det.-Constable Abbott said he accompanied Det.-Constable Douglas the second time, when they found one full tin of corned beef and three empty ones.

Charles Marsh, butcher, of Fitzroy Street, told the court that a 6lb. tin of corned beef was sent to the cafe on June 16th, and the following week another tin was supplied to defendant.

"NOT ENTERED IN RECORDS."

Frank William Cartwright, of the Ministry of Food, stated that he examined the food records, but the nine tins seen by the police had not been entered. When witness mentioned it to defendant, he said, "Of course not, because they were not there."

Defendant told the court, on oath, that when he took the police officers to the refrigerator on their first visit he opened the door, but the officers did not go into the refrigerator. At the time the refrigerator contained four or five empty tins which had been placed there by defendant's manager. It was not true that the officers took the top tin from the pile. He was out when the police called the second time and it was on a third occasion that he had said the tins had not been altered. Defendant told the court that such tins came from his grocer packed with butter.

Cambridge Daily News

OCTOBER
1945

13 THOUSAND NEW TEACHERS WANTED

" Universe " Education Correspondent

THIRTEEN thousand additional teachers will be needed by April, 1947, when the raising of the school-leaving age will mean an intake of 390,000 additional pupils, Miss Ellen Wilkinson, Minister of Education, told a recent Press conference.

It was urgently necessary, therefore, to increase the number of Emergency Training Colleges by about 20 in 1946 and by another 20 in 1947.

Miss Wilkinson said she was trying to implement the Education Act as soon as possible; to increase and improve technical education as a contribution towards recovery of our export trade; to see that no child was debarred by lack of means from having a course of education suited to age, aptitude and ability; and to secure that full effect was given to the provision in the regulations that admission to all grant-aided schools is made on the basis of merit.

She desired further to extend the training of teachers and to examine the content of education and give guidance for its improvement and development.

The main obstacles in the way of advance were the lack of trained teachers and the existence of large classes consequent upon this lack and upon the need for additional school accommodation.

Direct Grant Schools Must Stay

Speaking on direct - grant schools the Minister said that most of them were doing splendid work and that if forbidden to charge fees might decide to become independent schools and, having to raise their fees to meet such status, would pass beyond the range of ordinary people.

This was not the time to eliminate the Direct - Grant schools. Such schools, however, must set aside 50 per cent. of their places for non-fee-paying pupils; must have regard to the financial position of the parents of the residuary fee-paying pupils and where necessary must remit the whole or part of the fees, recovering the amount remitted from the Ministry.

Finally no child was to be permitted in these schools merely because parents could pay fees: admission would depend upon educational qualifications.

Special Agreement Schools Position

Most of the school accommodation for our senior pupils will have to be found in the non-fee-paying voluntary aided schools, modern or technical, and these will be almost entirely composed of schools which will be Special Agreement schools under the Education Act, 1944.

These Special Agreement schools for senior pupils were designed under the 1936 Act whereby local authorities were empowered to aid in the provision of buildings for the accommodation of senior voluntary school pupils by giving building grants of not less than 50 per cent. and not more than 75 per cent. of the cost of such buildings to the voluntary bodies.

Most local authorities decided to make agreements for the building of these schools with the voluntary school managers. Most authorities also agreed to offer the maximum grant of 75 per cent. building aid. Thus, Catholics were to have 289 such grant-aided senior (secondary) schools for 89,000 senior pupils. Very few of these schools were built and proposals made under the 1936 Act lapse under the new Act.

Proposals May Be Revived

Such proposals, however, so long as they serve substantially the same purpose as the original proposals, may be revived and revised under the terms of the Third Schedule to the Act of 1944.

There seems to be no doubt that voluntary school managers will be eager to revive the proposals. It is at the option of the local authorities to agree to such revival and revisal. Again, remembering that the place of the voluntary schools in the educational system of the country is dependent upon the willing co-operation of local authorities and voluntary school managers, it is reasonable to assume that requests for the revival of the proposals are already being presented by the managers and accepted by the authorities with the concurrence of the Minister for Education.

Any departure from such an understood arrangement would doubtless be regarded as "unreasonable" by the Minister.

DEBASED CHRISTIANITY

Bishop of Chelmsford on Cream Buns

" THERE is widespread in this country," writes the Bishop of Chelmsford in a letter to his diocese, " a debased form of religion which commonly passes for Christianity. It is a form of good-tempered benevolence and kind-hearted cheerfulness which is based upon the view that, if there is a God of any kind, he possesses in a superlative degree these good-humoured qualities and that easy-going tolerance which are generally regarded as the highest virtues to-day.

No Place for Sin

" But sin, righteousness, penitence, judgment and redemption, which are all keynotes of true Christianity, have no place whatever in this modern religion. The religious appetite is strong in all normal people, but the tragedy and the problem lie in the fact that this religion of cream buns and confectionery can appease the hunger for the healthy fare which only Christianity can give.

" It would be much easier to re-convert England (and the world itself for that matter) if religion was openly derided and persecuted. But the evangelizing of our people remains the supreme and urgent task for the Church to-day. and it is a blunder of a tragic character to regard the sentimental humanitarianism based upon vague theism, which is so prevalent in these days, as indicative that we are 'all Christians at heart.' How anyone can be Christian in another part of his anatomy we need not stop to inquire! "

CAMBRIDGESHIRES STILL ARRIVING

How Things are Worked
CAUSES OF DELAY
(" C.D.N." Special.)

UP to the present only a small percentage of the men of Cambridgeshire have reached home from the P. of W. camps in the Far East; and as some relatives may not understand the cause of delay and be getting a little anxious, it may not be out of place to explain the procedure in order to clear the air.

A boat may come in packed with troops, but it may contain only a very few men from our County. No boats have yet arrived with any appreciable number, and while some of them, like the Empire Pride and the Boissevain, included a good sprinkling of members of the Cambridgeshire Regiment, only a percentage of them resided in the County or the Isle of Ely.

What we had all hoped was that one boat would contain all the 1st Cambs., another boat all the 2nd Cambs., and another boat all the 287 Field Co., Royal Engineers. That was not to be. Colombo is the "clearing station." As soldiers, whatever their rank or whatever their unit, arrive there, they are assembled in groups, and as the boats arrive they are filled with groups to their full capacity.

Cambridge Daily News

Dundee Courier

Sunday Pictorial

" ANSWER TO ATOMIC BOMB "

Sir John Boyd Orr Wants World Wheat Pool

Sir John Boyd Orr, newly-appointed Director-General of the United Nations Food and Agriculture Organisation, told a conference in Quebec yesterday (says Exchange) that the organisation was the answer to the atomic bomb.

" If we cannot agree to work together to feed the world," he said, " then we cannot agree on anything."

A world-wide distribution of wheat to reach those who need it, most particularly in the Far East, should be their primary objective, and he suggested a world wheat pool which would guarantee a reasonable minimum price to producers.

Northern Echo

£10,000 MILLION MARK REACHED
Nation Saved Four Shillings In Pound

Out of every pound of private income four shillings went to the Government in voluntary savings.

This is disclosed by Sir Harold Mackintosh, chairman of the National Savings Committee, in a statement announcing that the £10,000,000,000 mark has been reached.

The money was used almost entirely in production of war weapons which brought victory, he says, and if to the four shillings in the pound saved is added another four shillings in direct and two shillings in indirect taxation, it meant that one-half of the private income of the country, a little less than £50,000,000,000, went to the Government during the war.

For the requirements of peace we were " starting from scratch," because the cupboard was bare, and we had now to save for prosperity and a full cupboard.

PROMISE TO G.I. BRIDES

WHILE a group of G.I. brides sat on the steps of the American Embassy in London yesterday and did their best to keep their babies quiet, two wives were admitted to interview Miss Louise Morley, of the U.S. Red Cross.

When they came out they said they had been given a promise that something would be done for the cases of immediate hardship.

Although no date could be fixed for the wives to travel to America, the deputation was told that it was hoped that transport might be available about January.

"Answer me, Eric—Have you been finding taxis for people again?"

Punch

Says She'll Unload the Meat Ships

MRS. Margaret Leadbeater, of Edgware, wants women all over the country to don dungarees and unload the waiting food ships.

The idea came to her suddenly yesterday morning as she stood in a queue outside her butcher.

"This is the last straw!" she suddenly said—just like that. "If the men won't unload the ships, why don't we women do it?"

And other women in the queue thought it a grand idea and said so.

Crack Shot

Mrs. Leadbeater taught more than 500 women to shoot in a Women's Home Defence force during the war. Dr. Edith Summerskill, M.P., Parliamentary Secretary to the Ministry of Food, was a colleague then.

And Dr. Summerskill has promised to bring Mrs. Leadbeater's dock labour scheme to the notice of the authorities.

"If Dr. Summerskill can't help up we shall go straight to the PLA and offer our services," says Mrs. Leadbeater. "And if they want us to lift sides of meat we'll do that, too."

Sunday Pictorial

LAVAL IS IN PAIN

May Not Get To End Of Trial

ALTHOUGH he has described him as "confident," Maître Naud, Laval's principal counsel, said to-day, that he doubted whether his client would be able to get to the end of the trial.

The water given him during the hearings contains drugs which the defence counsel obtained for him to alleviate pains caused by a stomach ulcer.

The defence also asked the Court to allow Laval's doctor to attend him before and after every session.

"STRAIN AND FATIGUE"

"Laval's health," Naud explained, "has shown a rapid deterioration since the beginning of the trial. The strain and fatigue of the long cross-examination with the pain of the ulcer have prevented him from sleeping.

"Comtesse Jose de Chambrun, his daughter, is allowed to bring him cigarettes every day. He smokes at least 40 daily, because his doctor says he is so nicotine intoxicated that he could not carry on without them."

Exeter Express and Echo

DOG WITH SQUINT

Sat on the bench

A WIRE-HAIRED terrier sat on a bench at the West London magistrate's court yesterday and wagged his tail, non-stop, while the magistrate (Sir Gervais Rentoul) decided who was his rightful owner.

Harry Gips, of Murchison-road, North Kensington, alleged that Mrs. Elizabeth Gills, of Pembridge-crescent, Kensington, had detained his terrier.

He said that he lost it more than four years ago. It was not until three weeks ago that he saw Mrs. Gills exercising the dog. He had been given the terrier just after it was born, and had fed it from a fountain-pen filler.

Pedigree produced

He claimed to identify it by a cast in the left eye, and handed a snapshot to the magistrate.

Mrs. Gills produced the dog's pedigree, and said that she had had the terrier since 1933. An operation was performed on the animal's left eye, and he had never been out of her care since.

After comparing the snapshot with the live exhibit, the magistrate said he was satisfied it was not the same dog. He told Gips that he had obviously made a genuine mistake.

The summons was dismissed, and Gips was ordered to pay 30s. costs.

Darlington and Stockton Times

Aussies Liberate Lancashire Nun

Sister Mary Cletus Miller, of the Missionary Sisters of St. Joseph, whose mother lives at Sale, near Manchester, interned by the Japanese with four other nuns in 1941, has been released by Australian troops, hopes to be home shortly.

Sister Mary Cletus went to North Borneo in 1939. In a letter to her mother she says that the community lost one nun by death, and that with the exception of one or two older nuns, all are in good health.

The Universe

TO DRESS OR NOT TO DRESS: *Evening Party Problem*

FOR those who go out o'nights the vexed question now is: Do we dress or don't we?   Do we go glamorous, or do we still dine in a suit? How do women feel about it, and what about the man's point of view?

And if change we do, what type dress shall it be? Full-blown, formal, and cut to the waist; high cut and sleeved; or a make-shift compromise that is low of neck and short of skirt? And what about the shops, what have they to offer?

First—and this is a certainty in the midst of many queries—evening gatherings, except the very formal, will be mixed and patchy for a long time to come. And I think it is this fact that should give us the key to the problem. The growing feeling for formalising evening gatherings is there, however, and will gradually become universal.

The Compromise

For most party occasions meantime the more general, and certainly the wiser choice, tends to a simple type dress with long or short sleeves, a long drifting skirt, and, by way of compromise, a front decolletage.

This, the shops tell me, is what most women in search of a party dress are after. Such a dress will see them through this transition stage with dignity and grace, and later, when backs and bosoms are bare again, it is a dress that will serve a dozen purposes, from charming house-gown to distinctive dinner-dress.

Materials? Crepe, rayon, velvet, wool—whatever you can lay lucky hands on.

By Phyllis Jenkins

The bodice may be very feminine, with heart-shaped decolletage—or it may be tailored.   I have seen such a tailored dress recently—light-blue crepe, tailored revers, three lovely crystal buttons closing the fronts, elbow sleeves, and charming detail—a cluster of palest pink tulips tucked through the tailored belt; a lovely dress to own.

Yet another variety of the same dress was in lemon yellow wool fastened through from throat to hem with self-coloured silken tassels.

For the young girl in search of her first real party frock I suggest something younger, less sophisticated, so why not a picture dress in some soft and lovely colour with fitted bodice and the new cap sleeves, and, of course, a full, long skirt marking a rounded hip line.

The men will fall for it like ninepins, for sure it is that they—so long as it does not mean battling with a white tie themselves—are weary of Mary in battledress and long for a return to the romance in clothes they all adore at heart.

For the more sophisticated and for all ages from eighteen to that important person the woman of forty and more there is the formula of a dressy cocktail suit or dress in an elaborate material such as lamé, satin, or velvet.

It is tailored, short of skirt, and, happy thought, might quite well be cut from a voluminous pre-war evening dress or cloak. It is a good garment to have by you, and so long as your legs are well-turned and your feet well-shod, can look extremely well and worldly wise.

Then, of course there is always the long skirt and evening blouse. This, too, can bear thinking about. But it needs careful handling and a sure touch or it will be tatty and dull.

Evening blouses should be fluffy, diaphonous and very feminine with jabot front maybe—lovely flimsy frail things that you can often make yourself from oddments. A little tailored jacket with sequin-studded revers and pockets will add style and save you the problem of an evening wrap.

Not So Good

The long skirt with its lamé jumper or jacket companion, easy as it is and obvious, I omit with conscious design just because it is obvious and easy, and has been done to death in the past.

In the same way I say no to the American-sponsored low-neck short-skirted party dress. I have not seen one, but am quite certain that it does not make sense.

To close, a word about long-dress deportment—a sadly neglected art. So many women fail to realise that long skirts demand short even steps—not the hearty ones that so well match their tweeds. It is a technique which needs to be tried out, studied, practised. The Victorians knew what they were about with their ridiculous "little mice."

Glasgow Herald

PEOPLE COULD—WASTE A LOT MORE MONEY... WE SHALL HAVE TO WORK OVERTIME

TOUGH JOB, TOO, NOW THAT PEOPLE ARE GETTING KEENER ON SAVING!

LEEDS BABY RESTORED UNHARMED

Taken by Girl Who Loved Dolls

It was a ten-year-old girl with a love for dolls who took away the curly-haired 15-month-old baby who disappeared from her pram in the busy shopping district of Briggate.

The baby, Mary Josephine Gallagher, an only child, was restored unharmed early yesterday to the mother, Mrs. Mary Gallagher, of Blackman-lane, Leeds. Police found Mary at an address in the centre of the city. There will be no court proceedings.

Mary's father works at Darlington.

Northern Echo

ATOMIC PLANES FOR CHEAP HOLIDAYS

Britain's Role In Air Transport

Atomic power may enable people of modest means to enjoy holiday trips by air to the shores of North Africa and use helicopter air services in Great Britain, said Sir Frederick Handley-Page in his inaugural address as president of the Institute of Transport in London yesterday.

Other wartime technical developments which promised much for the future safety, economy, speed and regularity of air transport were jet or gas-turbine propulsion, rocket power and radar.

There were also many instances where glider transport might be considered, such as where bulky equipment had to be transported across mountains or jungle to mining centres. They could land in restricted spaces.

For general freight the new types of aircraft would enable rates to be comparable with first class rail express, and no doubt the cream of first class shipping traffic would be skimmed by the aeroplane, costs being roughly comparable. Jet propulsion units burned cheap fuel, but the price of kerosene might jump if the demand went up substantially.

LOWER FARES.

Air transport may eventually have much to offer even the working classes. Already there are in being simple and relatively inexpensive aircraft which can operate at much lower fares than before the war.

The main lines of air transport would fly in the Northern Hemisphere, and, as its geographical centre, Great Britain had a special and vital part to play. Undoubtedly we should have regular trans-polar air services within a few years, perhaps leading to the development of those areas.

Within the British Isles there was much scope for air transport, and there could be alternative routes to those along the railway lines.

People in the West of England and Wales might like direct non-stop air services to Ireland and Scotland which did not pass through London, and East Anglia would appreciate quick communications with anywhere, he said.

We must not forget, too, that the perfection of the helicopter will notably influence our ideas of travel. A vehicle which can land or take off almost anywhere, is capable of speeds far higher than any surface vehicle, must open a new approach to internal air service.

The role of Great Britain and of the Commonwealth is to make the new age predominantly British, as our ancestors did the shipping age. In doing so we may claim to be serving humanity.

Dundee Courier

SHE'S IN AT LAST!

"Mary Ellen"

SHE'S back on the Council at last is "Mary Ellen" alias Mrs. Mary Ellen Lucas, one-time Councillor who has never relaxed

Popularly known as "Mary Ellen"; she is now once again Councillor Mrs. M. E. Lucas.

her fight to return to the Council Chamber.

This time she's in without a fight—unopposed in the East Ward, and few will deny that it's good to see her back.

She is well-known as an ex-Councillor as well as for her activities on many local bodies, including Maternity and Child Welfare, Housing Committee and Old Age Pensioners' Committee, etc.

Mrs. Lucas, who is a native of Taunton, came to Weston 38 years ago. Apart from her main policy, she also means to tackle the housing problem with virility.

"I do not like prefabricated houses," she told a "Gazette" reporter, "but we must house our boys when they come home."

Weston-super-Mare Gazette

Isle of Man Examiner

MARRIED AT FOURTH TRY

A "miracle man," as he is known to his friends, hobbled down the aisle on crutches at Doncaster Parish Church yesterday and was married to Miss Marion Henrietta Wilson, of Manor-drive, Doncaster.

He is Flight-Sergeant Alan Bailes, 20, of St. Ursula's-road, Doncaster, who was shot down on a night bomber raid, had twenty operations and finally penicillin to save his shattered legs.

Three times previously he has tried to get married and three times the surgeons have said "No" at the last minute.

Sunday Pictorial

ORCHARD STRIPPED BY BOY RAIDERS

DARLINGTON PLEA FOR STERNER MEASURES

Mr. Arthur Feetham, a Darlington County Magistrate and member of the Juvenile Court Panel, addressed Darlington Borough Juvenile Court on Tuesday, when four boys, aged between 12 and 14 years were charged with stealing growing fruit from his orchard at Gate House, Haughton-le-Skerne.

Mr. Feetham said that it was the third case in recent years brought in respect of his orchard. As a fellow magistrate he appreciated the difficulties in dealing with these cases, but unless some stronger and sterner measures were taken he did not know where it was going to stop.

The boys were returning from potato picking and used their sacks to put the apples in. He had 30 apple trees and the whole orchard had been stripped. Only two trees in the dog run and some pears had been left.

Mr. Feetham said that the boys should be taught not to do these things. Potato picking was something to be encouraged, but the entering of people's orchards was absolutely disgraceful.

Inspector Mansfield said that the total value of apples stolen was £5 12s, but other boys had also been in the orchard beside the accused.

The boys, who all pleaded guilty, were fined 10s each.

Good Character Wins Leniency

In view of her excellent character, a case of stealing a flag from a house in Swaledale-avenue against a 12-year-old girl was dismissed. A 12-year-old boy who was charged jointly with her was placed on probation for a year. It was stated that the boy had previously appeared for canteen breaking.

Three boys, aged between nine and 12, and a 14-year-old girl were fined 5s each, including costs, for trespassing on the railway. Inspector Ridsdale, L.N.E.R. said that the children were seen on the old Stockton and Darlington branch where they were dropping wagon doors. This was not only dangerous to the children, but much time had to be spent in closing the doors again.

Darlington and Stockton Times

AT JAP SURRENDER

Veteran Sailor at 21

Word has just been received that P.O. Ron Lucas, of Braemere, Porte-Chee Avenue, Douglas, was aboard Admiral Sir Bruce Fraser's flagship H.M.S. "Duke of York" at the Japanese surrender in Tokio Bay.

Although only 21 years of age, P.O. Lucas joined the Royal Navy in March, 1939, and is a veteran campaigner. He has taken part in raids on Norway; Russia-bound convoys; Normandy D-Day; Atlantic battles; Dakar; Madagascar; sinking of a commerce raider and capture of a Vichy convoy.

ATS GIRLS ANNOYED BY FRAULEINS AT DANCE

TRIAL PREPARATIONS IN NUREMBERG

AN INDIFFERENT PUBLIC

FROM OUR SPECIAL CORRESPONDENT

NUREMBERG, Oct. 26

Members of the international legal delegations already here are confident that it will be possible to open the trial of war criminals on November 20. A British officer, Major Neave, who served the indictment on the accused, is also responsible for producing the counsel selected, and where no nomination has been made it is probable that defending officers will be assigned by the court, as was done at the Belsen trial.

Alfred Krupp von Bohlen, the elderly titular head of the house of Krupps, is ill in hospital, and with the death of Ley the number of Nazis of the first rank interned in Nuremberg gaol is reduced to 21.

Outwardly in this shattered city there is nothing in the attitude of the people to suggest the great legal drama about to be enacted in their midst. They pass the massive palace of justice without so much as a second glance, as though unaware that the men who shaped their fate are there in the prison house behind —the men who brought upon them the destruction of the ancient walled city of Nuremberg which sprawls in desolation.

The court room itself is far from ready, the back wall having been removed to make more room and a gallery installed. Most of the accommodation will be occupied by the international Press, and in view of the stringent security problem involved the German public will not be admitted.

According to present arrangements the tribunal will meet on Monday to approve the final rules of procedure, which in their broad outline are contained in the international charter under which the court is set up.

The Times

ATS officers and other ranks in Luneburg, Germany, are angry. Last night they watched British officers take German girls into the officers' club for a dance—and they don't like the idea.

Some ATS officers also went to the club, but few went on to the dance floor because of the presence of the German girls.

The authorities who run the club recognise the feelings of the British girls, and they have laid down a rule that any British girl likely to come to the dance on Friday night must be warned beforehand that she is likely to meet with what some of them disgustedly call "Pieces of frat."

But ATS other ranks are barred because of the standard ruling on association of officers with other ranks—and the women now are really mad.

One good-looking Provost officer guarding women prisoners in the Belsen trial says, in fact:

"It's a bit thick after guarding that bunch of beauties during the week to see British officers escorting other German girls to a dance where our girls are forbidden to enter."

Any officer who takes a German girl to the dance must first give the girl's name to the club authorities.

ATS other ranks also want to know why they are not allowed to wear civvy evening dress for dances.

Sunday Pictorial

Ten Bananas— and Then Some!

SERGEANT Edward Hughes, U.S. Army, recovering from wounds in a British hospital, dreamed daily of one thing.

Now, at home in Philadelphia, his dream has come true.

On a large meat platter set before him was a "banana split," made with ten bananas, two quarts of ice cream, a quart of fruit salad, marshmallow, chocolate syrup, pineapple, nuts, cherries and whipped cream.

It took Sergeant Hughes an hour and a half to eat it, says British United Press.

Sunday Pictorial

"PUT WHOLE FAMILIES ON PROBATION"

New Method for Child Delinquency Suggested

By Our Own Correspondent

A suggestion that the present laws should be altered to allow a whole family to be placed on probation, not just one of the children, was made by the County Councils Association, giving evidence to the Curtis Care of Children Committee in London yesterday.

"Existing legislation" states the Association's report, "is based on the fact that a child needing care and protection must be removed from his natural family and placed in entirely different surroundings. The family life is thereby disrupted and parents are relieved of responsibility."

REGISTRATION OF FAMILIES TOO DRASTIC

"It would perhaps be too drastic and politically unpopular a course to provide for a system of registration of derelict or problem families which could thus be brought under the supervision of a welfare department of a local authority," it was stated. "At least, however, there should be a power to inspect and advise, and a duty should be cast upon local authorities to bring parents before the court in appropriate cases where they feel the interests of a child are detrimentally affected.

"This placing of the family on probation would call for the services of a social worker who could give practical instruction in homemaking, housewifery, parentcraft, housecraft, and the like arts, which are commonly little understood by parents of this class. The step might often be taken in preference to that of removing the family as a whole to care and protection, but consideration should also be given to the possibilities of removal of the family as a unit to care."

"This line of action," continued the Association report, "serves to place the guilt for children in need of a 'place of safety' where it so frequently belongs—with the parents."

Representing the County Councils Association at yesterday's meeting were Sir Joseph Lamb, Staffordshire; Sir James Aitken, Lancashire; Mr. R. Beloe, Surrey; Dr. C. F. Brockington, Warwickshire; and Mr. F. B. Mathews, Lincolnshire.

MONEY FOR REHABILITATION

Dr. Brockington thought that if local authorities had power to spend money on rehabilitating families starting to go down hill, many of the children would never become in need of care and protection.

The grave shortage of nurses in all hospitals and institutions was emphasised by Sir Joseph Lamb, who cited a mental institution which should have 140 nurses but had only 50 nurses. Some of those were married and hoping to retire when their husbands left the Services. In Staffordshire, he said, they were wondering if they would be legally entitled to refuse entry even to those who had been certified insane.

The Association also recommended that one local authority should be responsible for all matters connected with the welfare of homeless children.

Northern Echo

PETROL THEFT

Soldiers Piped It From American Lorry Tank

Three soldiers of an infantry holding battalion stationed at Foxley, Corporal Albert Leslie Hall, L./Cpl. Albert Millington, and L./Cpl. James Hugh Anderson, pleaded not guilty—before Mrs. Tomlinson (in the chair) and Mr. P. H. Alder-Barrett, M.B.E.—at a special Hereford City Magistrates' Court yesterday (Friday) to the theft of approximately 10 gallons of petrol from an American Army lorry the previous night.

Evidence called by Chief Inspector F. Wheatley was to the effect that just after 10 p.m. Special Sergt. A. Leighton was going to his home in Bath Street adjacent to the waste plot of land when he saw two of the soldiers pushing a private car alongside an American Army lorry. He kept observation from the rear of his house, heard the sound of a tank cap being removed, and the voice of one of the soldiers saying, "Here's the pipe." There was a strong smell of petrol fumes. He went to the police station and returned with P.S. G. Cousins. Two of the soldiers were then standing by the car, and there was a can, empty but wet and smelling of petrol, on the ground between the two vehicles. A piece of rubber tubing was protruding through the back canvas cover of the car, in which, between the seats, was a large metal drum containing approximately five gallons of petrol. When charged at the police station with the theft of petrol they had nothing to say.

Francis Parker and Lester Caratcasen, the American soldiers in charge of the lorry, said it was difficult to estimate what petrol had been taken from the tank, but the former said it was at any rate from four to six gallons; while the latter stated that the filter in the tank had been punctured.

Accused now had nothing to say except to question the quantity of petrol involved.

The Magistrates found the case proved, and after an officer had given them good Army characters, accused were each fined £2, and they were ordered to pay 5s. costs between them.

Hereford Times

MRS. NECESSITY'S FURNITURE

Good Housekeeping

THIS ENGLAND

A 5/- prize for the first entry in this column goes to C. Stupplef

Paste entries on postcard or slip of paper and give details of origin. Address to THIS ENGLAND, 10 Great Turnstile, W.C.1.

Canon H. S. Marriott asked whether Wilby could be placed on the priority list for timber houses if a further allocation were made. Wilby, he said, should have two because there were two very bad houses there. The occupants could be seen in bed, with their feet coming through the windows. They had to put umbrellas up to keep the rain off the beds. It was neither decent nor civilised.—*Norfolk and Suffolk Journal.*

Woman's Own

Youth Clubs

"Now the war is over the one thing that I really must thank it for is for drawing young people closer. For two years I have been a member of a Youth Club, mixing with people of my own age, and I can honestly say that I have never spent happier evenings than those sharing ideas, organizing concerts, playing games, getting to know people, and making really good and true pals. I am sure that people who read this letter and members of Youth Clubs will agree with me."—*K. L., Leeds.*

A Brutal Sport?

"I would like to air my views on boxing. It passes my comprehension how anyone can sit and watch two men lash each other until the blood flows. To me, it is a degrading and brutal spectacle, and the fact that it is all for money makes it all the more deplorable. But I now hasten to add that I think all boys should be taught the art of self-defence, but that only, and not later to go into an arena and, so to speak, make a Roman Holiday and pander to people of depraved taste. This candid opinion will make all the boxing fans smile, but civilized people will surely agree with me."—*Miss C., Newcastle.*

Demobbing Figures

"While reading a news flash the other day, I was surprised to learn that the clothes given to a demobbed soldier are worth in the region of £20. Service girls are given £12 10s. to cover their immediate requirements. Why this discrepancy in values? Already the girls receive only two-thirds of the men's gratuity and it seems rather hard that they don't receive even two-thirds of the clothes value given to the men. Isn't it time somebody saw to it that the Servicewomen have a square deal, or is everyone too far advanced in plans for the future to bother about the present?"—*H. K., Kent.*

Home-made Penicillin

"While collecting for the Red Cross a few months ago, a country-woman and I were discussing the good which science had produced out of the horrors of war. My companion mentioned Penicillin, and said she could remember her grandmother telling her how they used to put mouldy jam on wounds—a modern invention!"—*Miss G. C., Keighley.*

Book Borrowing

"I should be eternally grateful if some reader could suggest a plausible excuse for declining to lend a book. I would use it until it became worn out. It is not easy to say point-blank, 'No, this can never be called a loan, for I'm convinced I shall never see it again.' You might weakly submit that the volume does not belong to you, but fate will no doubt be against you and the book will be the very one you decided to autograph the same day you bought it. Some months ago I parted with a rare book, published in 1840—just borrowed for a few days you know! But it is gone for ever—left in an omnibus—so terribly sorry and all that sort of thing. The irony is that the borrower has presented me with a new novel 'to make up for the stupid carelessness'."—*Mrs. E. C., Edgware.*

Misplaced Humour

"I have read your article about people who have to wear glasses. You say no-one need look any the worse for wearing them. Is it fair then to the unfortunate ones, that when shown in films or described in books, characters who are meant to appear comic or half-witted almost always have on a pair of glasses? I know from experience that this can be quite embarrassing as well as annoying.—*Miss P. G., Yorks.*

Sharing a Garden

"The other Saturday afternoon, feeling I needed a breath of fresh air after business all the week, I went for a 2d. bus ride and then decided to walk into the country. After walking for about an hour, I came across quite a small house with a very beautiful garden. To my amazement, I saw a notice on the gate: 'Come in and rest awhile.' I was so impressed, I opened the gate and went in. There were three seats put in different angles each placed to give a different view of the garden. On one were six wounded boys from our local hospital who were enjoying a chat and smoke. When I came away it struck me that though the people in that house were not very well-off as regards this world's goods, what joy they were giving to others."—*Tired Worker, Leicester.*

BREAD ON RATION IF DOCKERS REMAIN OUT

Cabinet Minister Warns Of Food Ships Danger

BLAME PLACED ON STRIKERS

A member of the Cabinet last night confirmed that bread may go on the ration, but blamed the dock strike if it had to be done.

Miss Ellen Wilkinson, Minister of Education, said at Jarrow that unless the grain ships can be turned round quickly enough to get to Canada and away again before the St Lawrence freezes bread will have to be rationed this winter.

THE SUFFERERS.

She added that for the dockers to stay on strike in order to force the Cabinet to intervene meant that in every big dispute the recognised negotiating machinery would be scrapped.

Had the dockers considered not only what they were fighting for but whom they were striking against?

The dock employers stood to lose little, as they were the agent of the Government until the war situation was over. Nor would the rich suffer, for there would always be good food in London for those with money.

The whole weight would fall on the ordinary men and women, and especially the children, facing the most difficult winter.

Sir Ben Smith, Food Minister, said in the Commons on Friday that the world food shortage was such that some foods at present unrationed in Britain may have to go on the ration.

Dundee Courier

Isle of Man Examiner

RAMSEY TO HOLLYWOOD

Some years before the war, a 15-years-old brunette went on the dance band platform at the Ramsey Swimming Pool Ballroom and began to sing. Few of the people who heard her realised that it was the start of a star's career. Her name was Pat Kirkwood, and she lived with her grandparents, Mr. and Mrs. P. J. Carr, at Dreemskerry, Maughold.

Now she is in Hollywood, being feted by the companies whose names are household words, and making a M.G.M. film, "No Leave, No Love." They're giving her a "glamour course"-too — but she remains a brunette.

When the Manx Regiment was in Glasgow, Pat was there too, singing with Billy Cotton's band. Some of the boys went backstage to see her—and she quickly recognised Sergeant-Major Charlie Crellin from Maughold, who recalled how she used to sing as a youngster on the Manx Electric tram when travelling into Ramsey.

Darlington and Stockton Times

DAUGHTER FOR LADY BEATRICE SCROPE

The birth of a daughter to Lady Beatrice Scrope, wife of Mr. Ralph Scrope, at Stainton Grange, on Monday brings their family to five, of whom two are sons.

Mr. Scrope, who is agent for the Earl of Eldon's County Durham estates, is the second son of Mr and Mrs. Henry Scrope, formerly of Stonegrave House, Hovingham, and a brother of Mr. Richard Scrope, of Danby Hall, Middleham. His marriage, which took place at Brompton Oratory in June, 1934, to the Earl and Countess of Mexborough's second daughter, united two of the oldest Yorkshire Catholic families.

Incidentally, today is the eighth birthday of Mr. and Lady Beatrice Scrope's second daughter. Their elder son was four early this month and the younger will be three on January 4th, the day after her father's 41st birthday.

DUTCH CHEER IKE
Lunch With Queen Wilhelmina

Genl. Eisenhower, who is chief of the U.S. section of the Allied Control Council for Germany, arrived at The Hague to-day, and was greeted by cheering crowds.

Exeter Express and Echo

M.P.s' HOLIDAYS

How some of them spent the recess which has just come to an end

by Susan Garth

IT would be a relief to find a member of the New House of Commons who would say, "Holiday? Yes, had a splendid time. Never gave a thought to the constituency . . ." But, of course, nobody seems to say this even if it were true (and, of course, it's unthinkable!) I haven't spoken to every single M.P. of the whole 600 odd, but I have spoken to a few dozen and the story is the same. Work, work, work . . . all answer about 30 letters a day. Here are a few things said to me by the re-assembled M.P.s which I put down in an effort to present a picture of what an M.P. is like when he is not at Westminster. . .

Quintin Hogg, M.P. (Conservative)

"I've spent two weeks on a farm helping to get in the harvest. I was gathering the wheat and carting muck around the place. Not my farm—I haven't got one . . . And then I get about thirty letters a day. And all of them to answer. And for the last three weeks I have been back at the Bar—working very hard . . . But it's a great life—if you don't weaken. I write a lot for the Press, too, you know."

The Leader

Jenny Adamson, M.P. (Labour)

"I am at my Department (Ministry of Pensions) every day dealing with disability and other pensions; war service grants—and my orphans." (3,000 war orphans, to whom she is foster-mother.) "I want them to get the same chance in life as boys and girls with mothers and fathers to look after them.

"I took time off from the Ministry of Pensions to take a corset deputation to Ellis Smith at the Board of Trade. I am trying to get good corsets for the middle-aged and older women with more comfortable figures. They haven't been able to get a decent corset since we went to war. But Mr. Ellis Smith is sympathetic (Hugh Dalton was, too, when I went to him with the same trouble) ; and he is trying to help us. There are so many things women are short of—other garments even more intimate than corsets.

"Then there is housework. I can cook with anybody . . . I am not one of those people who think it infra dig to do the housework. . ."

Twelve Women In Atlantic Hop

The largest party of women ever to fly the Atlantic non-stop—12 members of the British Red Cross and the Order of St John, bound for New York to augment the Red Cross Mission there—arrived yesterday at Dorval Airport, Montreal, in a British Overseas Airways Liberator from Scotland.

Miss Catherine Gillman, staff commandant, was in charge of the party, which included Lady Maureen and Lady Meriel Brabazon, daughters of the Earl of Meath.

Dundee Courier

HOW MUCH IS A LETTER WORTH?

TO you, the writer, at home a letter may mean an extra task, an hour's leisure lost, another chore to be packed into an already overburdened day. To the waiting recipient across the sea, that same letter is transformed into a messenger of love, a signal of hope, a gift beyond price. Melodramatic, do you think? But any chaplain, any welfare officer, any soldier, sailor, airman almost, would tell you of homes shattered and lives blighted because letters did not come, or said the wrong thing when they arrived.

Here, in the security of our island, with the lights up and the wail of the sirens a thing of the past, we are at last beginning to realise that the war is over. In H.M. ships, and at R.A.F. stations and Army camps; in far eastern waters, in Burma, India, Malaya, and in places nearer home yet still far away, the slaughter has indeed stopped, but the separation endures and becomes harder to bear.

Battle is brutal but exhilarating; garrison and occupation duties, or routine patrols, are safe—but enervating. It becomes harder to maintain morale; fears of being forgotten, jealousies and suspicions of those at home, grow irrationally but dangerously.

So, wherever your menfolk are stationed, write often, and tell them what they want to hear—that they are not forgotten and that no one can take their place, and that though the cessation of hostilities has brought you relief from anxiety—joy, even—complete happiness waits for the day when they will be reunited with you once more.

Good Housekeeping

Hereford Times

Northern Echo

NOVEMBER
1945

PIT SENDS BEVIN BOY TO VARSITY

By Eric Bennett

NOTTINGHAM, Saturday.

BARRY GREEN is a Bevin Boy. Like thousands of other lads he hated the thought of going down the pit. Unlike some others he did not object, run away, or shirk the dirty work.

Now he looks like digging his way through the coal face to a university degree. And he is earning more than £8 a week at the age of 19.

Just over two years ago Barry Green, son of a London business man, left Preston Manor County School, Wembley, and began work in a City office.

He had volunteered for the Navy, had been passed A1, and was waiting for his call-up papers, when his number came out of the hat for the mines.

It was heartbreaking news to him. But he decided to tackle the job as keenly as if he had been called up for the Navy, on which he had set his heart.

In February 1944, after his month's preliminary training, Barry went to Clifton Colliery, Nottingham. He tackled everything that came his way.

"He was a weakling when he came," Mr. William Morrell, the mine manager, said. "Look at him now. Hard and fit as a fiddle."

It was not easy for Barry. He had to get used to "miner's knee," to strange ways and new mates. He suffered from boils

Sunday Express

Norwich Stage and Screen

"WHILE THE SUN SHINES"
—At the Theatre Royal

One of the biggest comedy successes in the West End during the war comes to the Theatre Royal next week, when Barry O'Brien is presenting "While the Sun Shines," by Terence Rattigan—successful playwright of the equally popular "French Without Tears" and "Flarepath."

The plot of this play is negligible, for given the initial impetus of a situation where an English Duke is an able seaman vainly trying for a commission and engaged to a W.A.A.F. of equally aristocratic connections, its development concerns only the attempts in cosmopolitan wartime London of a very Free French Naval Officer and an engaging American lieutenant to wrest his prospective bride from him. Nevertheless, the amorous propensities of our fighting allies provide perfect material for Rattigan's acute sense of the topical, and the sparkling dialogue—always refreshing and sometimes delightfully witty—makes this one of the most entertaining of shows.

Norwich Mercury

Jolly well BETTER thanks!

NEURALGIA
attack soon over

It was a devastating attack too! I just couldn't think or do anything, but, thank goodness, only for a short while. Actually, Beecham's Powders soon put me right. Aren't they just wonderful? I think they are, and I do most strongly recommend them. Quickly absorbed, Beecham's Powders are speedy in action. They are also fine for Headaches, Rheumatic Twinges, Colds, Lumbago, and as a pick-me-up at any time.

Prices in Gt. Britain (Incl. Purchase Tax)
Cartons of 8 Powders 1/4.
Single Powders 2½d. each.

BEECHAM'S POWDERS 2½d EACH

Exeter Express and Echo

Television Chief

The B.B.C. has appointed Mr. Maurice Gorham to take charge of the television service when it is restarted.

JAP EMPEROR'S SACRIFICE

Art Collection To Buy Food For The People

Emperor Hirohito has advised the Japanese Government that he has decided to offer his personal art collection to finance the importation of urgently needed food, it was learned in Tokyo to-day.

The Empress has offered her personal collection of jewels for the same purpose.

"BILLIONS OF YEN"

No official comment has been made on the value of the Emperor's collection or the Empress's jewels, but it was suggested that they were worth "billions of yen."

Hirohito's personal art collections are at present housed in the Uyeno Imperial Museum at Tokyo. They were not removed to safety during the war.

Cabinet members refused to speculate whether the Empress intended to include her crown among the donated jewels.

The Cabinet has decided to issue an appeal to all members of the Zaibatsu—big business combines—and of other wealthy Japanese families to follow the "unprecedented" example of the Japanese rulers.

Exeter Express and Echo

MISS DEBORAH KERR MARRIED

ROMANCE WHICH BEGAN IN BRUSSELS

Miss Deborah Kerr, famous film actress and Mayfield personality, was married on Wednesday at St. George's, Hanover Square to Squadron Leader A. C. Bartley, D.F.C. and Bar, who fought in the Battle of Britain.

Miss Kerr, daughter of the late Capt. A. C. Kerr Trimmer and Mrs. K. R. Kerr Trimmer, of Mayfield, met Squadron Leader Bartley at a dinner in Brussels, where she was entertaining the troops.

They announced their engagement on the anniversary of the day when he was awarded his D.F.C. in 1940 for shooting down eight German planes.

He is the eldest son of Sir Charles Bartley, a former judge of the Calcutta Court, and Lady Bartley, of Swanbourne, Bucks.

Miss Kerr wore an elk-skin dress with heart-shaped neck, long skirt and train and long tight sleeves. Her head-dress, also of elk-skin, was trimmed with ostrich feathers.

The famous Group Capt. A. G. ("Sailor") Malan, D.S.O. and Bar, D.F.C. and Bar, was best man.

Kent and Sussex Courier

EXTRA RATIONS FOR CHRISTMAS

SUGAR, CHOCOLATE, BUTTER AND MEAT

Britain is to have bigger rations for the Christmas and New Year festivities —extra sugar, more meat and butter and a larger allowance of chocolate and sweets.

Sir Ben Smith. Minister of Food. announced his "Christmas present" at a Press conference on Tuesday. As a result of our having done "rather more than was absolutely necessary" to meet the agreement on the reduction in fats and sugar, he said, it would be possible for him to make the following additional rations available for Christmas in England. Wales and Northern Ireland and for the New Year in Scotland :—

1 lb. of sugar;

4 ozs. of chocolate and sweets for everybody;

6 ozs. of butter and margarine, of which not more than 4 ozs. may be taken as butter;

6d. worth of carcase meat, and 4d. worth of canned corned beef. Vegetarians entitled to cheese in place of meat would get an additional six ozs. of cheese.

The additional meat will be available in England, Wales and Northern Ireland in the week beginning December 16th, and in Scotland in the week beginning December 23rd. The other rations will be available at any time in the four weeks period beginning December 9th.

GIFT PARCELS CONCESSION

"I have a little food in hand," said Sir Ben, "and I have decided that the simplest way to distribute it is by making these small additional quantities available for Christmas and the New Year" He also announced that by arrangement with the Board of Trade it had been arranged to exempt gift parcels from abroad sent to individuals from the necessity of import licence when these did not exceed a maximum weight of 11 lbs. The previous gross weight was 5 lbs.

While the additional rations, particularly of meat, promised for Christmas are considerably in excess of last year it has to be borne in mind that last year's additions were in the nature of a bonus over and above a comparatively high ration standard. This season's additions are supplementary to rations which have been severely cut for some months and merely replace to some degree the reductions consequent on the operation of these cuts.

Norwich Mercury

"The situation in Venezuela is very confused."—*B.B.C. news bulletin.*

Why pick on Venezuela ?

Punch

Cries of "Oh !"

"Position of trust required. Cashier desires change."

Advt. in daily paper.

Punch

"*You're back in A.R.P. again, learning how to cope with atomic bombs.*"

Punch

So this is peace !

A frayed temper is a sure sign that the body is exhausted and needs building up. Luckily, cod liver oil — the only unrationed priority food — is easy to get. Take digestible, sea-fresh SevenSeaS daily as a mealtime ' extra '. It's much richer in essential fats and vitamins than butter.

STANDARD OIL : Vitamin A 20,000 I.U.; Vitamin D 2,500 I.U. per oz.
CONCENTRATED : Vitamin A 60,000 I.U.; Vitamin D 6,000 I.U. per oz.

PURE SevenSeaS COD LIVER OIL

Standard Oil 2/6 and 4/6. Concentrated Oil 1/9. Concentrated Oil in Capsules from 1/9

Glasgow Woman's Letters to Hitler

From DANIEL DELUCE, Associated Press Staff Correspondent

BERLIN, Wednesday.

Hitler received lunatic letters from five continents, but the most insane of any found in the Reich files by Allied investigators were written by a Scotswoman, who called him " My best beloved."

Hitler's psychopathic charms are reflected in these epistles from a Glasgow woman which astonished both the German and British police in 1936.

The letters were scrawled on blue-tinted stationery. The writer first disclosed that she had had a vision of an assassination attempt by three foreigners, and added, " Please take care of my hero, for I must have thy personal safety. How can I comfort thee? I come into thy arms a little while." She signed herself " Your little frau, Jean."

Report To Gestapo

A black folder recovered by investigators from the Chancellery ruins in the Wilhelmstrasse provided the official solution to this strange one-way love affair.

It contained a report from the Glasgow police to the Gestapo headquarters identifying the writer as the daughter of a prominent suburban family married to a professional man of local standing. But the report admitted that she was regarded as " eccentric and peculiar in manner " by her acquaintants.

Glasgow Herald

THE ART OF LETTER-WRITING IS NOT DEAD!

DURING the past few years, millions have been made happy by the written word. Thousands in the Forces have found joy and consolation in putting their thoughts on paper. Letter-writing has proved a boon to all.

The Makers of Basildon Bond believe that many of these Forces' letters deserve permanent record. To do this, and to encourage the art of letter-writing, a competition has been organized for the best Forces' letters written during or since the war. To win a prize, the letter need not be a " literary " effort, need not even be grammatical. "Fine" writing alone doesn't count. *No correspondence will be entered into ; every effort will be made to return all original letters.*

BASILDON BOND

BRITAIN'S MOST DISTINGUISHED NOTEPAPER

SALE OF PAINTINGS AT NORWICH

Pieces of Lowestoft China Also Offered

Paintings by artists of the Norwich School and several pieces of Lowestoft china, among other art objects, were sold by auction at Norwich Corn Hall on Wednesday. More than 100 paintings were sold in what was the largest auction of its kind in Norwich in recent years.

A small oil by Crome, " Thorpe on the Yare," fetched the highest price, £54. A Lowestoft mug, size 3½ inches, inscribed " A trifle from Lowestoft," was sold for £36, while two Lowestoft teapots brought £13.

A painting by an artist of the Dutch School, Adrien Brouwer, one of Frans Hals's most talented pupils, brought the second highest price for pictures, £46. "Normandy View," ascribed to J. S. Cotman, sold for £30, while two paintings by David Hodgson (Norwich School) fetched £31 and £19 respectively. Another Crome landscape went for £29. The largest sized picture in the auction fetched only 10s.

Among other painters of the Norwich School represented were Stannard, Thirtle, Miller Smith, Bagge Scott and Ladbrooke. Some of the pictures were ascribed to such famous names as Rembrandt, Raphael, Rubens, Gainsborough, Poussin and Turner, but the auctioneers, Messrs. Clowes & Nash, were careful to announce that the paintings were " by or after " the artists mentioned.

Norwich Mercury

STARVATION IN EUROPE

Mass Meeting at the Albert Hall

WIDESPREAD concern in this country about Europe's starving millions was given forcible expression at a mass meeting which packed the Albert Hall on Tuesday night, and overflowed into the nave and crypt of a nearby church. Proposals that Britain should send a large proportion of its war reserves of food—four and a-half million tons—to Europe, and that the Government should sponsor a scheme for the voluntary sending of food and clothes, were enthusiastically applauded.

"We serve notice on the Government," declared Mr. Victor Gollancz, who organized the meeting, "that if the general rations of this country were to be raised so long as there is acute distress on the Continent, this would be regarded as a grave affront to the national conscience."

What the Soldiers Say

The Archbishop of York, who presided, maintained that, though Germans were to blame for the evils that had fallen on Europe, it was wrong that the guilt of the wicked men who were the leaders of Germany should fall on innocent people. "That certainly is the feeling of our soldiers, the men on the spot."

"The victorious Allies," Dr. Garbett added, "will stand at the bar of history according to the way they answer the cry that comes from these hungry people in such tragic circumstances."

Among the seven M.P.s who addressed the meeting was Sir Arthur Salter, whose account of the situation was none the less harrowing because it was dispassionate and based on statistics. He insisted that starvation is not an inevitable result of the war. Raw materials are in ample supply, and there are more than enough cargo ships to transport them where they are most needed.

"If Germany goes down in chaos," said Mr. Michael Foot in a speech of passionate oratory, "the whole of Europe goes down in chaos too. We can fight against famine as we fought against tyranny."

A Crawling Belsen

Mr. R. R. Stokes concentrated on the need of stopping the expulsions, at any rate during the winter, and made a special appeal to "our friends the Russians" to stop "this villainy." He said that British soldiers in Europe described the roads crowded with refugees as "a crawling Belsen."

Lieut.-Col. D. R. Rees-Williams, formerly chief legal officer in the Berlin area, described how deeply affected the British troops in Berlin are by the sight of hungry children pressing their faces against the canteen windows.

Church Times

SOLDIER BOUGHT BUS TO HOUSE SICK WIFE
—And Lost Life Savings

THIS is a story of the housing shortage—with a difference. It is the story of a soldier who lost his life savings on a bus he bought in a last bid to find accommodation for his sick wife and two small children.

Arriving home on leave, Mr. H. C. Higgs, of Hanworth Road, Hounslow, found his wife ill. Because she lived in an upstairs flat she used to go downstairs to cook.

To go on doing this was dangerous, said the doctor.

She had to be moved to a downstairs flat or whatever could be got.

So the soldier sunk his life savings in an old bus, intending to convert it into living accommodation. He took it to his mother's place in New Heston Road, where his wife would have cooking and sanitary arrangements at hand.

Then he applied to Heston and Isleworth Council to sanction his move. He was so confident. As soon as permission was granted he could get an extension of leave to make the bus a home.

At Tuesday's Council meeting the Medical Officer of Health reported that the bus roof leaked because of the removal of interior fittings. There was no door—boards had been placed along the roof edge and above the lower windows to shed water from the roof and sides when it rained.

In his opinion the bus was not fit for human habitation.

The Council refused Mr. Higgs' application.

Kensington Post

FOWL STEALING CHARGE

At the County Magistrates Court on Wednesday last week, a father and son, George William, and Fred Dale, of 42, Bank Terrace, Kidsgrove, were charged with stealing three cross-bred hens from a farm at Brereton, and also with attempting to steal 56 hens from a farm at Smallwood. They pleaded Guilty.

Supt. G. H. Durnell said that at 10-30 p.m. on the 8th. November, Thos. Mellor, Brookhouse Farm, Smallwood, went across the field behind his farm, and on nearing the hencote, heard a noise from among the fowl. He saw a man standing by the cote and another inside with a flashlight. He shouted to them, but they ran away. He fired a shot in the air with the gun he was carrying, thinking this might frighten them but they ran all the faster. He made a search, and found two cycles behind the hedge. One had a bag attached, containing two hens, which were warm and freshly killed. The other had a hen in the saddle-bag, in similar condition. P.C. Williams was informed and he, together with Mellor and another man, kept watch over the cycles until at 11-45, George Wm. Dale returned for his. He was taken to Holmes Chapel Police Station, and when charged, said he had got the fowl from a farm down the road. He said he was sorry it had happened.

Corroborative evidence was given by Thomas Mellor.

P.C. Williams said when he saw Fred Dale at Kidsgrove next day he said he knew nothing about it, and that he had gone to bed with a bad head as soon as he got back from work. When taken to Holmes Chapel Police Station and charged, he said: "I admit it, I did it with my father."

Aaron Penketh, Hill View Farm, Brereton, said he locked his hencote at 5 p.m. on Nov. 8th. It contained 50 fowl. On receipt of a message from the police next morning, he inspected the cote, and found three hens to be missing. Shown the hens found on defendants' cycles, he said they were his. He valued them at 30s each.

Fred Dale asked for another charge of stealing two hens, the property of George Hall, Brookhouse Farm, Smallwood, on the 28th.-29th. September, to be taken into consideration.

Mr. F. Griffiths, Kidsgrove, for defendants, said they were honest men, working for their living, and earning fairly good wages. Money could not possibly have been the motive. Perhaps, like many others, they might have been trying to supplement their meagre meat ration.

Supt. Durnell said this was the first time defendants had appeared on a serious charge.

The Chairman, Mr. H. Oakden, said the bench considered the case a very serious one. Defendants were liable to imprisonment but, as there were no previous charges, they would be let off lightly. He hoped the case would serve as an example. Defendants would be fined £5 with 10s. costs each.

Congleton Chronicle

BEVAN'S NATIONALIZATION PLAN FOR HOSPITALS WILL RAISE A STORM

ALREADY there are indications that a bitter House of Common's controversy will begin next year when Mr. Aneurin Bevan, Minister of Health, proposes to nationalize the hospitals in his comprehensive National Health Scheme.

The independence of over 1,000 voluntary hospitals will be fought for, not only by distinguished medical M.P.s on the Opposition side, but also possibly by some Labour Members who are closely associated with hospitals in various parts of the country, writes E. P. Stacpoole, the Press Association Lobby Correspondent.

FOR—

Critics of the voluntary hospitals have argued that it is undignified and unsatisfactory for them to depend on charitable collections in the streets, local flag days, penny-a-week schemes and similar efforts; and that the whole system should be rationalized so that the hospitals and their hundreds of thousands of patients know precisely where they stand.

To ensure the best possible medical attention for all it will be contended that the hospitals must be put on a unified basis of finance and administration.

Moreover, a unified system should secure better conditions for nurses and other workers.

AND AGAINST

Against the scheme will be the point that it will not work so well if the goodwill of the doctors is alienated.

It does not seem likely that the Bill embodying the National Health Service will be ready for some months.

In the new year it will probably be preceded by another bulky measure—the Government's social insurance plan.

Exeter Express and Echo

BUY HIM A SHARPEX STROPPER

WARTIME

Pifco **SHARPEX**

RAZOR BLADE SHARPENER **4/6**

Obtainable at Boots, Timothy Whites & Taylors, and all good-class Chemists.

NOVEMBER 5

After our hectic celebrations on VJ-Day, one would have thought all the fireworks and inflammable materials in the town had been used up. This does not seem to have been the case, for on Monday night our young people made a brave attempt at a return to the peacetime celebration of Guy Fawkes night. Two respectable bonfires were lit—one in the region of Cogie, and the other at the Old Town end of the Suspension Bridge—both of which burned brightly for an hour or two, and throughout the evening the explosion of "squibs" was heard up till a late hour. On the whole, however, the perpetuation of this questionable historical fact seems to have lost much of its traditional popularity during the years of enforced blackout. Or do we take unkindly to anything which savours of the noise of war?

Eskdale and Liddesdale Advertiser

Joyce's Appeal Dismissed: Judge on Passport Issue

William Joyce, sentenced to death at the Old Bailey for treason, stood stiffly at attention as he heard his appeal against conviction dismissed by the Lord Chief Justice (Lord Caldecote) in the Court of Criminal Appeal yesterday.

The judgment took only 25 minutes to read, and in it the Judge declared that the facts made it clear as a matter of law that Joyce still owed allegiance to the Crown when he began to adhere to the King's enemies by broadcasting.

Following the dismissal Joyce's legal advisers have decided to apply to the Attorney-General for a certificate to appeal to the House of Lords. Mr C. B. V. Head, Joyce's solicitor, stated:—" We have seven days in which to do this under the Act, and we shall definitely make an application."

The Court could not agree that Joyce's case was to be treated like that of a foreigner who once paid a visit of a few hours to this country.

Commenting that Joyce made application for the renewal of his British passport on the very eve of war, Lord Caldecote said—"A British passport is something more than a means of identification. It is plainly a protection in every sense of the word to the holder while he is absent from the King's realm."

As one point after another was decided against him, Joyce blinked, squared his shoulders, and gazed across the court. When the decisive words, " The appeal is dismissed," were uttered he gave a wan smile, nodded to a friend in court, and was taken away.

The main point of the appeal was that the local allegiance due from an alien continued only so long as he resided within the King's Dominions. It was also contended that no court in this country had jurisdiction to try an alien for an offence committed abroad, and that, on the facts proved, there was no case to go to the jury.

Lord Caldecote said it was clear that Joyce up to August, 1939, owed allegiance to the Crown as an alien resident—whatever that might mean—in this country and was here under the protection of the Crown. The proposition that an alien on leaving this country was not capable of committing treason by adhering to the King's enemies was a startling one. " It is one which this Court is quite unable to accept," he said

Lord Caldecote reviewed the authorities cited during the arguments, including the Resolution of Judges in 1707, and said that criticisms by Mr Slade, Joyce's leading counsel, of such meetings by judges might be well founded. But although the law as it stood then had been admittedly unchallenged for 250 years the Court could not hold that they were bound by it.

Joyce made application for the renewal of his British passport on the very eve of war, so that he had taken every step in his power to safeguard his right of re-entry into Britain, and meanwhile to ensure his treatment in any foreign country as a British citizen.

A British passport is something more than a means of identification. It was plainly a protection in every sense of the word to the holder while he was absent from the King's realm.

" We can find no justification for holding that because the appellant in this case is not a British subject, therefore, although he can commit the crime alleged in the indictment of being a person who has adhered to the King's enemies while owing allegiance to the King, yet no Court has power to try him because he is an alien.

" In our view the passport was capable of affording him protection even though it was obtained by misrepresentation, and it is quite immaterial whether the appellant availed himself of that protection or not.

" For these reasons we find ourselves in complete agreement with the decision of the trial Judge and substantially for the same reasons. The appeal is dismissed "

Glasgow Herald

Two Fined at Cromer Over Milk Sale

Summoned at Cromer on Monday for supplying milk otherwise than under the terms of his authorisation, Louis Stevens, Maryland, Montague-rd., Sheringham, told the magistrates he had been under the impression that he could dispose of surplus milk. He was fined £5, with £2 6s. costs.

Mrs. Blanche Watling, manageress of the Blue Danube Cafe, Cromer, was fined £3, with 4s. costs, for unlawfully obtaining four gallons of milk on September 6th.

Mr. R. B. Keefe, prosecuting for the Ministry of Food, said Stevens admitted he had delivered surplus milk to the cafe two or three times a week. This, defendant said, was milk which a British Legion canteen in Sheringham did not require. Mr. Keefe added that the cafe was registered for milk with another supplier. Stevens should have notified a Regional Milk Supply Officer when he had a surplus. Mrs. Watling had said she did not know she was breaking the regulations.

Stevens told the court it was impossible to regulate the supply. He sold the milk to the cafe rather than see it go stale.

Norwich Mercury

Bridport News

BRIDPORT PRESENTATION

A very enjoyable evening was spent at the Toll House Hotel, Bridport, by the staff of the Bridport Joint Food Office, together with representatives from the Lyme Regis and Beaminster Food Offices.

The occasion was a farewell dinner to Mr. D. W. Critchard, who has resumed his peace-time duties with Messrs. Roper and Roper. Reference to Mr. Critchard's excellent work as Food Executive Officer was made by Mr. A. V. Doy, Mrs. Fry, Mrs. Lambert and Mrs. Cramp, and the good wishes of all present were expressed. Miss Gape made a presentation of a silver tankard as a mark of appreciation from the three Food Offices.

FIRST INTO DENMARK

London Jewish Officer Led the Way

The first Allied soldier to enter Denmark was a Jewish officer in the British Army—Lieut George N. Mandelson, 1st Royal Dragoons, the son of Mr. and Mrs. H. Norman Mandelson, who live in Pinner.

Lieut. Mandelson was sent forward in an armoured car to see if the way was clear for the regiment to enter. The Germans were in possession but they did not attack him, and his regiment then came up. The Lieut. and his men received a tumultuous welcome from the Danes.

He joined the H.A.C., attached to the Royal Horse Artillery, before the outbreak of the war, and after O.C.T.U. he was given a commission in the 23rd Hussars, later changing to the 1st Royal Dragoons.

In North Africa he was badly wounded and twice blown up by mines. He was taken prisoner by the Italians, but escaped.

After serving right through from El Alamein to Italy, he then went to France on D-Day, attached to General Ritchie's staff. He was one of the first in Germany, being a liaison officer to the American Paratroops, subsequently being liaison officer to a Polish Corps.

His age is 24.

Jewish Chronicle

Duchess says Christian spirit needed in world

The world cannot be reconstructed successfully without Christian spirit and Christian ideals, the Duchess of Northumberland told her listeners when she opened St. Paul's Church bring-and-buy sale in the Masonic Hall, Alnwick, on Wednesday.

Introducing the Duchess, the Rev. G. H. Marshall said that they had made a good start with their sale, and he had already received £127 2s from the working party and about £15 in donations and subscriptions.

There was more in buying at a parish sale, the Duchess added, than by giving an offering for an actual gift. People who bought were giving an offering to the parish. They all realised that the church was their pillar and anchor.

Conditions changed

The Duchess said that it was two years since she had attended a similar sale, and conditions then were very much different from what they were to-day.

The situation had changed, and she was glad to be at the first parish sale to be held by St. Paul's Church after the war.

The Duchess also extended a welcome to the Rev. and Mrs Marshall, the new vicar of St. Paul's Church.

A vote of thanks was proposed by Mr P. W. Shelford.

Northumberland and Alnwick Gazette

HANDEL'S "MESSIAH"

OUTSTANDING PERFORMANCE IN OLD PARISH CHURCH.

Early this year Part 1. of Handel's "Messiah" was performed in Langholm Old Parish Church, and so well received was the presentation of this, the best known of all the oratorios, that in response to numerous requests, it was decided to do the whole work, and this was given in the Church on Thursday night to a very large and appreciative congregation of townspeople and many from the surrounding parishes.

On this occasion parts I., II. and III. were sung by an augmented choir of over sixty voices, while for the solo parts four principals were specially engaged.

The Rev. J. L. Cotter, B.D. briefly introduced the oratorio. The choir was very ably conducted by Mr A. C. Mallinson, A.R.C.O., L.R.A.M., to whose splendid tuition was due in large part the success of the performance. In all the difficult choral pieces there was never a moment when he had not the big choir completely under control.

Mr F. W. F. Routledge again presided at the organ and acquitted himself in that masterly fashion which has come to be expected of him.

The exacting soprano solos were brilliantly sung with the utmost ease by Mrs Dorothy Marshall. Seldom before has one heard the sweet music of "I know that my Redeemer liveth" sung with more moving effect. Tone and interpretation were something to be remembered.

The contralto on this occasion was Miss Grace Hush, an artist of outstanding merit, whose quality of tone and depth of feeling left nothing to be desired. Especially beautiful was her rendering of "He shall feed His flock."

Eskdale and Liddesdale Advertiser

Highgate launches a "Save Europe Now" Campaign

COMMITTEE'S CALL FOR SUPPORT

Hampstead and Highgate Express

A COMMITTEE OF HIGHGATE AND HORNSEY RESIDENTS IS BEING FORMED TO ORGANISE A CAMPAIGN IN THE DISTRICT IN SUPPORT OF THE "SAVE EUROPE NOW" CAMPAIGN. IT IS HOPED TO SECURE THE CO-OPERATION OF ALL LOCAL POLITICAL PARTIES, RELIGIOUS BODIES, YOUTH AND OTHER ORGANISATIONS, AS WELL AS PRIVATE CITIZENS

A meeting is to be held at 29 Cholmeley Crescent next Tuesday at which details of the campaign will be discussed.

The decision to launch the campaign was taken at a meeting held at the Co-operative Hall, Archway Road, last week, addressed by Mr. Fenner Brockway and Dr. A. D. Belden. In the chair was Mr. Hubert Wilson.

The following resolution was passed:

"This meeting of Hornsey citizens, having heard of the hunger in Europe and Germany, demands that the Government should, in conjunction with other countries, mobilise all food resources and transport to prevent the starvation of millions of people this winter."

Waiting For a Voice

Mr. Brockway deplored the continued expulsions from the Sudetenland and the area handed over to Poland. He emphasised that Europe's need for immediate help was not just a matter of practical politics, but a moral issue. It was not a question of nationalities, but one of human beings starving, he declared.

"The people of the world," he said, "are ahead of their spokesmen. They are tired of power politics and are waiting for the voice that will express their feeling and their longing for a true human and international spirit, freed from the old barriers of nationality, creed and colour."

He had hoped, he went on, that that voice would come from British Labour—and it was possible yet. There was a body of men and women in the House of Commons who were just beginning to make themselves felt.

"Sir Arthur Salter is the man who should be in charge of relief for Europe. No man equals him in his knowledge of the economic structure of Europe. He has stated in the House that Europe could be fed. If there were millions of British and American citizens in Europe to-day there would be no hesitation."

Mr. Brockway pointed out that there was actually a food surplus in the great exporting countries to-day. In the U.S.A. farmers had applied to the Agricultural Board for permission to reduce food production so that prices should not fall. In South America maize was being burnt as oil was scarce for engines.

"Fiendish" Old Ladies

Dr. Belden, speaking of the Atom Bomb, said:

"As a Christian Minister, I declare that to make an atom bomb is an utterly immoral act, for which the person responsible must give account to Almighty God."

He asserted that one million tons of food could be spared by Britain. It was foul hypocrisy to go on with our comfortable life while millions were starving beyond our shores.

"British women," he said, "after years of going to church, after years of saying the Lord's Prayer, will exclaim, 'I'd exterminate the lot.' You hear old ladies saying the most fiendish things. That's what the war has done to them."

DOGS GET HYSTERIA, RACES HELD UP

MASS hysteria broke out among the dogs at Coventry stadium last night.

The first race was declared void owing to hysteria among the six dogs.

The second race was announced as having only three runners, but a further broadcast said that those, too, were ill, and the race was declared void.

Six dogs in the third race were due to run, but two were withdrawn on the way to the traps and a third collapsed while being paraded. The winner (Cover Page) also collapsed.

Conditions improved for the fourth race, when all six dogs turned out.

Carried off

The winner of the fifth race (Sandy Lane) had to be carried off, and it was then announced that four out of the six dogs in the sixth race had caught the complaint.

The crowd of 10,000 took the incidents in a sporting spirit.

FOOTNOTE.—Hysteria is something of a mystery. Its serious nature is indicated by the fact that the N.G.R.C. have appointed a committee and are prepared to spend £100,000 on research.

The complaint affects dogs without warning and spreads rapidly. By placing dogs on a diet it is possible to get them normal quickly.

Sunday Express

ROAD BURDEN.

Mr. Roderic Bowen's Speech.

CONGRATULATIONS IN THE HOUSE.

Mr. Roderic Bowen, M.P. for Cardiganshire, speaking in the House on the second reading of the Trunk Roads Bill, made his maiden speech in the House. He described the Bill as a "timid step in the right direction" for the effect would be solely to increase the total mileage under the national system by 8,000 miles out of a total of 180,000, and in the 172,000 miles that remained were some of the most important highways in the country. Wales, in the Act of 1936, had only 376 miles of trunk roads, and in Cardiganshire the two roadways which provided the link between South Wales and Cardiganshire were not included in the first Schedule. Having referred to the limited scope of the Act, he passed on to speak of the conditions in Cardiganshire where the railway system was inadequate, and road transport was the chief means of the carriage of goods, and then pointed out that there was not in the county a mile of trunk road. The highway rate in Cardiganshire was 9/6 and the county rate 21/3. He compared it with Middlesex where the highway rate was 9d. The roadways on which this 9/6 was spent were built to carry horse and cart traffic, but were carrying heavy lorries conveying agricultural products and timber. During the past year alone ten million gallons of milk were carried over the roads of Cardiganshire, and he submitted that the maintenance of these roads should not be an intolerable burden upon the ratepayers but a matter of national expenditure. He urged the Minister to consider steps to alleviate the enormous financial burden borne by the rural authorities. In conclusion, he referred to redeeming features in the Bill, and hoped the Minister would bear in mind the need for a North Wales-South Wales trunk road.

Lieut. Commander Clark (Hutchinson (Edinburgh West) congratulated Mr. Bowen on his maiden speech, and said he had made a useful and comprehensive statement, adding, "His constituents are fortunate in having him to represent them here."

Cambrian News

WOMAN ON TOP OF AN EIGHT-FOOT WALL

How a woman was found on the top of an eight-foot wall, trying to adjust a pair of steps in the early hours of the morning was described at Clerkenwell Magistrate's Court on Tuesday.

Appearing on remand on a charge of being found in an enclosed yard at the rear of premises in Mansfield Road, Kentish Town, for an unlawful purpose, Mrs. Emily Medway, 37, of Mansfield Road, pleaded guilty.

She also pleaded guilty to stealing an enamel dish and a glass tray value 10s. belonging to Elsie Rose Pendrill, and a glass cutter and a drill value 10s. belonging to Percy William Gould. A charge of having housebreaking implements in her possession was not proceeded with.

Detective Sergeant Radford said that at 12.35 a.m. on October 30th Mrs. Medway was seen by a Mr. Kendall on the top of a brick wall outside 68 and 70 Mansfield Road. The wall was about eight feet high. She had a pair of steps which she was trying to place against a wall of 70 Mansfield Road. Mr. Kendall shone a torch on her and informed the occupier of 70 Mansfield Road, Mr. Hutchings. Mrs. Medway then walked back along the wall but fell off. She ran away, was chased by Mr. Hutchings, and eventually arrested by a police officer.

She had in her possession a glass cutter and a drill which had been taken earlier the same night from 72 Mansfield Road, together with a dish and a glass tray. Entry had been obtained through an unoccupied shop.

Mrs. Medway was a married woman with a 12-year-old son, the officer added.

A Mrs. West told the Magistrate that she had known Mrs. Medway for about three years. "She has been very kind to me in many ways," Mrs. West told the Magistrate. "I know she has not been very well recently. I would like to look after her."

Accepting this offer, the Magistrate made a probation order.

Hampstead and Highgate Express

GLAMOUR GIRL CONTEST

The Winner Comes From Exeter

MUCH interest has been shown by Exonians in the Victory Glamour Girl Contest which was arranged by Mr. Cyril Bartlett for the Lammas Fair Committee, as part of the Exeter Thanksgiving Week effort.

Over 600 people watched thirty of the prettiest girls of Devon take part in the finals of the contest at the Civic Hall, Exeter, on Saturday night. The finalists were picked from five groups which were held earlier in the week. Judges were Mr. and Mrs. T. C. Gwilliam, and Alderman and Mrs. F. P. Cottey. Presentation of the cup and prizes was made by Mr. F. P. Cottey.

The winner of the contest was Miss Joan Gray, 21 years old, blue-eyed, auburn haired, from 3, Sweets Cottages, Wonford, a close second being Miss Joan Creed, of 31, Cross Park, Heavitree, Exeter. Miss Brenda Collard, of 172, Monks-road, Exeter, was third, and Misses Brenda James, of Tiverton, and Beryl Morris, of 7, Prospect Park, Exeter, were fourth and fifth respectively.

Before the final was held Jack England and his dance band gave the audience three hours of modern dance music. Miss Anita Dee rendered several vocal solos.

It was announced that Miss Dorothy Ward, who was to have been one of the judges, was unable to attend at the last moment. Mr. Gwilliam offered his apologies for her absence.

The Mayor and Mayoress of Exeter (Alderman and Mrs. F. H. Tarr) and the Sheriff of Exeter (Mr. Harry Bradbeer) were among those present at the contest.

The proceeds of the dances and the contest will be given to the Savings Committee.

Exeter Express and Echo

Northumberland and Alnwick Gazette

J.P. warns cyclists of lights danger

The chairman of Glendale bench (Mr. Noel Villiers) gave an exposition of the danger involved and a warning after five persons had been fined at Wooler on Tuesday for cycling without lights.

"The magistrates generally are very perturbed and are from their experience very much alarmed at the increase of these cases," he said. "After many years experience on this bench I have always congratulated myself and others that we live in a rural district where people are mostly law abiding.

No alternative

"These are not criminal cases, but unless people conform to the lighting regulations there will have to be a very great change. There will be no alternative than to increase the fines very much —the penalties will be severe."

Mr Villiers said that some people might think these charges were trivial and the fines small. Therefore they were very careless. He felt bound to emphasise the importance of them, as their object was to prevent accidents which often resulted in people being seriously maimed, sometimes fatally. The regulations were as much for the protection of the cyclist as of the motorist.

Previous to the war there were something like 250,000 casualties in road accidents. Last September one and a half million licences were issued to motorists and there were also on the roads about 315,000 motor cyclists. They had no register of how many ordinary bicycles there were on the roads.

New road soon

As soon as things in this country got into normal condition and industry began to hum again, there would be a tremendous increase of motorists and cyclists. Therefore it was very necessary that they should conform to regulations.

He would urge that cyclists, when they came out at night, should have lights and see that their lights were in good order before starting out. Everybody knew how difficult it was in a fog at night to see a cyclist on the road who had no lights. Accidents were the consequence. He believed it was entirely due to the carelessness of cyclists. They took risks, which was very foolish.

A new code of regulations was to be brought in next year and there was no doubt that they would be more strict and rigid than at present. They wanted people to conform to them.

BRITAIN CAPTURES AIR SPEED RECORD

Jet Meteors Average Over 600 Miles Per Hour

FROM OUR CORRESPONDENT

HERNE'BAY, Wednesday.

Great Britain captured the world's speed record under the conditions laid down by the Federation Aeronautique Internationale here this morning when the Gloster Meteor IV. aircraft both exceeded 600 miles an hour as an average of four runs over the three kilometres (1¼ miles) course.

Group Captain H. J. Wilson did an average of 606 miles an hour and Mr Eric Greenwood 603. Wilson's fastest run was from west to east at 611 miles an hour; Greenwood's fastest run was also from west to east and was 608 miles an hour.

The aircraft and engine manufacturers, Gloster Aircraft, Ltd., and Rolls-Royce, Ltd., were studying the results here to-night in order to decide whether to allow the pilots to make further attempts, using more jet thrust.

Historic Importance of Trials

It is because these trials are being done in the region of the speed of sound, which is about 760 miles an hour at sea level and 15deg. C., that they are of historic importance. These British pilots in British aircraft are trying to penetrate the sonic wall for the first time. They are doing these speeds under rigidly controlled condtions, and therefore the results are not in any way comparable with the wild statements about speed that have frequently been heard in the past.

Compressibility and the shock stall are among the dangers they face. Some parts of both Wilson's and Greenwood's aircraft were shock-stalled, which means that all normal lift characteristics were upset during the runs But the shock stall did not develop over the whole machine. Had it done so the machine would have become unmanageable, and would either have turned upwards or downwards without the pilot being able to hold it.

Wing Commander Poulter, the meteorological officer brought down here for the occasion, predicted a wind from the sea with good visibility during the morning. That prediction was accurate, and at eight o'clock a weather flight was made along the course by a standard Meteor.

Mosquito Witnesses

About an hour and a half later Group Captain Wilson in his Meteor was airborne from Manston aerodrome. The two Mosquito witness aircraft for checking his height and seeing that the rules prohibiting the aircraft from rising higher than 400 metres (about 1300ft.) at any time were in position over the Isle of Sheppey and over Thanet.

Group Captain Wilson made a great sweep from his point of take-off, and aimed for the course as if he were throwing his machine along it. He had told me the evening before that all depended on this accuracy of aim, for if the aircraft was the smallest fraction off course it was impossible to alter it during the run. Then, trailing the long streamer of brown smoke, the Meteor rushed for the 500-metre marking point, running at not more than 100ft. from the water and dead straight.

It was the strangest spectacle I have witnessed. The aircraft was not very noisy, though the rushing sound of the jet engines seemed to fill the air, and, vaguely, to continue long after the aircraft had passed.

After going through the timed section and being recorded by the cameras with their tuning-fork timing apparatus, Wilson passed the Herne Bay pier and then began very gently to go into a right-hand turn. The aircraft is hard to turn at this speed, and the practice of both pilots was to turn right after going through the course and then bend round to the left so as to come in for their aim on to the course out of a left-hand turn.

Perfect Course

Wilson's runs were as follows:— A, 604 m.p.h.; B, 608; C, 602; D, 611. His course-keeping was perfectly accurate, each run being done, as it seemed, along invisible rails set in the air 100ft. above the centre line of the course.

After he had landed Group Captain Wilson expressed himself as satisfied with the runs, though he described them as trials and insisted that it would be possible to do still better if circumstances allowed.

It seemed impossible that two men could both fly such a perfect course at such a speed, but Eric Greenwood, in the yellow-painted Meteor nicknamed "Forever Amber," flew as well as Wilson and with a smaller variation. His runs were— A, 599; B, 608; C, 598; D, 607.

Plans for the future are to decide whether to allow the pilots more thrust and, if so, to make the necessary adjustments and then to try to set the record yet higher. Perhaps another 30 miles an hour might be possible, but the risks as the shock stall spreads increase. The Meteor was not designed originally for such high speeds, and it is a great tribute both to the designer, Mr W. G. Carter, and to the constructors that it has achieved them safely.

Entered for Record

Air Marshal W. A. Coryton announced that Wilson's speed is to be entered for the world record.

"We had hoped to go further," he stated, "but we had to come to a stop for the moment. Unfortunately minor defects have turned out on the aircraft. A fairing in front of the star on Britannia, where the air is taken into the engine, is affected. The rivets pulled loose."

There was no sign of damage to the other craft, but after inspection a decision would be made regarding another attempt.

The Air Marshal said he hoped that eventually they would reach the speed of sound.

Glasgow Herald

Some time ago the Gazette published the above photo, which had been sent to Mrs Wilcox, of Alnwick, by the photographer in the Middle East by mistake. It was recognised by his mother, Mrs M. J. Ryan, of Easington, Belford. L/C Thomas Ryan was one of the P.O.W.s released from the Far East and has now arrived home.

Northumberland and Alnwick Gazette

Men are STRONGER, KEENER

But women ARE MORE NIMBLE

WOMEN are definitely the weaker sex, so far as their jobs are concerned, according to a report to the Royal Commission on Equal Pay.

But, says the report, though women workers are "rather less efficient generally," are more often absent than men, and do not stay in their jobs so long, in one thing do they excel.

In work requiring nimble fingers such as typing and accounting-machine operating, they have ousted men almost completely.

And in the case of teachers, nurses and library assistants, women are men's equals.

Men workers, it is pointed out, tire less easily. Also, they have a keener sense of duty.

The report is made by a sub-committee of the Association of Municipal Corporations, representing 408 borough councils.

Sunday Express

TENBY TOWN COUNCIL USE HOUSING POWERS

OVERCROWDED FAMILIES ACCOMMODATED IN VICTORIA STREET

House Had Been Condemned For 27 Years

Tenby Town Council had no hesitation in exercising their special powers when a further case of overcrowding came up for consideration at Tuesday night's meeting.

The case concerned three families living in a house in Crackwell Street and was reported by one of the occupants who stated in a letter that ten people were sleeping in three bedrooms. Three of the women occupants expected their husbands to be released from the Services shortly and the matter was of extreme urgency. The house had been condemned twenty-seven years ago.

The Council gave the matter immediate attention and decided to move the families to a house in Victoria Street.

Tenby Observer

SIR OSWALD MOSLEY IN COURT

FIVE HOUR HEARING OF PIG CASE

DEFENCE NOT CALLED

After a five hours' hearing, Kingsclere Magistrates dismissed a case on Friday in which Sir Oswald Ernald Mosley, Bt., of Crowood Farm, near Marlborough, was summoned for permitting unnecessary suffering to be caused to pigs at Crux Easton House on October 5th by failing to provide adequate feeding and suitable accommodation for them.

When the decision of the court was announced, Sir Oswald, who had pleaded not guilty and conducted his own defence, was responsible for an outburst.

The Chairman (Lieut.-Col. A. de P. Kingsmill) said the Bench did not consider that the prosecution had proved the case, then to the defendant he said : " We do consider, however, that you should have been further aware of the state in which these pigs were, and should have taken earlier steps to see that they were properly fed. The case will be dismissed."

Sir Oswald : Am I to be subject to a stricture from the Bench if the case is dismissed?

The Chairman : That is the Bench's observations, that is all.

DECEMBER
1945

Minister's criticism of dances

Married people with families who go to dances frequently should find better places to attend, declared the Rev. W. Gainsborough, of North Sunderland, speaking at the annual soiree of Cheviot Street Presbyterian Church, Wooler.

The soiree was held on Thursday last. The first part of the proceedings was a tea served in the Church Hall by the ladies of the congregation. The meeting was held in the church, the Rev. G. A. Bannister presiding over a good gathering.

The speakers for the evening were the Rev. E. L. Lodge, Dr.Mus., minister of the West Church, and the Rev. W. Gainsborough, North Sunderland.

Mr Gainsborough took for his subject "Musts." Our whole life, he said, was made up of musts. We must work, we must pay our rates and taxes. We must send our children to school, and so on. During the war years we accepted many musts without complaining, but he believed there were now more difficult tasks to face to make peace. If ever a country was at the cross-roads, we were. It was up to every man, woman and child to do their best and face up to the problems that confronted them.

In the Church, said Mr Gainsborough, a great deal of harm was done by members of a congregation bickering and fault-finding with other members of the congregation. Also in this age young people would not take anything seriously in Church work and would not take part in discussions. It was the reaction from the war.

As far as dances were concerned, many married people, some with families, frequented these regularly. They should find more suitable places.

We were not free to do as we liked, but what we ought to do. This became very noticeable during the two wars and lack of discipline of the children had become one of the social evils of the day.

Dr. Lodge also gave an interesting address and brought greetings from the members of his congregation.

The musical programme comprised two solos by Mrs Singleton, "Smiling through" and "Bless this house," and Master Singleton sang "Say a little prayer" and "Silent night." Dr. Lodge gave two organ solos.

Northumberland and Alnwick Gazette

Here's Why YOU Waited

SOMETHING terrible's happened — the whole of Britain has been kept waiting by a slip of a girl.

Seven minutes after she should have announced the 6.30 a.m. B.B.C. Home Service programme "Bright and Early," announcer Andrea Troubridge gasped into the microphone "Good morning. The time is twenty-three minutes to seven. I am sorry, but I overslept."

While Andrea was feverishly clambering into her clothes, the engineers kept listeners amused. "The customers had to listen to seven minutes of Bow Bells," Andrea said yesterday.

Tonight she will go to bed worried, for this Dreadful Thing must never happen again. A girl keep someone waiting? Unheard of, sir, and totally dreadful.

Sunday Pictorial

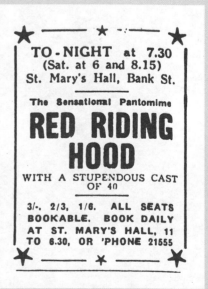

CRICKET LECTURE

Mr. Herbert Sutcliffe at Ripon

Mr. Herbert Sutcliffe addressed a crowded meeting of cricket enthusiasts in the Town Hall, Ripon, on Thursday night. Mr. J. M. Kilburn presided, supported by the President of the Ripon Cricket Club, Dr. A. C. Brown, the Hon. Secretary, Mr. A. F. Newton, and members of the committee. This was the first of a series of lectures and addresses which have been arranged for the purpose of stimulating interest in cricket locally, and, incidentally, supplying the club with much-needed funds. A collection made in the hall on Thursday night realised, with donations, the sum of £10.

Mr. Kilburn introduced Mr. Sutcliffe as one of the greatest cricketers who ever played the game. He would be remembered for one particular characteristic, and that was as a fighting batsman, a batsman who for Yorkshire and England was never better than when things were going wrong. We thought of him holding up his particular end hour after hour, and even day after day. He had won more successes for Yorkshire than anyone who ever played for the county, and when he set about it he was one of the most devastating batsmen. Nothing ever bowled yet could frighten him. The Club had secured for the series of meetings opened that night a trio of cricketers who would be remembered as long as cricket was played in Ripon.

Ripon Gazette

Wooler man wins £1,013

Mr Robert Carr, a Wooler shoemaker, has won £1,013 in a football pool contest. He successfully forecast three "draws" in his third attempt at the "pools".

Physically handicapped since birth, he has always been a keen supporter of football. He told a reporter that his "windfall" would be a great asset to him in later years.

Mr Carr is well-known in Wooler as a member of a local dance band.

Northumberland and Alnwick Gazette

Born 1848, still does own work

Warkworth's oldest inhabitant, Mrs E. R. Patten, of No. 1 The Butts, celebrated her 97th birthday on Monday.

Despite her great age she is wonderfully healthy and does most of her own housework.

She comes of country stock, being born at Charlton Mires, near South Charlton, Alnwick, on December 3, 1848, her father having been foreman there for many years.

She recalled how in her young days woman land workers toiled from 6 a.m. to 6 p.m. with only a two-hour break for dinner, for the sum of 9d a day.

On market days they used to walk to and from Alnwick, their produce having been sent in to Alnwick by carrier's cart, and provisions, etc., brought home in a similar fashion.

Farm butter in those days could be bought at 6d to 8d a pound, and eggs for 6d and 7d a dozen.

Married at St. Michael's Parish Church, Alnwick, she went to live in the Thropton, Longframlington, district, and later to Tyneley, near Chathill, before coming to Warkworth 16 years ago.

Northumberland and Alnwick Gazette

RUSSIA IS A FRIENDLY COUNTRY, SAYS MRS. PRIESTLEY

Back from a seven-weeks' tour of Soviet Russia with her husband, Mrs. J. B. Priestley in an interview with the "Express" when she came to Golder's Green last week to preside at a meeting of the Women's Forum related some of her impressions of that country and its people.

Hampstead and Highgate Express

The Russians, she said, are a warm-hearted and friendly people. The women, despite the fact that they are often employed at a number of jobs originally performed by men, are not hard, but extremely kind and concerned with their children.

"In the Soviet Union they look after their children magnificently, better than we do," she added.

She was amazed at the great interest and friendliness shown by the ordinary Russian people. Wherever she and her husband went, they were given enthusiastic welcomes, were especially at theatres, when whole audiences rose and cheered them for several minutes.

"The popularity of my husband in Moscow to-day is astonishing," she said. "Not only are they flocking to see his latest play, 'The Inspector Calls,' but there is a great run on his latest books, particularly 'Blackout in Gretley.'"

The feeling of friendship for the British people is not only very great in the cities, but in all parts of the Soviet Union. One woman Mayor of a little Caucasus village they visited threw her arms round Mrs. Priestley, embracing her and exclaiming, "Give my fond greetings to the British people."

No Exploiting of Sex

Mrs. Priestley pointed out that there is no exploitation of sex in the Soviet Union.

"There are no prostitutes in that country. The theatre is free from any suggestiveness likely to appeal to the 'tired business man,' and art is on a very high level."

She said that early next year it was hoped that the Moscow Arts Theatre would be visiting London "to show us how to play Tchekov and enable us to show them our British hospitality."

WHERE THERE'S NEED —
THERE'S THE SALVATION ARMY!

Teams of Salvation Army workers from Great Britain specially trained to cope with the problems of relief work are battling against appalling conditions of hunger, disease and homelessness in Holland and other liberated countries.

They are being helped by hundreds of trained Salvation Army Officers who have shared the trials of their countrymen in occupied lands during the war years, and whose knowledge of language and local need is a valuable asset.

MORE TEAMS MUST BE SENT OUT. £50,000 IS NEEDED QUICKLY.

Please send your gift NOW—marking it "Relief Work"—to General Carpenter, 101, Queen Victoria Street, London, E.C.4.

Member society of the Council of British Societies for Relief Abroad.

STRUMPSHAW

PLAY.—The nativity play performed in The Barn, Barnhill, Strumpshaw, included every child and Dutch visitor in the school. Senior scholars filled the main roles and junior shepherds, angels, villagers numbered over 50. The sum of £4 4s. was raised for the junior Red Cross funds.

Norwich Mercury

Peace on Earth
TO MEN OF GOODWILL

For the last two thousand years the world has heard the cry "Glory to God in the highest; on earth, peace to men of goodwill." It has sounded more poignant and more urgent at the end of each great war. But it has been said so often that I doubt whether the words today have any real meaning. We shall say them this Christmas. But will they be any more than an empty formula?

"On earth, peace to men of goodwill" —this is not really a trite phrase. If you go back through history and think of the great leaders of mankind—the philosophers, and the saints who have moulded civilization, Buddha in India and the Far East, Lao-Tse in China, the Greek philosophers, and, supremely, in our own civilization, Christ—you will find that they all had one great belief in common. It is that there are permanent and unchanging laws of right and wrong, of good and evil, which men will defy only at the price of suffering, strife and war. They all held that, just as there is a law of nature governing ordinary material things (for instance, water cannot flow uphill, or change its composition from H_2O), so there is a law of nature governing the behaviour of man. "Thou shalt love thy neighbour as thyself," or "thou shalt not steal," are as basic to human existence as the law of thermodynamics is to physics.

The great difference, of course, between scientific laws governing lifeless matter and the natural law governing human beings is that men *can* break the moral laws which bind them. They have free will. They can choose evil even though it contradicts their whole being. But what happens in nature when you break a law? What happens, to give a simple example, if you violate the laws of good health and expose yourself to infection? Illness and disease follow as an inevitable consequence.

Photo: by courtesy of "Picture Post"

BARBARA WARD

NOW A HEADLINE NAME AMONG BROADCASTERS, HAS WRITTEN THIS POWERFUL ARTICLE SPECIALLY FOR OUR CHRISTMAS NUMBER

Please do not think that I am wandering away from the men of goodwill and the peace that shall be theirs. What the saints and the philosophers are always trying to tell us is that it is as fatal for human society to break its moral laws as it is to break physical laws. The consequences of selfishness, disloyalty or violence are as inevitable as the consequences of disease or earthquake. Civil strife, fighting, hatred, and finally war do not just appear in society. They are thrown up by the behaviour of ordinary men and women in society, and they will go on being thrown up just as long as

men and women continue grossly to violate the natural laws of good and evil to which the conscience of mankind has always given witness. The cry "peace to men of goodwill" is not an empty formula. It has a terrible meaning. There will be peace only for men of goodwill. The men of evil will must always and everywhere sow seeds of war by their egoism, their violence and their bad faith.

This fact ought to make us see peace as a far more challenging and arresting adventure than the mere end of fighting. We are beginning now in homes and towns and factories and councils of state to lead the lives which will lead to peace—or war. Everyone is involved, for who among us knows by what tiny spark of ill-will or evil-doing the great train of disaster may not be set alight? If our family lives are rancorous and unfaithful, if our social life is riddled with exploitation and mass unemployment, if international relations are full of festering nationalism and imperialist rivalry, we are already on our way to war. There will be no peace, for there is no goodwill.

So this Christmas should be a time of dedication—of each of us to be a builder, not a destroyer, of peace. Each citizen by his personal and his social behaviour is paving a road—to war or peace. Peace will be built, like a coral reef, from the actions of an infinite number of men of goodwill so leading their lives that gradually their society becomes sane and sweet. This peace is not only the work of great statesmen. It does not simply turn on the decisions of Potsdam or Yalta. The best terms fail if there are no men to fulfil them. The worst terms can be thwarted if men refuse to carry them out. We are all of us the raw material of peace. And peace will depend upon our goodwill.

KILBURN YOUTH CENTRE MAY BE REVIVED

The Kilburn Youth Centre which, started during the war, had a membership of several hundred before it closed down for lack of suitable premises, may be revived.

The Hampstead Borough Youth Committee decided at its meeting at the Town Hall last week to try and find a new meeting place for the centre which met for a time at the Hampstead Health Institute and later in Kingsgate Road Schools.

GERMAN FIREARMS IN PUBLIC HOUSE

"MIGHT HAVE GOT INTO HANDS OF BANDITS"

Three German Army automatic pistols, a British revolver, and 307 rounds of ammunition kept in a safe by a Kentish Town publican were brought to Clerkenwell Court last Thursday when the licensee was charged with having them in his possession without a certificate. He was Harold Clifford Garlick, of the Gloucester Arms, Leighton Road, and he said he bought them from two soldiers on leave, who had been to Hamburg, and had presumably taken the German weapons from prisoners.

The Magistrate (Mr. Frank Powell) fining him £10 and ordering the weapons and ammunition to be forfeited, remarked that as there had been a possibility of their being sold again, they might have got into the hands of bandits.

Police Inspector Kelly said it was unlawful for British soldiers to bring weapons into this country, either as souvenirs or for any other purpose. One of the German pistols was a new weapon, introduced by the Germans late in the war.

They "Fascinated" Him

Garlick said that shortly after the defeat of Germany two soldiers came into the public house with the weapons and the ammunition. He wanted to buy one pistol only, but they insisted on selling everything, and he gave them £25 for it all, and a camera. The weapons and ammunition had been in his safe ever since, and no one else had access to them.

He did think at one time he might sell them, but had given up that idea, realising it would be a dangerous thing to do nowadays. He also thought he would throw three of the pistols away, as he actually only wanted one, but could not bring himself to do so: they had a fascination for, he said, they were fine workmanship.

Garlick was said to be a man of good character, who had taken over the Gloucester Arms on the death of his father. Mr. Powell said he had behaved in an extremely foolish manner.

Hampstead and Highgate Express

Dutch Guests at Norwich Insurance Party

For five hours on Saturday children of members of the Insurance Institute of Norwich, together with 39 Dutch children and their leaders, were entertained in the Norwich Union Life Office canteen. The children were welcomed by the president (Mr. C. Graham Harbord), and the events included ventriloquial and conjuring displays by Lawrenco, tea and Father Christmas, who distributed gifts to the 200 children.

Norwich Mercury

S IR,—Your correspondents who let their children of tender years do housework should remember that, as Wordsworth said, "the child is father of the man." Do we really want to bring up the rising generation to be fussy old maids, married Marthas, and husbands with a mania for running their fingers along ledges in search of dust?

Ealing, W.5   Henry Maggs.

As layers of fires I back our twins, aged three, against any toddlers in the kingdom.

Sidney B. Whimble.
234 Laburnum Crescent, Clacton

The Leader

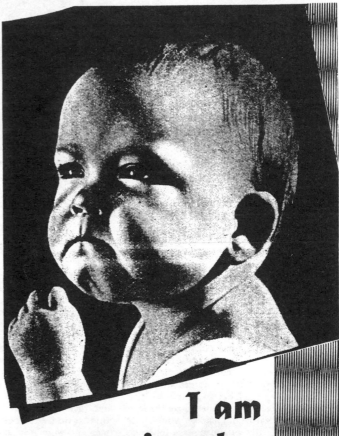

I am convinced...

Despite shortages and difficulties, there could be a happier Christmas for many this year .. with your help. Please send a gift today to The Salvation Army Christmas Fund, and do your part in making a merry Christmas for needy children and lonely old people.

GENERAL CARPENTER,
101, QUEEN VICTORIA ST.,
LONDON, E.C.4.

38/146

WEEK-END WIRELESS

TO-NIGHT

HOME SERVICE

3. 0—The Skull. A new story.
3.20—Salford v. Barrow. Commentary.
4. 0—Royal Philharmonic Society Concert.
5. 0—Backs to the Land.
5.15—Children's Hour.
6. 0—News.
6.10—Weather Forecast.
6.13—Sport, Talks, Announcements.
6.25—News from the North.
6.30—Northern Newsreel.
7. 0—Fred Harries Ensemble.
7.30—From the Army of the Rhine.
7.45—The Week in Westminster.
8. 0—Music Hall.
9. 0—News.
9.20—The First Mrs. Fraser.
10.45—Lighten Our Darkness.
11. 0—News Summary.
11. 3—These Passing Shows.
11.33—Southern Serenade.
12. 0—Big Ben. Close down.

LIGHT PROGRAMME

3. 5—Middlesbrough v. Preston. Commentary.
4. 0—Intermission.
4.30—Over to You.
5. 0—Call of the West.
5.30—Atlantic Spotlight.
6. 0—Radio Rhythm Club.
6.30—Shipmates Ashore.
7. 0—News.
7.15—Saturday Night Out.
7.45—Farewell, A.F.N.
8.15—World Parade.
8.45—Desert Island Discs.
9.15—Navy Mixture.
9.45—Sandy MacPherson at the organ.
10. 0—News.
10.10—The Man from the Country.
10.15—Music for the Fireside.
11. 0—Stan Atkins and his Band.
11.25—Melville Christie and Orchestra.
11.50—News.
12. 0—Big Ben. Close down.

TO-MORROW

HOME SERVICE

8. 0—News.
8.20—John Blore and his Orchestra.
8.50—Music from America.
9.30—Into All the World.
10.15—Beethoven. Piano Sonata in E.
10.30—Music While You Work.
11. 0—Music Magazine.
11.45—Royal Military School of Music Band.
 0—Northern Newsreel.
.20—Music for Reflection.
.50—The Week's Films.
 0—News.
1.10—Country Magazine.
1.40—Songs for Everybody.
2.15—Your North-Country Garden.
2.30—B.B.C. Sunday Afternoon Concerts.—5.
4.30—Polonius. (From Hamlet).
5. 0—Christian News and Commentary.
5.15—Children's Hour.
6. 0—News.
6.10—Weather Forecast.
6.13—Calling the North.
6.20—National Savings announcements.
6.30—Serenade in Sepia.
7. 0—This is Freedom.—7.
7.30—Fireside Talk.
7.45—Evening Service. From Hull.
8.25—Week's Good Cause.
8.30—The Man of Property. Play.
9. 0—News.
9.15—I Knew a Man—Lord Rutherford.
9.30—The Music of Coleridge-Taylor.
10.30—The Epilogue.
10.38—Time for Verse.
11. 0—News Summary.

(second column top)
11. 3—Manuel de Falla.
11.30—Sunday Nocturne.
12. 0—Big Ben. Close down.

LIGHT PROGRAMME

9. 0—News.
9.15—Rudy Lewis at the Organ.
9.45—Morning Melodies.
10.15—Family Favourites.
11.15—As the Commentator Saw It.
11.30—Music of the Masters.
12. 0—People's Service.
12.30—News.
12.45—Accent on Rhythm.
1. 0—Marches and Waltzes.
1.30—Kay on the Keys.
1.45—Transatlantic Quiz.
2.15—Music Parade.
3. 0—Children's Christmas Party.
3.30—Maurice Winnick and Orchestra.
4. 0—The Diamond Studs.
4.15—Sunday Serenade.
5. 0—Think on These Things.
5.15—Journey to Romance.
6. 0—Variety Band-box.
7. 0—News.
7.15—The Richard Tauber Programme.
7.45—Grand Hotel. Albert Sandler.
8.30—Tommy Handley in Itma.
9. 0—Sunday Half-hour.
9.30—Cyril Fletcher in Thanking Yew.
10. 0—News.
10.10—Talking With You.
10.15—The Twilight Hour.
10.45—In a Sentimental Mood.
11.15—Evergreens.
11.50—News.
12. 0—Big Ben. Close down.

MUNITION WORKER TURNS DRUDGERY INTO NEVER-ENDING JOY

Through Taking The Only Salts Specially Recommended For Women

Every woman in the country ought to read the amazing story of Mrs. P., who, in addition to 55 hours a week on heavy munition work, looks after a large house and her three small children.

For months she suffered terribly with kidney and bladder trouble. Then she read about Juno-Junipah, the only salts recommended specially for women. She tried them, and in her own words: "After three days I felt a different woman. Now, after two months, I look and feel twenty years younger, and enjoy my food without chronic indigestion. Instead of running one machine with great difficulty, I now *enjoy* running two, and I have nearly doubled my output. I would not be without your salts for anything. They have turned life from a dreary drudgery into a never-ending joy."

Why don't you try these special salts?

Juno-Junipah Salts are gentle. They prevent unwanted fat and clear the poisons out of the blood-stream without any harsh purging or griping. So they bring rapid relief to Rheumatism, Lumbago Sciatica, and other uric acid troubles. Moreover, they are the only salts to contain pure oil of Juniper, one of the oldest remedies for the Kidney and other troubles to which women are so liable, like Backache, loss of sleep, etc.

Take just a little Juno-Junipah in warm water every morning, and you'll be astonished how soon you begin to feel better and look better, too. Your pains will go, your complexion improve, and if you're overweight you'll be delighted at the way you retain the slim figure of youth.

Better Health and Looks
OR NO PAY!

So confident are we that Juno-Junipah will make any woman feel and look better, that here is an offer! Get a 2s. bottle of Juno-Junipah from any chemist to-day. Take it as directed, and if you aren't more than satisfied with what it has done he will refund your money without question. Obtainable from all chemists, including Boots, Taylors and Timothy Whites.

PRICELESS ART FIND— IN COTTAGE

SECURITY officers hunting for art treasures looted from Germany have found a priceless silver chalice from a German museum in a cottage in Hampshire.

The discovery was made after a search lasting for months.

Other loot worth more than £1,000,000 and intended for black markets in the Low Countries and Britain has been seized by military police and security officers on the western borders of the British zone in Germany.

Almost everything from cameras to super-sports cars worth thousands of pounds, and from German grand pianos to lorryloads of machine-tools, surgical instruments and museum pieces has come into the British net.

Though most of the smuggling has been done "privately," in some cases organised groups have been at work. These, to a large extent, have now been broken up, says British United Press.

In some cases officers were involved, and these have been court-martialled and received heavy sentences.

Smuggling of such things as grand pianos went on mainly from north German ports, with landing craft and transport planes acting as "delivery vans."

Sunday Pictorial

'HOT ICE BOYS' GET £3,000

Jewellery worth £3,000, belonging to Lady Alexandra Studd, was stolen yesterday in the latest haul by the London "Hot Ice" Boys, blamed now for £50,000 thefts in the past seven weeks.

The jewellery was taken in a raid on Lady Alexandra's home in Holland Villas-road, Notting Hill, W., by thieves who planned their movements to avoid domestic arrangements of the household.

Sunday Pictorial

Middlesex Aids China

County Has Raised £43,227

Middlesex people continue to express their sympathy for the suffering millions of China in practical fashion by contributing to British United Aid to China, the organization for the relief of distress among all parties and creeds. Up to the beginning of December British United Aid to China had received no less than £43,227 in contributions from the County. Local committees throughout the County have been largely responsible for this excellent result.

Here are the totals at the beginning of December for the principal centres:

	£
Harrow	4,266
Hendon	4,222
Finchley	4,179
Wembley	2,850
Twickenham	2,761
Ealing	2,441
Southgate	2,420
Hornsey	2,376
Enfield	2,234
Br'tford & Chiswick	2,007
Willesden	1,863
Edmonton	1,683
Heston & Isleworth	1,430
Acton	1,161
Tottenham	989
Staines	917
Ruislip & Northwood	865
Uxbridge	794
Southall	764
Feltham	733

The total for the whole country is now £1,637,859. Of this sum £1,345,600 has already been allocated by a special Anglo-Chinese Committee in Chungking, of which the British Ambassador is a member, to meet the most urgent needs of the millions of homeless, the orphans, and the sick and wounded.

Marylebone Mercury

LORD KIMBERLEY'S WEDDING

Gifts from Tenants at Big Party

To mark the recent marriage of the Earl of Kimberley, more than 300 tenants and friends were present at Kimberley Hall on Friday. They were the guests of Lord and Lady Kimberley.

Mr. H. A. Bowles, on behalf of the tenants of the estate, presented a silver salver, cheque and an illuminated book containing the names of the subscribers. The Countess was given a bouquet by little Marion Jarvis.

Mr. W. S. Blake proposed the health of the couple and in reply his Lordship said he hoped it would be possible to make this an annual event for the children on the estate.

Refreshments were served and the guests entertained by a London concert party.

Norwich Mercury

"*I talked him into it.*"
1939

"*I talked him into it.*"
1945

Punch

Grimsby Evening Telegraph

THE CHANGED CONDITIONS OF BRITAIN

1919. "And then, darling, as soon as I've found some sort of a job we'll set about choosing a nice little house somewhere near it."

1945. "And then, darling, as soon as we've found some sort of a house I'll set about choosing a nice little job somewhere near it."

Punch

"Itma" At The State, Kiburn

"Mrs Handley's Boy" With The Children

Tommy Handley made a personal appearance on Saturday morning at the Gaumont State, Kilburn, during the Junior Cinema Club's weekly matinee

Mr. Handley arrived while the community singing was in progress; tumultuous applause greeted his appearance on the stage when he was introduced to the children by the manager, Mr. Cheepen.

During the period he was on stage, Mr. Handley led them in the singing of the club song, with Rudy Lewis at the organ.

With his usual farewell — "T.T.F.N." — Tommy left the stage via the auditorium and was mobbed by the excited children on his way out, losing a coat-button in the process.

Tommy Handley told a reporter he would be unlikely to make any more films owing to the demands made on his time by broadcasting, etc.

Middlesex Independent

THE SCOTTISH WOOLLEN COMFORTS COUNCIL

Sir,—Owing to the closing down of certain Comforts Depots in Scotland some doubt seems to have arisen as to the necessity for the knitting of comforts for servicemen. The Scottish Woollen Comforts Council which deals with the issue of coupon-free wool and the distribution of comforts for Scotland wishes it to be known that comforts are urgently needed for the men in the Army and the Air Force and it strongly appeals to Scottish Organisations and knitters generally to help to supply our men at home and overseas for this our final winter. The Council gratefully acknowledges the magnificent work which Scottish women have done in the past and hopes this final appeal will meet with an immediate and generous response. Any information as to where wool may be obtained and types of garments required may be had from the Secretary at 11 Gloucester Place, Edinburgh, till the 26th November, thereafter at 60 Castle Street, Edinburgh.

R FINDLAY CRABB, Captain, Chairman of Executive Com.

Shetland Times

B.B.C. Announcer Resigns

HIS IDEAS "CONFLICTED WITH HIGH POLICY"

Mr. Joseph Macleod, the B.B.C. announcer, has resigned. His resignation will take effect in February.

A resident of Hampstead and one of the best known of the B.B.C. announcers, Mr. Macleod told the "Express" this week that he was dissatisfied with the B.B.C.'s post-war policy, which he characterised as "timid, unrealistic, and arbitrary."

"I am afraid that those responsible for policy are not in close enough touch with the spirit of the listeners," he said.

Mr. Macleod had been asked by his divisional controller to prepare a report on how he thought the Home Service programme could be improved. He spent eight days drafting it, only to learn that his suggestions could not be acted upon.

"Sense of Frustation"

"I wanted to change the actual content of the programmes, but I learnt this conflicted with the question of high policy,' he said.

His resignation, he added, had no political significance.

"I just do not believe the Government have any idea of the sense of frustration among the artists on the job from producer to engineer. The whole spirit of the B.B.C. needs changing.

"I have no immediate plans, but I may go back to theatrical production and the writing of film scripts."

∴ *Mr. MacLeod, who lives at Regency Lodge, Swiss Cottage, is 42. He was educated at Rugby and Balliol and has been called to the Bar. He has been with the B.B.C. for seven years. A vice-president of the Society for Cultural Relations with the Soviet Union, he has visited Russia several times and has written books about that country and its theatre. Left-Wing in politics, he was once Labour candidate for Huntingdon. His wife, also a Scot, was a Labour candidate for the Adelaide Ward in the recent Hampstead Borough Council elections.*

Hampstead and Highgate Express

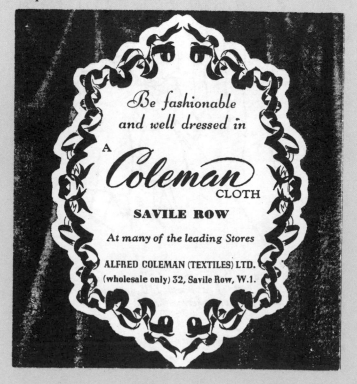

It's a Black, Not White, Christmas

IT'S going to be a Black Christmas. There won't be snow to make it white and the black market's on top. Last night's weather report said it would probably rain most of the holiday in most places.

From one end of the country to the other yesterday stories of the shopping racket poured in with just an odd gleam of honesty and goodwill to all men

But, first the story of hope. Great crowds left from all the main - line London stations.

PITY POOR SAMPSON !

IN New York they're having the biggest turkeys in years —at only 2s. a pound.

John Sampson, who hasn't been home to England for years, cables that there's not much of that Scotch whisky we're going without for the sake of the export dollars except in the bars. There are plenty of bars, all the same, he adds.

The turkeys New York's guzzling are a whole lot the Army fattened up to send abroad to the troops. Now the G.I.s are home, Ma and Pa and little brother and sister are getting them.

Other things John Sampson says are making him not quite so homesick as he might be are:

Cranberry sauce, tangerines, nuts, oranges, grapes, grapefruit, pears and apples.

Highlight of Hollywood's Christmas—they'll be starting on the celebrations just about the time we're beginning to think, maybe, there's going to be a hangover—will be the turning of a mile of the famous Boulevard into a "San'a Claus Lane."

There'll be a nightly parade of stars, movie cowboys, clowns, bands and actors

They were going home—and that was all that mattered.

And all the trains were not lut-going. Some came in bringing British Army of the Rhine men home on leave.

One hospital train discharged scores of wounded and limbless RAF men and as if by a miracle the milling crowds forced a passage and the wounded boys were given a clear way through

Londoners are blessing the skipper of the good ship Empire Mariott. It's docked with 1,100,000 oranges.

Party Pets

Holly, which Covent Garden dealers buy for 3d. a pound and sell for 3½d., was being offered in the street yesterday at 5s. a spray.

BUDGERIGARS and canaries fetched four guineas each —an all-time record. Some fools paid up to fifty guineas for bulldogs. Mice, guinea pigs and rabbits sold at boom prices."

Forty-five couples were married yesterday at Tottenham N., the registrar having to use four rooms for the marriage queue.

Those Empties

AND don't forget the empties. Milk roundsmen are leaving notices saying, " A bottle for bottle."

Lack of raw materials has put a brake on German brewing and there will be no extra beer for Christmas over the NAAFI ration of 3½ pints a week a man.

But all Army ranks travelling on the overland route to and from Britain, Mediterranean and parts east will have their Christmas Day dinner on the way. They'll get turkey, Xmas pudding, mincemeat, oranges, beer.

Sunday Pictorial

Fortitude

["The manufacture of men's full-length socks has been resumed."
Recent announcement.]

WE hitched our belts. We squared
  our jaws.
 Our shoulders plied the wheel.
Our lips were stiff. Our eyes were
  bright.
 Our hearts were true as steel.
We set our teeth. We stood our
  ground.
 We took it on the chin.
Our coats were off. Our loins were girt.
 We had the will to win.
We held the pass. We faced the blast.
 We steered 'twixt fearsome rocks.
All this we did, and now at last
 We can pull up our socks!

Punch

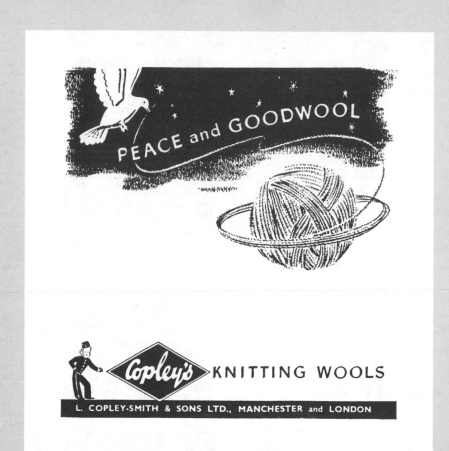